D0209192

TO THE MOON
AND
TIMBUKTU

TO THE MOON AND TIMBUKTU

A Trek Through
the Heart of Africa

Nina Sovich

NEW HARVEST

HOUGHTON MIFFLIN HARCOURT

BOSTON • NEW YORK

2013

This edition published by special arrangement with Amazon Publishing.

For information about permission to reproduce selections from this book,
write to Permissions, Houghton Mifflin Harcourt Publishing Company,
215 Park Avenue South, New York, New York 10003.

www.hmhbooks.com

Library of Congress Cataloging-in-Publication Data
Sovich, Nina.
To the Moon and Timbuktu : a trek through the heart of Africa / Nina Sovich.
pages. cm
Includes bibliographical references.
ISBN 978-0-544-02595-0
1. Sovich, Nina—Travel—Africa, Northwest.
2. Africa, Northwest—Description and travel. I. Title.
DT179.5.S69 2013
916.4040905—dc23   2012042643

Book design by Brian Moore
Map by Mapping Specialists Ltd

Printed in the United States of America

DOC 10 9 8 7 6 5 4 3 2 1

CONTENTS

To Florent

ATLANTIC OCEAN
MOROCCO
Casablanca
Marrakesh
Agadir
Tiznit
Goulmima
Tan Tan
ATLAS
Laayoune
WESTERN SAHARA
(Morocco)
Dakhla
S
A
EL DJOUF
(Empty Quarter)
Nouadhibou
Oudane
Atar
Chinguetti
MAL
Nouakchott
MAURITANIA
Timbuktu
Riv
Sénégal
St. Louis
Dakar
SENEGAL
River
Niger
Mopti
Djénné
GAMBIA
Bamako
Ségou
GUINEA BISSAU
GUINEA
SIERRA LEONE
LIBERIA
CÔTE D'IVOIRE

MTS.
TUNISIA
N
W
E
S
ALGERIA
LIBYA
H A R A
AHAGGAR MTS.
drar des foras
NIGER
Agadez
Gao
CHAD
Niamey
Marady
Zinder
Lake Chad
NIGERIA
BENIN
TOGO
CAMEROON

Part I

THE ESCAPE

1

Hotel in Dakhla

THE CABDRIVER ASSURES me his sister Salima runs a lovely hotel.

"It's a very good hotel, yes, very good hotel. No noise, no bother. Very clean. They have many, many Western tourists. Many women. Salima is a good woman."

He leaves me in front of a squat two-story building made of poured concrete that sits on the edge of the desert next to the army airport. The second-floor balcony is hanging off its anchor bolts, and the windows are murky with sand and pink goo that looks a lot like Pepto-Bismol. The only light in the hotel emanates from a first-floor pool hall that smells of fish heads and burned felt. Cigarettes, empty milk cartons, and black plastic bags skip down the street in the midnight breeze, accumulating in a huge pothole in front of the hotel. Clean, I suppose, is a relative term.

My cabdriver is, however, right on one count. There are women. Lots of them—standing in windows and doorways all down the street, lit from behind by candles and kerosene lamps into spectral figures of muslin cloth and cloying scent. Their bodies are round and their faces hard, but they beckon me with soft laughter and hennaed hands. I suppose a client is a client to a working girl — or after two weeks of travel through the Western Sahara, I have become sufficiently androgynous to enjoy their attention.

I've been nowhere places before — the northern reaches of Azerbaijan, the desert in Western Egypt, Sweden with its endless pine forests — but the Western Sahara doesn't even exist. At least not in a political sense. It's a land claimed both by the native Sahrawi population and the Moroccan government, which has occupied the country since the 1970s. Dakhla, its most southern city, would like to think of itself as a resort town, but as it is home to Morocco's commercial fishing fleet, its real allure lies in loose women and a sheltered port. I've landed in West Africa's version of Tijuana, a place purposefully kept lawless so soldiers and sailors can blow off steam.

Salima is indeed very nice, but highly suspicious. She pulls aside the night watchman and they speak in furtive, rushed Arabic, gesturing toward my black backpack. Under a green neon light that lends an aura of unreality, I paw through the contents to show her there's nothing inside but clothes and books. She asks for payment up front anyway and scribbles down every detail in my passport. When she finally hands over the key, her mood is dark.

"Look. The Chinese will come back tonight. You don't want any part of that," she tells me in weirdly idiomatic English. "I suggest you go upstairs and bolt the door. Don't come out until morning."

"What happens if I come out before morning?" I ask. It's an awkward question but I'm curious.

"Well," she says slowly. "Not good things."

"Not good things is vague." But she stares hard at me and frowns, until, finally unsure what else to do, I frown too. "I'm going," I say, and head toward my room.

"Best," she says.

There is a particular queasiness that comes from being warned by the proprietor of a hotel to avoid the public spaces in that same hotel, but the room, as far as seven-dollar-a-night rooms go, isn't half bad. The full moon shoots light through acrylic curtains, bathing the walls in a red glow that suggests a dark, almost Victorian velvet. There's a television, though it's bolted to the wall and covered in wire mesh, and in the corner is a broken wooden chair. It could be worse. I've stayed in worse, but I jam a chair under the door handle anyway and lie down on the bed without taking off my clothes.

Over the past few weeks, I have skirted down the fertile rump of Morocco into arid Western Sahara, rarely staying in a town more than a day or two and often catching taxis south before knowing my destination. I've eaten sheep brain sandwiches and hitched rides with soldiers and stayed in hotels almost as bad as this one. In order to cover half a continent in less than six months, I have moved quickly and cheaply. Now I've reached the edge of the world, or at least the edge of the Sahara, and it feels a little as though I'm paying a price for my hubris and an old, temporary exuberance.

At three a.m. the bordellos close for the night, and the street outside my window fills with fishermen from all over the world who have come to work the fertile waters off the western coast of Africa. Under flickering streetlamps, a group of Russian sailors tighten their brown leather belts and pass a bottle of vodka. Across the street, Chinese fishermen in thin beige Mao suits smoke clove cigarettes, while two Moroccan soldiers start a swordfight with pool cues.

My floor becomes noisy with drunk fishermen looking for their rooms. Someone retches and someone else tries my door handle. Men cluster around the pay phone down the hall, calling home with prepaid phone cards in fifteen-minute increments. They shout and laugh in Mandarin and Russian over thousands of miles of broken phone lines. I lie in my little bed looking at the ceiling and count the hours to sunrise in conversations that I don't understand.

At daybreak I say good-bye to Salima, who gives me a knowing smile and a slight pat on the shoulder. A small and rare moment of female solidarity. Then I make the long walk back to the center of Dakhla. At a café by the ocean, I order espresso and bread and try to defend myself against the frantic sunlight bouncing between the water and the desert. Through squinted eyes, I watch children walk to school in green-and-white uniforms and the sea throw up spray onto the boardwalk. I close my eyes, drink my coffee, and when no one is looking, rub butter on the dry skin around my nostrils.

For a moment I succumb to fatigue and allow myself to think about home. Thousands of miles north, in a warm and quiet Parisian apartment, my husband is sleeping under a down duvet with a pillow over his head. In an hour he'll wake up, pick out a dark suit, and shave while listening to Europe1 radio. Then he'll spend twenty minutes looking for his keys and leave in a rush. If I caught a flight now, I could sleep tonight with his hand on my hip.

Instead, I ask the waiter about transport south to Mauritania. He tells me that bush taxis leave from the outskirts of Dakhla, but warns me that the road is rough—no hotels, no gas stations, no cell phone reception, no natural sources of water. Sometimes the track is so thick with sand that the old Peugeots drive on the beach by the Atlantic instead—a beach, he warns, that is mined. He adds that his cousin is bringing fishermen across the border in two days, and I could join them for a reasonable fee.

I think about all the women who have made similar trips in the Middle East and Africa. Mary Kingsley, who walked through Gabon's jungle in the 1890s in black wool skirts, surviving hippo attacks and surging rapids. Alexandrine Tinné, who rode a camel across Libya in 1869 in a gallant, if foolish attempt to be the first European woman to cross the Sahara. Gertrude Bell, who counseled kings and prime ministers on the creation of Jordan and Iraq and climbed daunting Swiss mountains in her spare time. I see a photo of my mother, resplendent in mid-'80s Banana Republic safari gear, grinning up at the big green sign that marks the equator's passage through Kenya. None of these women would have turned back.

Then again, none of these women traveled absolutely alone as I do. I heave a great sigh and consider what lies ahead for me. Spotty transport, cheap hotel rooms, bad food, worse water. Searing heat during the day, freezing temperatures at night. A thousand more miles before I reach Dakar, Senegal, where the only person I know in West Africa lives. Every night I'll arrange new lodging, every day new transport south. Every evening I'll eat alone; every night I'll jam a chair under my door handle. Throughout it all, this relentless light will follow me, haunt me, and hound me into dark cafés and shadowy bus stations where no respectable woman should go.

I smile and shudder and try to suppress the gnawing realization that I have pushed myself too hard in the past couple of weeks, am too dazed and tired and lost, metaphorically and perhaps even literally, to keep going. I should return to France, where life is sad and gray but solid and predictable. I should go home to my very good husband and our quiet, ordered house; I should start up as a reporter again. I should have babies.

But even in my shattered, scattered fatigue, the idea of going home brings on a wave of despair so intense I feel momentarily nauseated. I turn my face up to the brilliance rising off the ocean. It blinds me behind my eyelids and the world turns to white light, crashing waves, and the cry of children. Their laughter tugs at my heart a little, but it's the sun that makes my eyes water. Tears mixed with rancid butter fall down my cheeks and disappear into the wool of my sweater. I beckon the waiter.

"Tell me your cousin's name."

2

Connecticut Childhood

MANY YEARS EARLIER, a handsome Swedish woman put on the *Out of Africa* soundtrack, poured herself a glass of Chablis, and implored her daughter to admire the sloping lawn of their Connecticut home as though it were the Serengeti itself.

"Nina, Nina," she said with long *a*'s that hinted at a singing Scandinavian cadence but were flattened by a smattering of English education. "Nina, you must come and see how beautiful the garden is."

I was thirteen, maybe fourteen. Young for my age, but old enough to sense that there was something inherently questionable about the *Out of Africa* soundtrack. Between the children's singing and the deceptively simple flute harmonies lay the theory that the gorgeous luxury of colonial occupation represented some sort of cultural apex. Denys's plane soared above the herds of antelope and the movie implied that beauty, no matter how it was come by, could imbue life with meaning and joy, even if it was at the expense of Africans. Even in my cosseted childhood I suspected that dangers arose there.

Nonetheless, Mother played it every evening, without irony, and she was aggressive about getting people to like it. My friends would come to the house, trolling for ice cream or Duran Duran records, and she herded them toward the back terrace where the stereo worked at full force and the garden lay in all its glory. *Do you like the new rhododendron tree? Isn't the light lovely? Have you heard this music? Have you seen the livestock?*

Livestock was a word she used often and liberally. In homage to Isak Dinesen she had fashioned our suburban house as a kind of farm, buying chickens and putting them in a coop-like enclosure by the big willow tree. When all but one of the chickens were eaten by a weasel and the brave survivor was bitten in the head by the neighbor's dog—giving it what appeared to be a very painful type of brain damage—my mother called on my father to "put it out of its misery." Donning his dentist's smock and carrying a fireman's axe, he set off that morning to do his duty, mumbling under his breath, "This isn't what I had in mind when your mother told me she wanted to move to the country." Still, he got the job done, good man that he was, and two weeks later, my mother got more chickens.

"Nina," she said again when I didn't respond. "Isn't it wonderful? Do you see how lucky you are to have a garden like this?"

I sighed. I knew this land so well. I had weeded, mowed, and raked it through every season. This garden felt like a prison and the midsummer haze that hung over it a kind of sticky glue that slowed both body and mind. Even in my adolescent grump, I had to admit, however, that it was lovely. The sun setting behind the tall oak trees in the back cast soft yellow light onto a runway of Kentucky bluegrass. The edges of the pachysandra plots were precisely cut, and the new lovers' bench by the greenhouse glowed with fresh white paint. Martha Stewart, then just a caterer down the road known for her good (but not outstanding) mushroom cap hors d'oeuvres, would have been proud of this garden and could have called it her own.

"It's a good garden, Mom," I said, hopefully with enough resignation to convey victimhood.

"You should help me tomorrow then," she said brightly. "There is weeding to do."

"No."

"You need the pocket money," she said firmly. "You need to get dirt on your hands."

My mother grew up in Stockholm and, as far as I could tell, spent her childhood playing marbles in poodle skirts and watching Doris Day movies. Her obsession with "working the land" was something she had picked up in the States. Like many immigrants, she seemed to choose her American traditions randomly. Working the land she endorsed, but eating Doritos, watching TV, or my getting a new car when I turned sixteen were out-of-the-question American indulgences.

"I'll never have a garden. All you do is work on the garden. It's mindless," I said, peevish.

"Oh, Nina," she said. "You don't mean that."

Then she looked stricken, setting her hands on her hips in a gesture of tough but beaten resignation. She was brilliant at playing all the cards in her deck—guilt, persuasion, fear, and plain old coercion. I released another stifled yet still pointed sigh, but it was useless. I would end up spending Saturday sitting in a field of weeds with Cecil, the gardener from Jamaica, who wore a wool hat even in August and seemed, even to my naive eye, unnervingly content to arrange flowers all day long.

I didn't understand for many years why it was so important to her that I work in the garden. In the full flush of teenage rebellion I thought it was driven by her desire to control me. Then I thought it was a last-ditch effort to teach me the values of industry. Later still, I thought it was some mangled attempt to spend time together. I was well into my twenties and far from home before it occurred to me that she was trying to teach me to be happy with the world I would most likely inhabit. The world of safe and predictable suburban conformity.

My mother, however, was poorly suited to this job, as she was herself profoundly ill at ease in Connecticut. Most aspects of wealthy suburban life clearly irritated her. She had no patience for tennis games and country clubs and charity events. Wives as a general class of people bored her. She detested small talk, calling it a "fake American invention," and had the uncomfortable habit of speaking her mind in any and all situations. That's not to say she didn't have friends. I'd often come home to my mother sitting at the kitchen table with a cup of coffee, talking to another woman, usually in Swedish, with a kind of coiled intensity. Three hours later, I'd come back to the kitchen and they would still be there, hunched over their coffees, like characters in a Bergman movie. Very often they discussed politics or social issues, but usually they reverted to what I came to think of as Swedish talk—the profound and relentless exploration of their own interior lives. Here, in short, bitter sentences nearly devoid of adjectives, they would put everything on the table—disappointment with America, alienation from their children, fear of getting old. Needless to say, this sort of intensity didn't work well among the breezy, noncommittal women of New Canaan.

To say she simply detested being a housewife was an oversimplification, however. She clearly took some satisfaction from these relationships, as she did from working in her garden, but very often the monotony and falseness of others around her would weigh until she looked nearly broken with the effort of living. Always something of an insomniac, she would become nearly sleepless, prowling the house late at night, picking early-morning fights with my father, then watching old movies in the afternoon, curled up in an exhausted clump on her prized English sofa.

My father went about his business, as he always did, pulling steady twelve-hour days at his dental practice and avoiding his restless wife by spending evenings at the gym. I was away, floating through a succession of boarding schools, inspiring no one with my academic performance and tendency to get caught smoking cigarettes behind the library. Finally, something would break in her. Fed up with New Canaan, fed up with the monotony, she would leave.

Her leaving was both more grand and less serious than it sounded. She didn't leave permanently; she just took trips, long sojourns around Africa, the Middle East, and South America. First it was Egypt, then Kenya and Tanzania. Later Jordan and Israel and the territories. Then Argentina, Chile, and Uruguay. Sometimes she traveled with my godmother, Ensaf, but often she took organized tours and cruises. This was, to put it mildly, unusual. New England housewives in the 1980s didn't travel alone. They rarely spent a night away from their husbands.

My father, who seemed to like being alone as much if not more than being married, never protested. When she got home the tenor of the whole house lifted. Tanned and confident, she laughed more easily and was easier to be around. We would sit around the kitchen table, my mother and father gazing at each other with a sparkle in their eyes, and look at the pictures. There was my mother standing by the Ngorongoro Crater in a safari suit with hundreds of tiny white clouds drifting behind her in the evening sky. There she was outside the Al-Azhar mosque in Cairo looking laughingly at her stocking feet. There she was leaning over the railing of a ship, the wind blowing through her blond hair as she looked out at the foggy, craggy Falklands.

It was like everything in her soul that was big and bold and colorful expanded on these trips. She could be almost poetic in her description, lofty in the aspirations a country or city set for her. "Cairo's a good city," she said. "I could go back, but it's crowded and dense and desperate. It rumbles. Even at night when you go to sleep you can feel it churning beneath you, as though it isn't content."

After a while, when she had traveled enough to know, she came to love Africa best. She made it sound as though the Serengeti and the wide open spaces of the Sahara lay open to God. There it felt like the lid of the world had been pried off and a route to the sublime had been revealed. Lift your face to the sky and the unflinching blue could only reflect the divine. Turn your eyes to the dunes and purify yourself by letting your gaze run a thousand miles without landing on an intrusion. In that golden tub of light and heat, the pain and fear and simple smallness of the world became unraveled. In those deserts and savannas, the life she lived was written in bold, historical strokes.

It was magical and infectious and divine, but it never lasted, in part because she never went away for long enough. Two or three weeks didn't allow for true revelation or thought. In no time at all, the vision, the subtleties of the continent, fell away. A fog of resignation and depression returned to cloud her vibrant self. Soon she was back in the garden, plugging the virtues of suburban life. Home was where the truth lay, not aboard a jeep careening through the Serengeti; I needed to find meaning there. Then the *Out of Africa* soundtrack was back on and the wine bottle was open and she was imagining again that with the right music, a lovely home, and a well-appointed garden you could imagine you were, if not in Africa, at least some other place.

Family opinion holds that when I left Connecticut and vowed never to return again, it was in retaliation to suburban conformity and by extension my mother. I had rebelled against the white picket fence, the pervasive quiet of those heavy New England nights. Most important, I had rebelled against both of my parents' great efforts to encourage me, their only child, to have a family.

This is patently untrue, however. If I were to draw a direct line from my Connecticut childhood to the hotel full of drunk Chinese fisherman in Western Sahara, Mother would be standing there like a slightly inebriated traffic cop directing the way. She encouraged me to go. She laid the path. *Go now,* she whispered to me at night in my dreams. *See the world, see it all, then see it again.* The overriding lesson of my childhood was that travel was the only thing that could ever make a woman happy.

3

First Freedom

SUDDENLY, THE HOUSE is full of gold-leafed papyrus and onyx bookends depicting squat, pudgy pharaohs. Mother is back from a three-week cruise down the Nile and is raving about the epic statues of Abu Simbel and the sultry peace of Aswan. Sensing opportunity, I am holding out a brochure for the American University in Cairo.

"It's only a semester and actually cheaper than Mount Holyoke," I tell her.

She looks at the brochure and spins it across the table to my father. They laugh and he nods appreciatively. I've been lobbying to go to the Middle East for a while now, and my father appreciates persistence.

"You can go. You should go," she says. "This is the sort of thing that one gets out of their bones at an early age. Especially in America."

"You didn't get it out of your system," I say pointedly. I don't want her to think that Egypt is the end of it.

She frowns. "No, but visiting Germany was a big event in my day," she says. "You wouldn't get anything out of your system either if you spent all your summers picking strawberries in *Germany.*"

I have just spent a summer studying French outside Paris—snooty students, arrogant teachers, impossible standards of beauty, and far too much rain. If I hated France I am destined to hate Germany. No, I am done with Europe.

"I don't want to go to Germany," I say evenly.

"Of course not. Never. But your father *is* going to take you over there. Cairo is no joke." Then, as though I didn't get the message, didn't understand the sheer importance of what she is trying to say, she repeats, "Cairo is no joke."

My father takes two weeks off of work and flies me to Egypt. There we discover that my mother has booked a cruise down the Nile in a luxurious boat with the Scotts, my father's friends from dental school. They spend much of the vacation sitting on the deck, watching Egypt float by and talking to my father about housing prices and college tuition rates. I signal my disapproval by sitting alone in my room and hanging back from them in the souk, but no one notices. My trip of independence and exploration has been turned into a family vacation. By the time my dad boards a flight for the States, I vow never to travel with family again.

But family, whether I liked it or not, had been up to that moment my entire life. I wake the next morning in the university dorm room with a knot in my stomach and a fluttering heart. I am all alone, in a strange land and very far from home. For the first time I have really gotten what I want, to be away from the all-watching eyes of my parents, and yet I am crippled by anxiety. It is all so overwhelming, the options so endless. I can ride horses around the pyramids at midnight, using the moonlight as my guide. I can take the overnight train to Aswan in the south or spend the weekend snorkeling and smoking *shisha* in Sinai. Every day I face the prospect that something will happen to me that has never, ever happened to me before, and might never happen again.

This bounty has the effect of turning me into a nervous wreck. I am either timidly reading in a corner of the common room or trying to make friends with such ebullience I frighten away both the Egyptians and the Americans. I become a deeply strange presence on campus.

Nevertheless, I come to love Cairo in a way that I have never before loved a place. I credit the city with bestowing on me the only small moments of happiness I find in those months. Especially in the morning, the purity and lightness of the desert makes the minor sufferings worthwhile.

I rise at dawn, woken by the sound of sheep braying outside my window, and slip down the stairs, past the sleeping security guard and out onto the tall steps that lead onto our leafy street. It is cold, always surprisingly so, and I wrap my only sweater tighter around myself and consider whether I should finally buy that pair of wool socks. Then I set off.

At midday, Cairo is a chaotic nest of animals, racing cars, food carts, beggars, impromptu construction sites, and elevated four-lane highways. It's a crumbling, exhausted megacity fighting to survive the desert. In the morning, however, it's still a village. The mist off the Nile mixes with smoke from cooking fires and sand to make a gentle fog. Wrapped in long woolen scarves, people eat plates of oily beans and chat quietly. The flower vendor unpacks his flowers. The man who makes *kushari* from a cart sorts the chickpeas, rice, and lentils. Old men sweep the steps of the graceful colonial buildings and throw sudsy laundry water into the street. And enough people catch my eye and nod hello that I can practice my Arabic and wish them a morning of flowers, hearing in return that they wish me a morning of light.

There is magic and alchemy in that walk. The perceptions

move slowly inside me, mixing with loneliness, alienation, and sheer nineteen-year-old naiveté, to become a kind of alertness. I feel, though I have been stripped of many comforts, that Cairo is bending toward me just enough to make me feel whole and light and strong. I have managed to find peace despite my alienation, despite my great social failure at school, and I take pride in that. It is all so simple, just a walk through a city that is beginning to waken, but it teaches me that some of the real delight in life lies ahead of me, in unexpected places and things.

Once I reach the end of Zamalek, I cross the Nile toward the center of town. The transport boats are running at that hour but the tourist feluccas haven't opened yet. The sun is just beginning to pierce the haze, promising another warm winter day. I head for a café near the university where my friend Paul, a fellow student, is smoking a cigarette and drinking coffee. I like Paul so much that it is okay he is my only friend in Cairo. He offers me a cigarette and asks me whether I want to play backgammon. I nod and light a cigarette and order coffee. When I inhale, the smoke rushes to the tips of my fingers and right down my neck. For a moment my whole self tingles.

That feeling—bravery, solitude, the tug of longing for home—becomes the defining moment of my adulthood, haunting me for years to come, driving me to challenge myself in the same ways. It becomes the feeling I seek over and over again later in my life when I escape the US to live in Pakistan as a researcher and the West Bank as a reporter. The bitter sweetness of travel fills me up and makes me feel whole. It becomes the only antidote to the intensity of my small family and the powerless sorrow that is woven into suburban life and woven into me.

Travel becomes the thing that defines me. I am no one's wife. No one's mother. Barely a daughter. I am alone in the world and content in my solitude. With tremendous relief—the relief of someone who doesn't really thrive on unpredictability—I realize how I will live. I will become a reporter and spend my life traveling the world, writing about people who don't have their stories told. For as long as I can, I will sculpt my life so that it feels as though I am walking through the streets of Cairo, and that the world is a strange and wondrous place.

Oak Tree

THEN I FELL IN LOVE.

"What brings you here?" he asks. He has serious brown eyes and is very tall, bending toward me in a way I interpret as patronizing. I straighten my back, slide my feet farther down into my red clogs so they at least feel more like real shoes.

"I'm a reporter."

"A journalist?" he says, surprised. "To cover the speech?"

I hesitate. "Sure."

Strictly speaking this isn't true. I came to the speech of French politician François Bayrou because I am just out of graduate school, broke, and under the impression that there will be free food at the soiree. Yet I have reported before and I plan to go back soon. It is a lie but a small one.

"And you work here in Boston?" he asks, again bending toward me a little.

"I used to freelance, the West Bank, a little in Azerbaijan, but that's only emotionally sustainable for so long." I say this with a knowing tone, hoping he'll laugh. He doesn't.

"Now I'm done with school and just trying to decide where to go . . . I was thinking Indonesia, maybe Afghanistan, but I want to get some experience at a local paper first, so I'll hang around Boston a few months."

He smiles slightly and furrows his brow. He is impossible to read but keeps looking at me with those intense eyes. I drink more wine.

"I look forward to reading your articles," he says eventually, letting his eyes linger a moment on the clogs. "I'm sure they will be very, very good."

I'm about to say something caustic to this, something so self-deprecating that it wanders into the territory of self-loathing, but when I look up his eyes are crinkled at the edges, deep and warm. He smells like coffee and cigarettes and the faintest whiff of red wine. Suddenly standing next to him feels like lying down under a big oak tree in a forest—all is muffled by fallen leaves and fresh moss. All is safe.

Then he bows a little and lightly touches my shoulder.

"We should have a drink sometime," he says.

Three days later he sends me an email and invites me to dinner. He arrives at my door in a silver Buick LeSabre with a red interior that he has rented just for the occasion. We sit outside in the cool and salty Boston summer and talk about politics and newspapers and the introduction of the euro. He shows a deep intelligence that is free of arrogance or conceit. He laughs easily at my jokes. At the end of the evening, he pulls the Buick up to my front door and offers a curt nod. I stand uncertainly at the door, key in hand, realizing, with only the vaguest cognition, that I am being courted.

"Next weekend?" he asks, leaning over to the passenger car window.

"Sure," I say.

Four years later, we marry.

Bread Crumbs in Paris

SAVE A FEW SHORT, unhappy trips to France as a child, I had never before lived in continental Europe. I suppose when I moved to Paris to be with Florent I thought it would be like New York or London—busy, work-oriented, diverse. If it was a slower sort of place—I heard people enjoyed three-hour lunches and a thirty-five-hour workweek—I could approach it as I did Cairo. I would observe and appreciate, savoring the small wonders of a city known for its beauty and savoir faire. In either case, I would find a niche for myself; I was good at moving abroad.

It quickly became apparent, however, that Paris and I didn't get along. I found the city a deeply conformist place, with inhabitants who were very adult and practiced in the art of living but emotionally distant from their own lives. Children did not run in the streets. Fathers did not run out for milk in their sweatpants. No one snacked between meals. Judgment, designed to bring people into line with the accepted practice, was a kind of national tic. The baker squinted his eyes at a patron's unkempt hair. A neighbor would audibly gasp at the sight of a woman wearing clogs. If a hostess failed to produce an appetizer, guests whispered in alarm—*C'est bizarre! C'est bizarre!*

Perhaps centuries of war and invasion have wearied Parisians of change. Perhaps they truly feel they have found the key to life. In either case, there was no room for sudden shifts in temperature. No room for individuality or difference. All was smoothed and even and predictable, gray and cold just like the weather. It couldn't have been more different from the warm collegiality of the Cairo streets—the unassuming eye contact; the spirited morning hellos; the chaos of yelling, joyful children.

Yet I had chosen to live here and I loved my husband very much, so I did try to be a good wife. In some ways I still heard my mother's voice in the back of my head telling me to roll up my sleeves and get dirt on my hands. Get into the culture, I thought. Learn how to be French. Thus I acquainted myself with the seasons of the cheeses, buying pungent Mont d'or in the winter and sweet chèvres in the summer. I studied French every afternoon and night and took my first stab at cooking, making boeuf bourguignon in honor of Florent's native province of Burgundy. After a few months, I found a job as a reporter at Dow Jones in Paris, covering French financial news. I tried to find friends.

But the same walls, the same incompatibilities, kept smacking me in the face. There was a reason I never learned to cook before the age of thirty-two. My wandering mind let every one of those glorious stews burn on the stove. There was a reason I didn't own anything, had never accumulated anything in my life but some khakis from the Gap and a wooden desk. I had lived in concrete houses with cockroaches the size of rats and no hot water. I had a great tolerance for ugliness. Things, at least the acquisition of things, had never occurred to me. Paris was undoubtedly beautiful, but that sort of stiff, formal beauty was lost on me.

For a while I hoped the job would save me, but being a financial reporter was difficult. I had started out my reporting career writing personal stories about Palestinians under occupation or Azeri refugees. Now I lived in a world where a hot story consisted of Société Générale's third-quarter revenues. My performance wasn't just judged on the minutes it took to release a story, but the *seconds*. Life became a series of professional failures as I translated press releases incorrectly and missed big stories. Some days I was so rattled by work I wouldn't go home until very late, preferring instead to sit in the café around the corner from my apartment.

Friends would have helped, but that also seemed an impossible task. French women breezed in and out of each other's lives, a *bisou* here, a drink at a dinner party there, but didn't seem to value female connection. They focused on their children and husbands. In hindsight I probably wasn't the best company, but at the time I couldn't see that. *They are annoying and retrograde*, I thought. *It's like living in the fifties.* With a bitter smile of recognition, I thought of my mother's habit of sitting at the kitchen table with a Swedish friend for hours on end. No wonder she longed for the strong, honest friendships of her countrywomen. No wonder she occasionally lost her patience, picked up her skirts, and headed off to Patagonia. It was terrible to live in a different culture and feel constantly judged, never up to standards.

Under any other circumstances I would have just left and made another life for myself, but now I was married. This fact alone made me meet the morning with dread. I had made a promise and I was trapped.

So, inevitably I suppose, my husband and I fought. Many young couples argue, but our fights were tinged with a kind of weariness I associated with long and burnt-out marriages. *You don't care about my life, my career,* I heard myself saying. *You don't care about helping me to adjust to this place.*

It was a culture shock unlike any I had ever experienced, and it was made worse by the fact that I strongly felt I needed to integrate into French life. I needed to make my life here a success and to be a good wife. It all needed to be so wonderful and the love between us so strong that I could forget the life I had left behind. Plus, there wasn't a moment to lose. Florent counseled me to slow down, to enjoy the city a bit, to stop spending my evenings pouring over French vocabulary, but I wouldn't listen.

One Saturday afternoon I found myself in the supermarket holding a little black dictionary and a wicker basket. Bread crumbs, bread crumbs, bread crumbs, I thought. Why was there no word for bread crumbs? I found a woman, midforties, walking through the aisle with a clipboard. I would ask and explain. She would help me.

"I need bread," I said in French. "That is dried. Which you cook with."

She looked at me blankly.

"You know the tiny small morsels of bread that you put on the meat to make it take the butter?"

Her eyes grew wide. Alarmed.

"Small morsels of bread. Very small. Like pebbles on the beach. Smaller, smaller."

"Non, non," she declared, hand up. *"On n'a pas cela. Ce n'est pas possible."*

"Do you not make bread crumbs?" I shouted. "Does everyone make their own? Is that even possible?"

She backed away, horrified. I started to cry, holding the little wicker basket for dear life. In a land without bread crumbs, how could happiness ever be achieved?

So many times I had lived abroad. Not just Cairo and Lahore, but Baku and London. I had always adjusted, made friends, and gotten by. Paris seemed insurmountable. I could only think it was because I was married. That I was married to someone I still loved made it somehow worse. I couldn't leave him, and I couldn't bear the notion of staying. The heaviness and inescapability of the life I had constructed for myself weighed on me. Every morning I woke with dread. My freedom was gone forever, and I had given it away.

6

A Victorian Traveler

When victorian women broke with convention to travel to Africa or the Middle East they often cloaked desire for adventure in dutiful purpose. Gertrude Bell, who went on to counsel Churchill on the postwar composition of the Middle East, originally went to Persia to care for her uncle. Mary Gaunt began to travel to make money as a writer after her husband suddenly died. One of my favorite travelers, Mary Kingsley, went to West Africa to gather specimens of fish and fetish, often in the form of small wooden statues revered by animists. Her father had been a gatherer of African wildlife, and Kingsley, wanting to continue the esteemed tradition, followed in his footsteps after his death. In her exuberant, self-effacing book *Travels in West Africa* she writes:

> It was in 1893 that, for the first time in my life, I found myself in possession of five or six months which were not heavily forestalled, and feeling like a boy with a new half-crown, I lay about in my mind, as Mr. Bunyan would say, as to what to do with them. "Go and learn your tropics," said Science.

She was thirty years old at the time and had lived a strange, secluded life. In a house outside London, where the shutters were permanently drawn and no light or air allowed inside, she nursed her chronically ill mother. If she left, as she did once for a weekend in Paris, her mother retaliated by veering toward death. Meanwhile, her father spent as little time at home as possible, exploring the South Pacific and the Americas in the name of science and coming home only occasionally to terrorize the household with his bad temper and distaste for English domestic life.

Mary's father was from a fine English family with roots back to the thirteenth century. His relatives had been priests and doctors, writers and explorers. Mary's mother, however, had been the cook, whom Mr. Kingsley had only deigned to marry four days before Mary was born. Mary was a legitimate child, but just barely, and she grew up in a kind of class netherworld, not quite her father's daughter, not quite a servant. She received little formal schooling and spoke with her mother's Cockney accent her whole life. Nevertheless, by the time she reached adulthood she was curiously well educated. Deeply intelligent, a genius even, she fed her intellect on books she pilfered from her father's vast library. There she read Darwin and Spinoza and taught herself geography, math, and Latin. She dreamed of a world that existed outside London, outside her father's indifference and her mother's spasms of depression and illness.

Her long confinement, lack of formal education, and working-class heritage could have relegated her to a miserable spinsterlike existence, but then, in her late twenties, something unexpected happened. In rapid succession, both her parents died. She found herself with a small pot of money but no husband, no children, and no expectations tied to position or class. She took the first steamer she could to the Canary Islands and on to West Africa.

To some she said she went as a lark and to others she said to pursue science, but of course when you read her *Travels in West Africa,* as I did my first year in France for no reason at all other than an abiding interest in Africa and Islam and women and travel, science doesn't play much of a role. There are exciting hippo attacks on the Ogooué River (present-day Gabon) and terrifying boat rides over rapids and even a humorous incident when she falls in a hole lined with spears and is saved by her voluminous black silk skirts, but little mention of her scientific purpose. When she wakes up in the middle of the night to find that her guide, Kiva, has been tied up by creditors and faces certain horrible death, she writes:

> I dare say I ought to have rushed at him and cut his bonds, and killed people in a general way with a revolver, and then flown with my band to the bush; only my band evidently had no flying in them, being tucked up in the hut pretending to be asleep, and uninterested in the affair; and although I could have abandoned the band without a pang just then, I could not so lightheartedly fly alone with Kiva to the bush and leave my fishes. . . .

There are the fish, flopping around at the end of the paragraph, so to speak, distracting her from her real purpose, which appears to be killing people in a general way with a revolver. That's what she was like. Swashbuckler first, scientist second. She was an adventurer, pure and simple, who also liked to be alone or in the company of strangers. She was compelled by a sometimes unreasonable desire to see things that few had ever seen. And she was determined to do it on her own terms, eschewing the companionship of Europeans en route and at least trying to stay away from the missionary men who might be considered benefactors.

Of course Kingsley and almost all the other women who

traveled at that time were spinsters or widows. Married women did not leave their husbands, and they certainly didn't do it to spend months on end in the white man's grave that was West Africa.

Thankfully, in the hundred or so years that had passed since Kingsley did her travels, life for women had changed. We could travel now wherever we wished, married or not. Supposedly we could have it all.

Except . . . the dynamic seemed surprisingly consistent. Having it all seemed to consist of holding down a job at Dow Jones, making sure the house was stocked with food, and preparing myself for the inevitable and slightly dreadful prospect of children. Duty came first, joy second. Unless I traveled for work, which I hardly ever did, I was expected to stay by my husband's side and earn my keep. I actually had far less freedom than did my mother, who still retained an aura of the Victorian lady with her cruises down the Nile and Abercrombie & Kent tours. She traveled for pleasure, while I was a working girl who needed to explain my moves in professional terms.

Societal pressure in large part kept me in Paris, but that first year as my marriage tottered and my decisions seemed fogged by indecision and apathy, I began to care less and less what people thought. I was unhappy and my career as a financial reporter meant very little to me. I wanted to travel one last time, both to be alone and to get closer to the original reason I had entered journalism in the first place; to write about Islam and politics. Perhaps in Africa I could again be in the company of women whose laughter and warmth I missed so much in France. If, in the course of this trip, I could figure out a way to bend my loner personality to the strictures of marriage, all the better.

. . .

Then magically one night my husband seemed to reach the same conclusion. I couldn't help but feel it was my fourth attempt at Julia Child's boeuf bourguignon that triggered it. I had called him at work and made him come home at seven thirty to taste my magnificent creation, but I drank while I worked and half watched television at the same time and lost track of where I was in the recipe. The result was not good.

"It's incredible," I said, tasting the stew. "It tastes almost alkaline."

Florent put down his fork, imperceptibly pushed the plate away, and reached for the wine. "No, no. It's not so bad. The meat is tender. Did you forget salt?" Then he frowned a little at the edges and looked at me with that patronizing air I once found so comforting and now just sort of resented. "I don't understand why you are cooking all the time. There have to be better ways for you to spend your time."

Florent loved food, and this remark made me feel guilty, but before I could say anything he went on.

"I'm just saying that if I had wanted a French wife I would have married a French wife," he said flatly.

"This is because the boeuf bourguignon is bad."

"No. It's just . . . what are you doing?" he asked, folding his fingers together so it felt like more of a declaration.

"I don't know. I'm being wifey, I guess."

"You should stop. I married such an unexpected woman. A woman in red clogs at a formal dinner who was on her way to Afghanistan or Indonesia or wherever . . ." The memory of our first conversation made him laugh a little and he leaned back in his chair. "Where is she? Where is my explorer?"

It seemed a rhetorical question, so I let it hang in the air as he got up from the table to go outside and smoke a cigarette. I watched him in his solitude under the Parisian drizzle and thought of his life with me gone—standing up in the kitchen eating cheese sandwiches late at night, watching soccer in his underwear, drinking wine and smoking cigarettes on our small balcony. He loved to be alone, my man. It was what drew me to him so many years ago. In this love of solitude, we were kindred spirits. Now he wanted me to go. Something in him had changed. He was beginning to harden toward me. I had become his wife but not a partner, nor a friend, and in that lay a kernel of disappointment.

7

Nowhere

SOMETIMES WHEN I CAN'T sleep at night I hum a little of the *Out of Africa* soundtrack to soothe myself. I can't help it. It's wired into me, like a three-note lullaby.

Naturally, when I considered traveling, I thought about Kenya first. I could spend a couple of months in Nairobi, then a few more near Lake Victoria, perhaps on a farm. This would be a beautiful introduction to sub-Saharan Africa—the Serengeti at dawn, cheetahs drinking from a water hole, white linen dresses, safari hats, copious amounts of gin . . .

"Sounds like a vacation," said Florent.

"Oh no. It's not a vacation," I said. "It's more like an expedition."

"Then maybe save the gin and tonics for another time."

Point taken, I considered the other end of the comfort spectrum—Mary Kingsley's route, down the Ogooué River. This trip would be incredibly difficult. I would have to paddle the river in a canoe, braving rapids and crocodiles and suspicious locals.

It wasn't the hardship that threw me so much as the notion of spending two, maybe three months in the tropics. The jungle, for all its beauties, was dark and constricting. Kingsley talks of intense heat, humidity, and inhuman mosquitoes. She is constantly hacking at foliage with a machete in order to get above the growth to see something, anything. This felt disturbingly like living under the Parisian cloud cover in January.

Kingsley did talk about doing an expedition up the Niger River, but abandoned the plan without a real explanation. I had never been to that part of West Africa, but it appealed to me. The Niger is farther north than the Ogooué and much of it runs through the Sahara desert. Here lay hot sun, endless space, caramel-colored sand dunes. I had seen desert like this in Western Egypt. It had been terrifying in its brutal emptiness, yet breathtakingly beautiful.

I took out a map of West Africa, huge and crinkly, impractical, as big as my bed. These were the maps overland travelers in Land Rovers used to cross from Morocco and Mali in their jeeps. At the center lay a brown-eyed Sahara, as big as the continental United States but barely touched by towns or cities, much less roads. Here and there lay a slight fringe of green, an oasis perhaps, offering hope. The national boundaries of countries that crossed the heart of the desert — Mali, Mauritania, Algeria — were more often than not completely straight, implying a random colonial allocation of land. On the Sahara's southern belly lay the Niger River. I scanned the map looking for someplace, any place that I knew. Taoudenni, Siwa, Tamanrasset. It was all so foreign, so far away. My heart fell a little. I couldn't go someplace where I didn't recognize a thing.

Then I saw it. Tiny, improbable, hovering just above the Niger River on a lick of land between the desert and the Sahel. A place I recognized but didn't know at all, and my father's voice calling to me from childhood.

· · ·

"All the way to Timbuktu I had to go to get your milk," he proclaims, depositing the carton on the kitchen counter with a definitive clunk and shaking the snow off his coat.

It's December and a school night and I am already in my pajamas. I want hot milk with honey before I go to sleep because I have a sore throat. Mother is upstairs reading in bed. She calls down from the bedroom.

"You all right, Steve, was it bad out there?"

"Fine, fine," he calls back. "They salted so it was all right, but I had to go to Vista,"

"Vista!" she exclaims. "Good God. Well, you're home now. Nina, milk and then to bed."

"All right," I call, exaggerating my froggy voice to elicit sympathy.

"The A&P in New Canaan was closed," he says to me, having lost his audience upstairs. "So I went to Vista. But it was fine." Vista is over the state line in New York, a world away.

"You said Timbuktu," I say. I'm at that age where I demand firm answers to all my questions no matter how inane. *Timbuktu* is a word I haven't heard before, but it sounds so good. Tim-buk-tu. I flick the nice hard consonants off my teeth.

He drums his fingers absently on the table, trying to remember where the small saucepan is. The snow is very heavy outside now, falling on the apple trees and hiding them. It distracts him for a moment.

"Timbuktu," I insist.

He looks at me quizzically, as though he has no idea what I am talking about.

"That's just an expression," he says finally, remembering.

"Well, what does it mean?"

"It's in Africa, Africa," he says finally finding the saucepan and pouring in the milk. "Far away. In the Sahara. It's the farthest away you can go."

He turns on the stove and I consider this. I know where Africa is, vaguely, but I have never been there.

"Have you ever been there?"

"No, no, see, it's very far away. You can't go there. I'm not sure it's even a real place anymore . . ." His voice trails off and I can tell he's reached the end of his expertise. "It's like the moon. It's nowhere . . . a nowhere place, at the end of the earth."

"Is it near Tipperary?" I ask. It sounds like Tipperary. My father and I have songs we like to sing in the car. One of them is *It's a long way to Tipperary, it's a long way to go. It's a long way to Tipperary, to the sweetest girl I know.* We like to sing it over and over again until my mother puts her head against the passenger-side window and closes her eyes.

He laughs. "Tipperary? No, that's in Ireland. Or is it Ireland? I don't know. Good question. But those are two very different places." He pours the milk into a glass, then adds a tall steel spoon to absorb the heat and a big dollop of honey.

"Drink your milk now," he says firmly. "And to bed. I don't want you missing school tomorrow because of this throat thing."

I dutifully drink my milk. He comes up to my room with me and tucks me in, kissing my brow and making sure that all the windows in my room are firmly shut. When he turns off the light, he stands in the doorway.

"Goodnight, Ninutchka."

"Goodnight, Daddy."

I remember blue winter light filling my room. The moon drifting upward of the tall dark fir trees and its light bouncing off the snow and casting shadows. Slowly it took its place high in the sky, the valleys and mountains etched upon its surface in darker shades of light. It was so far away and so beautiful, so exotic yet accessible. How would I ever get to the moon? How would I ever get to the dream places that people only ever talked about, but never visited? *Timbuktu . . . as far away as the moon.*

Now it was on my map, the only place I had ever really heard of in the Sahara, a place at once unknown and so familiar. In that moment something crystallized for me. I had lost the dream of Timbuktu and I wanted it back.

The furious, intractable contradictions of my life rushed at me. I was a wife who wanted to be alone. An American stuck in Paris. A romantic who ground out copy on the revenue growth of French telecom companies. A free spirit jammed into French bourgeois life. Every day I woke up and lived a life that did not suit me. Every night I tried to forget the easy joy and peace I felt in places like Cairo and Palestine. I was hollowed out. The sheer discomfort of my marriage and Paris and working at a newswire were causing a long, slow war of attrition against my sense of self. I felt like I didn't really exist. I was so unlike myself, I couldn't believe anyone could see me.

Out there lay deserts and mountains, a harsh and empty terrain that would demand firm decisions, bold character strokes. Would I be a housewife or a warrior? A girl or a woman? A saint or a survivor? Like the Victorian explorers who traveled there for glory—Mungo Park, René Caillié, and Alexander Gordon Laing—men who died excruciating deaths at the hands of their guides, who never reached their goals or were never taken seriously, the thrill lay in both the journey itself and the hardship of it. I could test myself out there. I could be changed. I could come home a tougher, kinder, and more patient woman.

Along the way I would get my dreams back—all the fragmented images acquired during a life of seeking out stories of the African continent. Babies tied to the backs of their mothers; green and gold cloth; slowness and smiles; red earth; village fires; market women; and clean, silent, endless space. The moon and Timbuktu. This was the Africa that could fill up my soul. I would pour its beauty into me like wet cement until I was made solid. Then I could be seen again. Then I would exist.

I thought of all those trips my mother took when I was a child. Because she never went away for long enough, these trips seemed to fizzle just short of real revelation and experience. She never resolved her conflicted opinion on duty and motherhood and marriage, nor did she challenge these institutions to which she was committed. It felt like every trip she took was like a beginning—exciting, lonely, filled with hope—but stopped too short, before the conflicted, confusing middle, before the satisfaction of an end. Thus she never figured out what she wanted and was never able to demand from my father the kind of life she felt she deserved. In short, she never really got to the place where she could fight for her own happiness.

She paid the price. We paid the price. And I didn't want a marriage like that. I should either be in or out. I should either love my husband enough to stay in Paris or I should ask him to give up his company and move. I should have the strength to craft a life that reflects my own needs and desires. We should be strong enough to make a marriage that isn't like the others we have seen. And for that to happen, at this particular time, I must go.

8

My Fishes

ON HEARING THE NEWS that I will travel alone overland through West Africa, my mother helpfully sends along the State Department's travel advisories which boil down to a series of stern warnings. *The security situation in north, west, central and southern Mauritania remains uncertain. Travel situation north of Niger River extremely dangerous. Travelers advised to avoid Agadez at all costs. Al Qaeda affiliates thought to be working with local Tuareg tribesmen. Situation in Zinder remains fragile.*

Many warnings are based on a long-running war between the central governments of Mali and Niger and nomads called the Tuareg, who move across the Sahara by camel and jeep, indifferent to national borders. Known for their blue head scarves, haughty demeanor, and centuries-long history of raiding desert towns, the Tuareg claim that both governments ignore their poverty and have been slow to fill promises to integrate their young men into the military. Some even want an independent state of their own that would transverse the Sahara from Niger to Burkina Faso.

At the time of my travels in 2007, the situation was exacerbated by Libya's strongman and leader, Muammar Qaddafi, who fancied himself a modern-day desert warrior. He armed the Tuareg just enough to keep the rebellion on a slow simmer and to destabilize the governments of Mali and Niger. He had his hand all over the Sahara, people said, and was the real power broker in towns such as Timbuktu, which relied on his oil money to keep the schools open and the town's central generator running.

It was Qaddafi's support that led to the most serious Tuareg rebellion to date, one that nearly split Mali in two. In the early 1990s several Tuareg leaders deserted from the Malian army, then raided a military post in Kidal, deep in the desert, as well as the cities of Timbuktu and Gao. Without much of a fight the army retreated, and the track to Timbuktu (for there was no road) became so infested with bandits that aid workers couldn't gain access. A cease-fire was called in 1995, but the area remained so lawless that US government officials became worried that al-Qaeda in the Islamic Maghreb, until then working out of Algeria, would move down into northern Mali and use it as a training base. Suddenly it seemed as though the Sahara could be turned into a stateless hosting area for al-Qaeda, akin to Afghanistan and Somalia.

With US army help, Bamako's government did finally retake the region. Aid workers returned, as did some semblance of the Malian army. But the combination of profound poverty, government neglect, Libyan and Algerian interference, and rising Islam continued to keep Timbuktu unusually isolated. I could get there, but it wouldn't be fast and it wouldn't be easy.

Ease, however, was not what I was after. I was after challenge, and in this I again consulted Mary Kingsley. She prided herself on the economy of her travels, taking postal boats and river pirogues when available, and once selling all her clothes along the river to pay her way. In this way she managed to not only preserve the family finances but also to protect herself from thieves who might mistake her for a wealthy target. Then as now, it seemed the best way to travel was as cheaply and modestly as possible, taking public transport whenever possible and relying on the kindness of women to guide and protect me.

I had great faith in the company of Muslim women. Generalizations were impossible, but for the most part I found that Islam's encouragement of modesty and separation of the sexes worked well for foreigners. In my early twenties when I traveled alone in Jordan or Pakistan I usually found a worried bus driver hustling me over to the oldest, most respectable woman and saying something to her along the lines of "She's all alone. Do something," to which the matriarch would nod and take me under her wing. For the rest of the trip I would be at her beck and call—this often entailed holding her bag on my legs while she chatted with her friends—but at least I was protected and safe. No one messed with women like this in the Middle East, thus no one messed with me.

I hope the same thing would happen to me on this trip, and it was with a hint of nostalgia for those tough but kind women that I choose to start the trip in Morocco, an African country also anchored in the Middle East. I would fly into Casablanca, then dip through Western Sahara into Mauritania, then to Senegal and Mali and across to Timbuktu. I would allow Providence to guide me and not rush the trip with timelines and schedules. If I found a place I liked I would stay there for a week or two. If I found a place I didn't I would move on. I had spent so many days and nights working at the wire, stressed about the seconds and minutes it took to put out a story, I didn't want to have those constraints now. I would find a way to tame time.

I spend the next few weeks planning out the trip, reading up on Kingsley, but it is the process of stripping down my life that is a great delight. I stop highlighting my hair and getting pedicures. I put away the wine and cigarettes. I close the French books. I quit my job at Dow Jones. I give up on trying to please

Florent (yes, in my own way I had been trying to please Florent) and cooking elaborate Burgundian dishes. I stop trying to be a wife.

One evening, I lay out three long-sleeved shirts, two pairs of khaki pants, two pairs of underwear, two bras, sunscreen, and a wool turtleneck on my bed. I look at the clothes with tremendous relief. This is what I will take with me. This and four books and a small black backpack.

Mary Kingsley looks up at me from my bed. On the front cover of her book she is wearing a black silk dress that buttons up to her chin, long sleeves and puffed shoulders. Around the top of her prim face is a strict black bonnet with small flowers at the temples. She wore this outfit every day she traveled in Africa. She wore it when she walked through leech-infested marshes and streams, when she walked twenty-five miles a day through the jungle in 110-degree weather. Kingsley had a strict sense of propriety and dressed like a spinster in mourning for her entire adult life. But under her bonnet, her face is pretty and her expression is full of suppressed life. She looks like she is about to burst out laughing or make some scathing remark. I wonder, if she were here sitting next to me in this graceful Paris apartment, if she would tell me I should stay home with my husband or go out and find my fishes.

Part II

WESTERN SAHARA

———

9

Coffee in Casablanca

THE BIG BLACK MOOR who runs things at the Mauritanian consulate in Casablanca clearly hasn't issued a tourist visa in a while and is thrilled to accommodate.

"So, you! You, you, you," he says in a booming voice. "You're going to Mauritania! This is exciting. How are you going?" He shuffles papers on his brown desk and waves away an assistant bearing a tray of coffee cups. When he finds my application he slaps the desk and reads it at a distance like a man in need of glasses.

"I see here you are going by way of Western Sahara. How exciting. Just write down your vehicle number here and I can give you the visa today."

He slides the paper across his desk and taps the box where I am to write my license plate number. For a moment I consider jotting down random numbers but decide lying probably isn't the best way to start out a six-month trip through Africa.

"Well . . . I don't have my own car."

He deflates ever so slightly before some thought cheers him enough to plug on.

"Ah well, traveling alone . . . what an adventure. This is what you want, right? Adventure? How marvelous!" He pulls out my passport and stamps a one-month visa. As I admire the handsome seal, he scribbles some numbers and letters under VEHICLE REGISTRATION and slips my application into a huge pile of papers. It appears I have an SUV registered in France after all.

"Bon voyage!" He waves happily. "Think fondly of us!"

I wish all the embassies in Morocco were this accommodating. Like Ingrid Bergman in *Casablanca,* I have come to the city by a shabbier ocean in search of transit papers. Niger, Algeria, and Mauritania all require visas, and I was told in Paris by a seasoned Africa traveler that Morocco was the place to get them. Were it only so. Most of the consulates are small and overrun by migrant workers desperate to avoid expulsion from Morocco. The officials are unhelpful, bureaucratic, and suspicious of tourists. The guy at the Algerian consulate actually laughs in my face when I apply for a visa.

"Come back in three days," he says. "If you want."

I've been trying to get a visa to Algeria for two months and even the outside chance of success has kept me in Casablanca. I try to relax into the unexpected delay, telling myself I have all the time in the world, months and weeks if I want to travel this enormous continent. Spontaneity, changes in plans, flexibility are all the point, but in the morning I wake up in a dingy hotel room, unsure what to do and strangely lethargic. Breakfast takes an hour, arranging my small bag perhaps another. I like to read a little in the morning and write if I can to clear my head. That leaves another eight hours of daylight to fill. I wanted to be yanked out of my structured world, but now that I have, I feel useless.

The feeling of uselessness creates panic, which in turn spurs frantic activity. I decide on sites I want to see in the city and hire a guide, Mohammed, whose brown leisure suit nicely matches the brown leather seats in his Mercedes. Though charging the handsome sum of forty dollars a day, Mohammed has decided that talking is well beyond his job description. He flat-out ignores me when I try to discuss the weather, first in hearty French, then tentative Moroccan Arabic. When that fails I launch into classical Arabic—a version of the language that only exists in writing and news broadcasts—which causes him to fairly melt into the driver's seat with embarrassment. Though my Arabic is rusty (I haven't studied since my midtwenties) I'm confident my courteous and innovative phrases will win him over. After all, how many American tourists can say *It is necessary to circumambulate the Ka'ba seven times* in eighth-century Arabic?

Mohammed is unimpressed and stares dully at me in the rearview mirror. After traffic holds us in the city center for thirty unscheduled minutes, he stops in front of a café and waves me out of the car.

"Qahwa," he says, pointing to a gray coffeehouse full of Moroccan men in polyester suits smoking unfiltered cigarettes.

I nod enthusiastically. What a great chance to meet locals, really feel the pulse of the city. As I walk in the front door, Mohammed throws his body in front of mine, panic etched into the lines on his pudgy face.

"No, no, no. You take your coffee there," he says in Arabic, pointing to a swanky cafe a few doors down.

"I," he says, hand to chest, "I take my coffee, here."

I've spent enough time in the Middle East and South Asia to know the drill when it comes to coffeehouses. Nice girls, respectful girls, do not clutter up the male sanctuary. Therefore, he will go to his coffeehouse, occupied by men who occupy themselves all day long with dominos and strong political talk, and I will go to my coffeehouse where French and Moroccan girls sip Italian espresso and bounce in their chairs to club music.

I think with fondness but also embarrassment back to my days as a student at the American University in Cairo, when I often skipped class to spend long afternoons in coffee shops with my friend Paul, playing backgammon and smoking Marlboros. I was nineteen, and honestly believed the Egyptians could sense my deep appreciation for their culture and didn't mind my crashing their cafés. I still remember the way old men in long cotton smock *galabeyas* looked away when I walked in the door. They were embarrassed for me, the same way I'm embarrassed for women who wear translucent shirts with no bras to Christmas parties. Once the codes of decency have been broken, it's very hard to think about anything else.

I know the coffee shop is off-limits, and Mohammed is beginning to make increasingly frantic gestures underscoring this point, but a part of me still resists. In the past fifteen years I have become a reporter, sometimes a good one, and have learned it is better to ask forgiveness than permission. I've crashed private birthday parties, questioned defendants on their way into court, and interviewed CEOs. Once I even broke into an assisted living center in Norwell, Massachusetts, to interview seniors about changes to the zoning codes. Some of my stories have in their own small ways changed the course of events. Now I can't go into a coffee shop?

Mohammed insists and he's not a small man, so I turn on my heel with as much dignity and drama as I can muster and march down to the café for foreigners and rich Moroccans. Satisfied, Mohammed trundles into his hole in the wall, orders a coffee, and starts up a game of dominos that lasts roughly four hours.

I find a corner table, order a four-dollar espresso, and watch the life of the café unfold. The waiters, resplendent in long white aprons and smart black ties, cluck over Moroccan girls in jeans and firm little head scarves pinned under their chins. The *plongeurs,* sweaty from washing dishes in the kitchen, come out to smoke and steal looks at the girls, who ignore them. The alley cats, sensing opportunity, sneak past the *plongeurs* and head for the kitchen, where they are beaten away by a furious French cook who orders everyone back to work. By midmorning the mist that floats in off the cold Atlantic has lifted and the city is bathed in warm winter light. It's not all bad to be tucked into a café in Casablanca with nothing at all to do.

We go on like this for two days, Mohammed and I. He comes to get me in the morning. We drive around, get caught in traffic, get frustrated, and go for coffee. Sometimes he drops me off to see things like the Hassan II Mosque, huge and impressive, but strangely empty of worshippers, or the Habous Quarter, a reproduction of a seventeenth-century souk that sells lamps and tapestries, but Casablanca isn't a city for tourists. It's Morocco's commercial center and striving very hard to be European amid the country's slow-moving Islamic resurgence. Many of the coffee shops I visit have security guards on watch for suicide bombers, and Mohammed trails me in the car when I walk the boardwalk by the Atlantic. Although the city seems to levitate on a permanent bed of sea mist, the tension in the café is palpable, and after a while unbearable.

Still, when the Algerians tell me they will not be issuing me a visa out of Morocco or any other country save my own, I'm a little sad to go. The city has a vague air of melancholy to it, like Coney Island in the off-season, and I feel pleasantly wistful here. Mohammed, who knows the contours of my trip but none of the details, believes I have been in the city far too long and tells me one day there is a good train to Marrakesh. One morning he picks me up at the hotel for the last time and drives me to the central station. Everything is fresh and cool and smells vaguely of salt and palm trees. It's disarming and hopeful, and I think even Mohammed feels its beauty because there, in the neutral territory of a transit station, he relents. He orders us coffee from one of the outdoor stands and we drink it together in the early-morning haze, leaning on the hood of his Mercedes.

10

The Cold Atlantic

For a week i tumble south, leaving behind books as I read them and staying in hotels that cost five or six dollars a night. Bedtime is the sound of the communal toilet flushing and traveling salesmen snoring through plywood walls. Breakfast is egg sandwiches on street corners with the vegetable vendors and thimbles of strong sweet tea. Every morning, I rise with the sun, head for the bus station, and wait for transport south. Sometimes a bush taxi leaves at eight a.m., sometimes one doesn't appear until late afternoon. I become someone who is always in a rush yet always waiting. One day I spend seven hours at a bus station watching two boys sew together burlap grain sacks to make an awning for their roadside restaurant. I drink orange juice. I close my eyes to doze. I think about home. I read my book, but I cannot fight it—boredom wells inside me until it becomes like a fresh unwanted organ, pumping and seizing and spitting out bile, threatening to burst right through my abdomen and kill me.

I am traveling fast now to get out of touristed lands and into the desert. I reckon that once I get to Dakar it will be relatively easy to get to Mali, then to Timbuktu. I leave the possibility open of getting to Timbuktu through Mauritania, however; though looking at the map it seems as though this will be difficult, possibly dangerous. Have patience, I tell myself. Kingsley didn't always know where she was going either. She waited until she reached the outer port and then decided whether to travel by river or land.

Yet patience is the one thing I don't have. Driven by months of studying French and working at the wire and trying to adjust to France, I feel that speed is important. Yet I won't rent a car, so I keep to the slow bush taxis and buses and try to make time by never staying in a town more than one night. My encounters with Moroccans become a series of small, sharp gasps of cordiality. I accept tea from the bus driver, who has eight children and would like his son to go to school in the States. I chat with the traveling salesman who after failing to sell a sweet fruit drink in Mauritania is having better luck unloading it in Morocco. I share lamb tagine with three fishermen.

"Are you married?" one of them asks me. He has stopped at this restaurant by the side of the road because his truck has broken down. We are the only customers, so the proprietor has put us around the same big plate of couscous and lamb tagine, which we are eating with our fingers.

"I am," I say, a little startled. I have worked side by side with colleagues in France for a year and never discussed where we live, much less our romantic status. I forgot about the intimacy of other cultures, the intimacy of the road.

"Ah." He nods pleasantly. "Where is he?"

"France."

"Ah," he says again, offering up the best piece of lamb, a morsel of fat flecked with meat, on a crown of his dirty black fingernails. "And why is he in France, while you are here?"

I take the meat and swallow it; it tastes a little like diesel oil.

"He has other aspirations," I say.

He quickly switches to French, then Arabic, to consult with his fellow fishermen. *Aspirations, aspirations?*

I smile. "He has other things to do."

They smile, confused. "And the children?"

"There are no children."

This leaves them stumped in silence. No children. Then one says something to the other in swift, incomprehensible Moroccan Arabic. They all nod at each other and look back at me with true pity in their eyes. When the leader speaks to me again, his voice is soft, filled with understanding.

"Have you come to see a doctor?"

It is the only possible reason I would be traveling alone, and this conversation, or a variation on it, happens over and over again, with men, women, and children. I am an indigestible oddity, something either to be pitied or scorned. Even women, whom I expected to rely upon to look after me on this trip, to take me under their wings, seem wary of me. It is not that they aren't used to women traveling alone, it is that I have reached a certain age. A twenty-year-old backpacker makes some sense, a thirty-four-year-old one less so.

I learn quickly to say that my husband is waiting for me in the next town and that children are on the way. Kingsley advised this when she traveled through Gabon, when, to her intense irritation, Africans constantly asked her if she was married. She found it simply easier to say yes than go three rounds over why not. Nevertheless, people are still watching me, judging me. So I travel even faster. Sometimes getting to bed at midnight, then up at five, hoping to get into a part of Africa where I might be so unusual people simply don't know what to think.

I drop south. Flat farmland gives way to rolling red-brown hills divided into plots by bright green hedges of cacti. The hills turn to flat and stony desert. The sky, smudged by fog rolling in from the Atlantic, loses its royal blue and settles for a vague gray. The air is tinged with rosemary and henna, and once we leave Agadir, the quiet becomes real, deep, and satisfying. Occasionally a goatherd comes into view, but the land is empty, as though everyone is on the bus, venturing from one metropolis to the next.

Soon we are out of Morocco. By bus, taxi, and car I have traveled some nine hundred miles. I have left behind the day-trippers, the hippies, the four-star hotels and plush golf courses. I have entered the western side of the Sahara, where caravans once plied the coast, bringing slaves and gold to Europe from the heart of Africa, a place tied physically and spiritually to Timbuktu.

By the time I arrive in Western Sahara, I've also stayed in some wretched hotels and slept no more than thirty hours the whole week. I'm exhilarated and exhausted, but rest is still a ways off. It is still a thousand miles from Nouadhibou, the fishing port in Mauritania where I am planning to stay for a week or two. As if to give me one last chance to abandon the plan, the bus driver stops and lets all the passengers out at a small gas station for an hour-long break. Some go to eat, many to pray in a small mosque next to the gas station, and I idle around the door, unsure of what to do.

There is nothing here. I don't mean that lightly or with judgment. There is just very little. No trees. No buildings. No birds or wildlife. To my right, the desert runs hard and rocky and without interruption for three thousand miles east to the Sudan. To my left it falls with stunning swiftness into the Atlantic Ocean. There cold, green fast-moving currents throw up mist that becomes a curtain around the edge of the African continent. The place feels menacing, unnaturally empty and quiet, like two enormous planets brushing past each other in space.

My skin is covered in a thin layer of damp salt, and I take the sweater out of my backpack. It's cold and windy here. I'm hungry. For two days I've only eaten oranges and bread because I always arrived in hotels too late for dinner and left too early for breakfast. Next to the mosque is a small shop selling French bread and sardines. The shopkeeper looks on skeptically while I hold the cans in both hands and try to decide whether the metric weight is inaccurate. Finally I settle on the big can, which is fifty cents more. With the bread I spend two dollars and feel grimly satisfied by my austerity. Mary Kingsley budgeted roughly one pound for every five miles in Africa. I am spending far less.

I am traveling more cheaply than I ever have before, but I don't see an element of self-punishment in it, though others would certainly later make that argument. I enjoy my deprivation, even feel superior about it. In paring down my life like this I want to remind myself how little we actually need. There is also, however, a tinge of vanity to what I do. I want Florent to know how frugal I am. See how wise a traveler I can be. See how I am costing us nothing by being here. If he knew how rich our lives could be with less, then perhaps we could leave Paris and I could live the life I always wanted. We could move to Africa and forget about striving for status and wealth in terrifying cities like New York and Paris. We could forget about the mortgages, the children, the retirement accounts, the flat-screen TVs and minivans that seemed tied to getting older. We could go hole up somewhere, just the two of us, and live a quiet, meaningful life. I could teach English at a local school. He could start a business, giving Africans good, stable jobs. We would work hard, but not fourteen-hour days. In the mornings we would drink coffee and talk, in the evenings go for long walks in the equatorial sun. We would be happy with less. We could be above it all.

I leave the bus and walk across the road to the edge of the cliff. As I get closer I can hear the sea, rolling in a half mile from shore over sandbars and jagged rocks. I pull the neck of my sweater up to my ears as though thick wool could protect me from the nihilism of this place. I look up at the sky, and the gray streaks of clouds seem close enough to touch. Then, because hunger and fatigue have made me feel numb and I don't like that feeling at all, I squat to the ground and scuttle toward the rim on the backs of my hands and feet like a crab. The wind rolls over the top of my body, throwing mist into my nostrils, and I let my legs dangle over the side.

It's three hundred feet down. I can feel the wind whipping up the side of the cliff and jostling my boots, shaking them like a hand shakes when held out the window of a car on the highway. On the beach below, two ships rust in the waves. An oil tanker with Cyrillic letters on the side that has been picked over by metal scavengers, its railings, windows, and cranes gone, and a container ship that is half-buried in the beach. Despite their immensity, they look small on the long white beach and light enough to be moving inland on a crest of mist and waves.

Then the wind lets up a little as if gathering its breath and I lie down, looking up at the shredded clouds hustling their way toward the hot interior of Africa. Not in a lifetime of being alone have I ever actually been so alone. No friend or family member knows where I am. Even the bus driver barely registered my existence.

I could throw myself into this cold foreign sea. No one would ever find me. It would be a clean act of self-annihilation, curiously pure and honest and well reasoned. Shouldn't the world be relieved of another person trying to build a life? Another person who would, upon building that life, end up happy in that bland, voiceless American way? What a thrill just to jump now and never do that, or worse, never to strive to make my life into something of which I was proud and which suited me. What a relief never to make those hard decisions that could cause me to feel that, in a world of remarkably similar women, I was different, I did exist, I did matter.

Who really would miss me? My parents. Florent. People I love who have never hurt me. I sigh heavily, and the strong wind carries my small protest away. I long for the dramatic gesture, but not one tinged with cowardice and defeat.

I start to crawl back from the edge. The wind is even stronger now and as loud as an airplane and I am careful to pull my legs over the edge with my arms. Suddenly I catch sight of two European men in white cotton sweatshirts sitting on beach chairs about fifty yards along the cliff. Behind them two white Winnebagos shake in the wind as though preparing for liftoff. One of the men stands up and waves, but he's not waving at me. I look behind me and see two French women in flowered pants and floppy sun hats running toward me. They are stumbling over the rocks and yelling soundlessly in the wind like characters in a silent film.

This is somehow terrifying. They run toward me, crazy, frantically yelling, holding on to their hats, flailing their arms. One of them comes right up behind me as though she doesn't see or care about the cliff at all, and I quickly drop my torso down onto the earth, hoping it will make it more difficult to throw me off the edge.

"Don't jump!" they shout in English, leaning in over me. "Please, don't jump!"

I look up at their overfed country faces.

"What?"

"Don't jump!" they yell, carefully looking to each other for support, wondering if I speak English.

"I'm not jumping," I say with some irritation. Is there no escape from the constant meddling of the French? "I'm just looking out at the sea." To prove my sanity, I sit up and throw a wave off at their husbands. They stand up and cheer me with what look like plastic cups of red wine, then sit down abruptly.

"What were you doing? This is so dangerous! *Vraiment effrayant!*" the women exclaim.

"I was experimenting," I say, but I guess my French translation is lousy because they just look at me reproachfully. "I was just thinking," I sigh.

This they will not accept, and they pull me back from the cliff and march me back to the gas station. I am now firmly, inescapably in their care, and I recognize a well of untapped maternal instinct flowing toward me. They direct me to a corner table, where they unpack lunch. There they have laid out a feast—smoked Savoy ham, Reblochon, real French bread, a bottle of wine, and bars of dark chocolate. It's a French holiday picnic transported to southern Morocco with retirement dollars and a Winnebago.

They begin to talk, in unison, like people who have known each other since childhood and take some pleasure in their quirkiness. They are best friends from Rennes, where one was a teacher in public school and the other worked in her sister's traiteur. They are retired now, and every winter they drive from France through Spain, into Morocco, and then to Mauritania, Senegal, and Mali. For all the homemade sweaters and flowered pants, they are remarkable travelers.

"Have you been to Timbuktu?" I ask when they start gushing about Mali. If they have been to Timbuktu I'm turning around right now and going home.

"No, no," they say in horror, shaking their index fingers at me. "That is too far. Far in the desert, and there is no road."

"Soon we are going south to Mauritania to be in the sun. *Mauritanie est magnifique!*" one of them says as she slathers cheese onto bread for me. "But we hate Senegal. Too much corruption, too many people pulling at your clothes. It costs one thousand euros just to get the car into the country."

They chirp and sing, comfortable drinking their wine right next to the mosque. All day long they eat and walk and knit their grandchildren sweaters while their husbands fish. Not so different from life in Rennes, they explain.

They've been pretty much everywhere in Africa without Africa affecting them at all, yet they have a quiet, almost stealthy sense of danger about the place. On one hand they praise the sun and sea, on the other they warn about the Moroccan military and the separatist Sahrawi. They actually seem to cherish the lawlessness of it. I think about the ships rotting in the seas. This must be the only place on earth you can abandon an oil tanker without anyone noticing.

"Franco used to vacation there," they say over each other, going for unison. "He just needed to be clear of Spanish things so he would come here for some holiday. So many nice places he could have gone in Spain but he came here. It says something, doesn't it?"

They giggle together.

"Imagine running into Franco on the beach in Africa."

"Imagine," I say, unsure whether running into a Fascist dictator on a beach is a good or bad thing in their estimation.

"He used to come here because he could do things in Africa he couldn't in Spain."

"Like what?" I ask.

"Things . . ." they say breathlessly. "And now that he is gone, the Moroccan army goes to the Western Sahara to play. At least this is what we have heard. We avoid the cities in Africa and we *vraiment* avoid the Moroccan army, but when you get there you will see."

"What will I see?" I ask.

"Western Sahara is so attractive because it does not really exist."

11

The Bleak Desert

LIKE MANY PEOPLE, I learned about the desert from the movies. When I was sixteen my father took me to the Ziegfeld Theatre in New York for a special screening of *Lawrence of Arabia,* all four hours of it, and I became enraptured not only by Lawrence's kooky quest to lead the Arabs to independence but the sheer gorgeousness of the desert itself. Half the movie seemed to be shots of thousand-foot sand dunes and rose-tinted light and honorable Bedouins taking tea by oases. The drama was cemented by soaring theme music and lingering shots of Lawrence, wearing quite a lot of black kohl, squinting into the distance and looking determined.

This became my image of the desert, as the movie *Charade* with Audrey Hepburn became my image of Paris. And even as I got older and realized that life rarely imitated the movies I found it hard not to hope, just a little, that make-believe would mesh with reality.

I search for my *Lawrence of Arabia* desert, hope for it. After leaving my friends from Rennes, I get back on the bus, determined to press on, down into Western Sahara. Here the land is flat and rocky with small pools of salty water left from sporadic showers. From behind some rocks poke tufts of green, but even the camels wandering seemingly without owners look askance at these bits of vegetation. It is neither full-on desert nor green savanna. It feels like the moon.

As the bus trundles on, ever farther south, I open my book on the Sahara, helpfully titled *Sahara,* and read about this place I am about to enter. It is notable only for its extremity. The land is entirely non-arable. It rarely rains. The nomads are viciously independent. Besides phosphorous and fish, and perhaps oil or natural gas, there are no natural resources.

Yet Mauritania, Morocco, Algeria, and the native population of Western Sahara, the Sahrawi, have squabbled over this land among themselves for the past forty years. Although Morocco occupies the Western Sahara, the land's international status has never been formally established. I am entering one of the few patches of land left on the earth that isn't a country. The West Bank and Gaza are others. In a political sense, at least, this country doesn't exist.

For much of the twentieth century the Western Sahara was occupied by the Spanish, who used it as a playground of sorts. Stories have it that, just as the French ladies reported, Francisco Franco used to come here to blow off steam, though exactly how that manifested itself is unclear. After he died in 1975, Spain handed the territory to Morocco and Mauritania in a politically disastrous manner, neither establishing a native-born government nor sanctioning the annexation of the land by any of its neighbors. Over the next ten years UN agencies dithered over the sovereignty of Western Sahara while Morocco consolidated its control by sending in three hundred thousand settlers in what became known as "the Green March." These civilians were intended to outnumber the Sahrawi and make it impossible for the Western Sahara to gain independence through referendum or for Mauritania to take control.

The Sahrawi formed a political unit called the Polisario

Front and attacked both the Moroccans and the Mauritanians throughout the late 1970s, becoming such a nuisance that the Moroccan army pushed them into the eastern part of the country (a place so waterless that even the Bedouin avoid it) and built a 1,700-mile sand berm to keep them out. The wall, supposedly visible from low-altitude space, is mined with thousands of cluster bombs and manned by Moroccan soldiers. It's probably the most dangerous place in this part of West Africa, certainly the most militarized.

I knew the situation was tense, but I didn't know to what extent. As soon as we cross the border into Western Sahara, it feels like a police state. The bus is stopped at random checkpoints and Moroccan soldiers come on board to inspect our papers. About every fifty miles, I am asked to step off the bus and fill out a form with my address, destination, and passport information. Each time the soldiers ask me what I am doing here, where I am from, and where my husband is. I tell them he is waiting for me in the next town, but it's clear they don't believe me. They keep me in one of their little huts by the side of the road, asking questions, trying to trip me up, until the bus driver comes in and says he's going to leave without me. The soldiers look me up and down in a naked, predatory way, but let me go. They must be terribly bored. Bored soldiers are never good.

At Laayoune, the capital of Western Sahara, I decide to stop for a couple of days. I will have a proper meal and shower before I make my way across the border. If I was feeling removed and alienated before, Laayoune only serves to harden the emotion into outright fact. I am apparently the first five-foot-ten blond American to come along in quite a while. Several waiters knock on the door of my hotel simply to look at me and say hello. The hotel is a huge, cavernous affair, empty of patrons and with very little food, so I make my way to the bar, hoping to get something I can at least drink. There Pakistani and Nepalese UN peacekeepers, stationed in Western Sahara to observe the Moroccan army, are getting sloshed in total silence. When I walk in, the entire room turns to stare at me, and I quietly walk back to my room.

Sooner than I want, the next day I head back to the bus. The need to keep going is driven by the old habits of a wire reporter. Rather than stop and think, look around and reconsider, I have become used to filing the story and moving on. Somehow or other I see the trip as an effort in productivity. Each day that passes feels like an accomplishment and I am used to this false validation. I want to sleep every night and know I worked, even if the working is just moving south. It doesn't occur to me that in the months I travel alone in Africa, perhaps the last months I will ever get to do this in my life, there are better ways to feel good about myself.

I move south. The desolation outside Laayoune becomes more stark. Even the small herds of camels who wander the desert turn their backs on us as we drive by. I strain to see something, anything in the distance—a building, a ridge, a factory—but my eyes grow tired. Finally, I stop looking out the window and stay inside the bus at rest stops rather than face the desert. I long for confined space, a book, the TV, Florent's eyes across a pillow.

I had imagined a broad, liberating desert with rose-flecked sand dunes and clean, sweet air, something that would turn my small world of European concerns into grand gestures. Out here, I hoped the parts of me that were timid and parochial would die in favor of a brave, worldly Nina. This is what my mother promised when she talked about Africa's wide-open spaces, the lid of the world being pried off, a route to the sublime revealed. This desert doesn't aid that goal. It doesn't fortify but leaves me raw and undernourished. After two weeks,

I want to be swaddled and bound tight enough not to feel the outside world. I am tired, hungry, lonely. Confused. I have not found my *Lawrence of Arabia* desert. I have no sense that either victory or peace will come to me.

This was how I felt when the gesture came.

12

The Love of Home

"ARE YOU TRAVELING ALONE?" she asks in perfect American English.

I am sleeping when she touches my shoulder and I turn my weary eyes toward the source of the question. She's probably twenty years old and is wearing jeans, a pink T-shirt, and a matching jean jacket. Her heart-shaped face is ringed in black hair that's been styled into a shoulder-length feather cut, and her eyes are very black. As she talks she removes her earphones and the music of the Senegalese rapper Akon wafts through the bus. She is heartbreakingly pretty, like a heroine from pre-Islamic love poetry, more gazelle or desert fox than human girl.

"The bus driver thinks you are traveling alone and therefore must know what you are doing. We decided I would ask."

When I look up the entire front of the bus is looking at us, not all of them kindly. There have been three checkpoints this morning and I have probably slowed this already excruciatingly slow bus down by an hour, hour and a half.

"My name is Iman. I too am traveling alone. It is a pleasure to meet you."

I too am traveling alone. Her English is like Florent's—formal, almost Victorian. On a Tuesday night over sandwiches: *Would you be so kind as to pass the salt?* His language never slides, never cuts corners.

"My name is Nina. I am going to Dakhla." I brace myself for the inevitable questions. Where is your husband? Your children? Instead she seems more intent on redirecting the bus's focus away from me.

"Mssafer bouhdo."

The rest of the passengers turn back to the front of the bus, inexplicably sated.

"Dakhla is among the most beautiful places in Morocco," she says. "We have a wonderful bay for windsurfing and swimming and soon it will become one of the most well-known places in Europe for tourism. The beach is the best."

I picture for a moment the long white beach outside Laayoune with its rusting oil tankers and the creeping cold sea. Nothing short of death would make me get into those waters.

"You love your home," I say.

"I do!" she cries happily, just at the thought. "I miss it all the time. I cannot wait to finish my studies."

I like Iman's enthusiasm. It's nice when pretty girls are above ennui and teenage cynicism. I also feel a wave of warmth for her clear and uncomplicated relationship with the notion of home. I have admired cities and towns, enjoyed the rhythm and feel of a culture, but never really become attached to the place I lay my head. I suppose that kind of investment always made me feel queasy and claustrophobic, as though I were back weeding my mother's garden, with no obvious way to get out.

She takes my momentary pensiveness as a sign of passive warmth and comes and sits next to me. She shows me her telephone, which plays music, and talks about her classes at the university in Agadir. As the oldest of five children, she is the prodigy and the darling, a girl so talented even her father, a colonel in the army, couldn't deny her a university education.

Her brilliance also meant that she could not study languages as she wanted, but a far more prestigious line of work, engineering.

"I learned English by reading English books in the morning before class," she says. "But I never speak. Do I sound all right?"

"You sound good, actually."

She taps her head quickly on my shoulder and giggles.

"After French and Spanish, English is my favorite language."

Her physicality is disarming. While she talks she rests her hand on my leg, driving her forefingers into my knee when searching extra hard for a word. She wraps her arm around my shoulder to point out the camels outside and clasps my hand to make sure I'm listening. I'm grateful for the attention and for her warmth. Her uncompromised sunny disposition is like a comforting blanket I can wrap around myself to shut out the Sahara.

"I like Akon and Beyoncé and finding out what celebrity lives are like," she says.

"Which celebrities?" I ask.

"The big ones," she says simply.

She is eager to show me the Western Sahara and discreetly points to a Sahrawi woman behind us. Iman writes *melfha* in my notebook in Arabic, which is the name for the long strip of brightly colored cloth that Sahrawi women wrap themselves in, head to toe. She is impressed that I can read the letters, and leads the bus in making little *tutt*ing sounds to alert me to interesting developments. *Tut, tut!* "A camel!" she says, as though I had come to the Western Sahara for the wildlife. *Tut, tut.* "Europeans!" She points to the white campers with French and German license plates that cluster by the road like a flock of sea birds.

Her eyes grow wide when I tell her about my trip, even

wider when I tell her that my parents live in America and my husband in Paris. Surprisingly, she finds that I am so far from my mother the saddest fact of all. She tells me that her father brought the family to the Western Sahara in the 1980s and lived in Morroco for part of that time.

"It was horrible," she says.

"For you or for her?" I ask.

"For both of us," she exclaims. "My mummy. All alone with all my terrible brothers!"

The bus ride stretches out all day and into the night. Iman dozes, and when she does I keep an eye on her and her things. I marvel in the fact that I have had to come to Africa to feel like I am back in the camaraderie of a woman's college. When she wakes we share oranges, and as I root through my knapsack to look for crackers my book *Sahara* falls out. Iman picks it up, flips through it, and groans.

"I've seen this movie," she says. "The movie with Penelope Cruz? Is the book good?"

"Oh no," I say, a little distraught. "It's not a novel, it's a history of the Sahara. Sort of a topological history with bits of . . ." She pulls her hand through her hair and looks at me blankly, clearly bored. "Never mind."

"Victoria Beckham is too vain," she says, ignoring entirely the previous line of conversation. "For that reason I do not like her, but she is hoping for a fourth child. That is interesting. Do you think she is vain?"

"She is certainly vain," I say.

"You are not vain," she says critically, decisively.

"No, I am not vain, not about the way I look anyway."

She looks at me curiously, as though trying to compute other types of vanity.

"It's odd because European women are very pretty, very careful about themselves on television, but not in real life."

"It's really not fair to compare me to Victoria Beckham. Not fair to her either. We're different . . . types."

"Yes, you are different types." She picks up the book on the Sahara again. For all her obvious abilities, I don't think it's ever occurred to her to really care about anything besides her family and pop culture.

"You should keep that," I tell her. "I have another in Paris. I ordered a paperback copy by accident."

Like a little girl at Christmas she holds the book to her chest and exclaims, "Thank you so much! I will read all the words and look up the ones I don't know in my dictionary. Thank you so much, Nina."

She is very well bred to thank me for a book she clearly doesn't want, but I also feel I have done something small to guide her away from the life of a pop princess turned soccer player's wife. When finally the bus arrives in Dakhla I'm sad to see her go. Iman is sad too and she invites me over for dinner. I am about to accept when I catch sight of her family, standing at the edge of the bus station. Her father gives Iman three hard kisses on each cheek while her mother hugs her from behind, smoothing her hair with her hand. Clearly she is cherished, as she should be. Iman points to me across the crowd, but her father frowns deeply. She looks up at him with pleading eyes and he shakes his head. Before she has to come over and explain, I disappear. I don't want to take anything away from her precious hours with her family. As my taxi pulls away, I can still see her looking for me, worry in her eyes.

13

Trumping Comfort

BEFORE I ADOPTED the sedate comforts of a Parisian life, I lived in some places that by any estimation were truly appalling. There was the house on the edge of Lahore with only three hours of electricity at night, cockroaches the size of mice, and no steady source of hot water. I froze in the winter, baked in the summer, and it always smelled of propane gas. Then there was an apartment in Baku that sat atop a ten-story concrete Brezhnev-era building on the edge of the Caspian sea. The apartment was nice enough, but at night the wind blew so hard that I woke in the morning with ringing in my ears, as though I had been to a rock concert.

The worst was perhaps my house in Ramallah, where I lived for nearly two years in the late 1990s. It lay just beyond the Israeli-Palestinian checkpoint in a sour and muddy depression, next to a nurse's college full of gossiping teenage women. They giggled all night, screamed all day, and stole things out of the yard. The house itself, a square concrete affair with a flat roof, had a decent kitchen and three bedrooms, but it constantly leaked. All through the cold, damp winter, rain dripped down the walls until the interior was crusted with mildew. I used to lie in bed and look up at the splotches of black mold on the ceiling and find animal patterns. In November it was a lion, by March a big blue whale.

When spring came, the rain stopped and the house got better. The gully in which it sat dried out and small tufts of grass sprouted in the yard. Wildflowers appeared and the grape arbor in the backyard blossomed. As the summer got hotter, the arbor became the place I had dinner with friends and coffee in the morning. Eventually I strung it with Christmas lights so when I walked home from work late I could see it from the top of the hill, glittering.

All of Ramallah glittered then. Families returning from the United States and Britain in hopes of a better future with the Oslo peace accords had taken up residence in the old Palestinian town. Coffeehouses, jazz bars, and Italian restaurants were opening everywhere. European aid money poured in, opening new schools and hospitals, but also craft museums and art house cinemas. At night long lines of hip young Palestinians, many of them born and bred in California or London, would stand outside the theater waiting to see a Bergman or Kurosawa film.

It was a vital, hopeful time in the history of the Palestinian-Israeli conflict, and although I had arrived to study Arabic at Birzeit University, I quickly abandoned the plan to live in Ramallah. I found a job working part-time for an Arab member of the Knesset and another job freelancing for a Palestinian paper. I made one thousand dollars a month, which, with a roommate, was more than enough to cover my expenses.

The work was interesting and hard, but because I was neither Arab nor Jewish I could easily move between both worlds. One morning I would wake up and take the service taxi into Jerusalem, where I would meet my friend Yael who would take me to Tel Aviv. We would go into the Knesset and work on speeches in Hebrew and English for our MP. At night we would go back to her house in Tel Aviv and roast kebabs in the back-yard while her friends drifted in and out, talking about politics. The next day it was up to Nablus, a Palestinian city set high in the hills, where I would do things like interview a local man for a story on family-run Palestinian businesses. He would take me around his dark, cool factory in the old city and explain that his family had been making a particular soap from one olive grove for three hundred years.

Every day I woke up in my dank, moldy house and pondered what new wonder the day would bring. Then I would put on one of three dresses I had—the black one was beginning to fray at the hip, I noticed—run my hand through my hair, and step out. On weekdays I left at nine and was back at six, and then one day a week, Friday or Sunday, I rested. The bustling city would fall nearly silent and I would sit on an old sofa under a mulberry tree and study Arabic until I was dazed and placated with the effort. When I closed the book, if I was lucky, someone would stop by. Sasha, bringing a bottle of wine and some meat, singing hello and heading to the kitchen to cook. Maybe Richard or Sophie after that. We would eat and drink and talk, bound by the sense that we were living in the middle of history and for once history was moving in the right direction.

I knew it wasn't sustainable. At some point one can't live on one thousand dollars a month. I needed a real job, a real life, so I left, went to graduate school, learned how to be a reporter. I did the responsible thing and became so busy I didn't have time for regret. My sense of loss was helped by the knowledge that things in the Palestinian territories changed after that. The Second Intifada started. The wall went up. Yet, often when I tried to fall asleep at night and couldn't, I would think about the clear, bright sun of an olive orchid in Nablus or the humid languor of the beach in Tel Aviv. Some days I just thought about the whale-shaped mold above my bed. I missed even that.

It was this early experience with travel that informed me, made me value certain things on the road to Timbuktu. The intimacy of women was high on the list. Iman dug her fingers into my knee as she talked, lay her head on my shoulder and giggled, and it reminded me how easy it is in the Middle East to enjoy the company of women. The culture was structured to put walls up between the sexes, and though both men and women paid the price for that, it also had the effect of drawing women closer together. Iman trusted me instinctively. Even if she couldn't bring me to dinner at her house—and I think I understood why her father said no—I looked forward to what I hoped would be the first of many gentle encounters with women in Africa.

Ramallah also taught me the value of experience over comfort. Ever since I had first visited Cairo as a teenager, been so very homesick and yet learned to love the city, I had suspected that my love of a place stemmed not from pleasure or joy, but from the tinge of loneliness and even the fear each day brought. I associated apprehension with learning and by extension an affirmation that I was living my life correctly. I never felt quite comfortable in Cairo and I never expected to, and this helped sharpen my senses. I began to appreciate small pleasures—my friendship with Paul, the misty walk to school—and to dismiss dangers and annoyances as irrelevant.

It is with this perspective, this belief, that I enter Dakhla. I expect the road to bring burdens and inconveniences. I expect to feel lonely and out of sorts. This is how I am—wide and bright to the world. This is how I will see how other people live and how I will emerge more open-minded and wise.

But Dakhla isn't like the other places I have been. It isn't Ramallah or Beirut. It isn't even Lahore or Baku. It is a nowhere place in an occupied country caught between the desert and the sea. It is a place where Moroccan soldiers in reflective aviator glasses pass through town in armored SUVs. Where

Chinese fishermen in Mao suits stand around outside the pharmacies smoking heavy, fragrant clove cigarettes and hacking blood into handkerchiefs. Where Russian sailors sing, recklessly drunk at midday, and native Sahrawi are few and far between.

It is a place I should turn back from, where the mold on my ceiling would be the least of my problems, but I ignore this. The prospect of going home is too dreadful, too humiliating, and I haven't yet learned to turn back when I have had enough.

That night I check into Salima's hotel. Soon I am sitting by the boardwalk on an unnaturally bright morning rubbing butter on the dry skin around my nostrils. I am wondering whether Mary Kingsley would have turned back, and concluding no. I am thinking that I need to find transport across the border to Mauritania, a border that is mined, nearly trackless, and nearly devoid of human life. And I am asking my waiter a question.

"Tell me your cousin's name."

14

Slow Fear

THERE ARE TWO TAXIS leaving for Mauritania that day. One is a white van that usually transports bottled water and cigarettes but has been co-opted for human transport. Someone has laid a carpet on the floor and thrown in a flashlight, but the interior is basically a dark, empty box with a rear sliding door that opens from the outside. It has no windows, no air conditioning, and no way for passengers to get out if the driver has a heart attack or abandons the van before the border. I poke my head inside and two small, very round Sahrawi women blink back at me like badgers in a hole.

The other car is a silver Peugeot that has 438,768 miles on the odometer and so much body rust that from a distance it looks made of iron latticework. The interior has been stripped of every possible car accoutrement (radio, door handles, side panels), leaving a shell of hard black plastic and seats that sag so low it is difficult to see over the dashboard when sitting in them. The driver is a man named Hamda who fishes during the week and drives passengers between Mauritania and Morocco on the weekends. He seems very pleased to have me aboard.

Hamda is small, shorter than I, and extraordinarily thin,

with cheekbones that jut out half an inch underneath his small black eyes and flaps of skin that hang in folds under his chin. He is a Moor, born in Mauritania, and like most of his countrymen wears a *daraa,* a long sleeveless blue tunic with gold embroidery on the front. The daraa is a very beautiful piece of clothing, designed to billow in the desert winds and shine under the strong light, but it is also meant to be worn over a suit of clothes or long cotton pants, sort of like a doctor's lab coat. Hamda wears only boxers underneath, which means that he has to constantly fiddle with the fabric so it will cover his body. No sooner does he arrange the tunic than a blast of wind from the sea rips it from his shoulders. Frustrated, frantic with irritation, and inexplicably surprised by this turn of events he stops whatever he was doing to spend five minutes setting the daraa straight. Then another gust tears it off. It is both funny and painful to watch, and I suspect Hamda could increase his productivity by a good 30 percent if he gave up the daraa completely, or at least wore trousers underneath it.

The daraa is a source of pride for the Moors that live in this region, however, a sign of their heritage and masculinity that they would no sooner discard than their wives or children. For Hamda it also serves a purpose in that it seems to absorb a great deal of his nervous energy. In a culture where men seem to take long, steady strides and conserve quickness for hunting and warfare, Hamda bounces between objects. First he bangs away on his engine a while, then bums a cigarette from a fellow driver, then trots off to the edge of the desert to pee, then runs back to bang on the engine before stopping midbang to boil a pot of water for tea. Between stops he fixes his daraa and makes smart-ass comments to his fellow drivers, who either ignore him or flick their cigarettes in his general direction.

"Your car is tired!" he yells at the drivers of other, better cars.

"My car is tired? Your car is tired!" one of the drivers yells back.

Then, infuriated beyond all logic, Hamda responds.

"I have two wives, and you . . . *you* find comfort in your mother."

He's a pitiful little man, but he's also my ride, and apparently a good guide through the minefields near the border and the bandits that lie in wait near the long, hard beach.

"I am a man in whom many have placed their lives," he tells me proudly as I hand over the extortionate sum he demands in order to secure a front seat to myself. "You will have no worries with me."

Initially I have no worries about Hamda. All morning I sit in the front seat of his car, reading my book and drinking little cups of sweet tea. I watch Moorish women buy tickets for the women's van, and congratulate myself for booking a ticket with the boys. At least I won't have to drive to the border in utter darkness, clinging to the walls every time we hit a bump.

I do, however, have some mild concerns about my fellow passengers, three Mauritanian fishermen who sometimes work the iron ore mines at Guelb el Rhein. All are single, illiterate, smelly, and deeply religious. I know this because at one point or other they all stand very close to me, tell me they are good Muslims and ask to see my book on West African history. After flipping through it they say they can't read but like to look at the letters on the page. One of them a tall, cross-eyed fellow with a poorly repaired cleft palate, is particularly worrying. He stares at me all morning, then around noon suddenly and inexplicably reaches his hand through the front passenger window, grabs my book, and throws it into the road. I'm so startled I simply get out of the car, pick up the book and go back to reading as though he were a daft two-year-old. It's then I notice the large indentation and sickle-shaped scar above his right ear, a scar so deep and red it looks as though he's either had brain surgery recently or something big and heavy has fallen on his head.

It seems too difficult to change cars or spend another night in horrid Dakhla, however, so when we finally leave at one thirty p.m., I am relieved. The terrain, which I didn't think could get any worse, immediately does. Fine white sand scuttles across the road and any pretense of vegetation disappears. The ocean pounds the edges of the beach and the fragile car shivers as if in fear. It's two hundred and sixty miles to Nouadhibou, and I assumed, despite the poor-to-nonexistent road, we would get there by nightfall. Yet Hamda is only driving fifty miles per hour.

"Doesn't the car go any faster?" I ask him.

"Wait until the wind is behind us," he says. "But we aren't going to make the border tonight. You can spend the night with us."

"In the desert?" I whisper.

"There is a hotel by the border, for the truck drivers. We might make that. We might not."

After that a deep dark feeling sinks in. The desert softens a little into dunes and Hamda turns on the radio, piped-over longwave from southern Morocco. The Peugeot sputters along and the three men in the back seat keep counsel among themselves. Every once in a while a truck, often with license plates from Senegal or Algeria, passes us on the road and Hamda tries to stop it by frantically waving his arms. Twice, drivers pull up alongside us and Hamda makes smoking motions with his two fingers. Both times the drivers laugh and keep on going and he does not get his cigarette.

Over the next hour, his mood worsens. First he bites off his fingernails, then he turns the radio on and off, then he scratches the rubber coating off the steering wheel with his thumb. He turns on one of the fishermen behind us, speaking very quickly and angrily in Arabic until the man hands over a bottle of water. He drinks half the bottle and throws the remainder out the window.

Then, I suppose, because he has nothing else to do, he turns on me.

"Neena. Neeenaaaa. Neeennna." He screeches my name over and over again. When I smile as though enjoying the joke he shoves his face in mine and says it louder. "Neeennna!" He turns around to get the others to say it too until the car is full of my name, sung obscenely, angrily. They laugh and I look out the window at the ocean. By the shore is a little hut made of stones, and a man fishing with a net. "Neeena must be married to a fisherman because all she does is look at the sea," he sings.

"I would like an American wife. Wouldn't you like an American wife?" he asks the others. They all nod and clap.

"I'm married," I say feebly, too quietly. Then again, "I said I'm married," but it does no good. They keep saying my name over and over again, like children in a schoolyard. I open my book and Hamda snatches it from me and throws it into the back seat.

"Neena, Neena!" he shrieks.

Ignoring Hamda, I pull out my camera and start flipping back through pictures. I find a good strong one of Florent's face and turn around to show the men in the back seat. As I hoped, they stop singing my name and marvel at the digital camera.

"This is my husband and here are my children," I say, showing pictures of my husband's nieces and nephews. They are transfixed. One of the fisherman, a younger man with a weak moustache, asks me my religion. I'm happy to answer but then Hamda pulls the daraa above his head, exposing his bare stomach. The display of flesh shocks and quiets everyone so Hamda can begin the hazing again.

"No husband, no husband, there is no husband!" he screams. Delighted, the other men begin to repeat the phrase over and over. "No husband, no husband." Hamda leans over to inspect the radio and rests his hand for just a moment on my thigh.

It's agonizing to travel at forty miles per hour while struggling against full-on terror. Slowness amplifies fear by adding frustration. If only we were going fast, I wouldn't feel so emasculated, and neither would Hamda. I try to distract myself and contextualize panic by thinking about all the other scary things that have happened to me. There was that very bumpy flight over the Atlantic where the stewardess screamed. Or the time my boyfriend drove through a West Bank checkpoint and the Israeli soldier trained his rifle on us. My relationship with God is estranged. That can't be good.

But terror can only last so long. Eventually, it's replaced by simple dread. That dread is matched nicely by the sudden, if inevitable, breakdown of the Peugeot. Hamda loses control and we veer off the road into a ditch, coming to a complete stop in sand so soft it covers half the tire. The smell of tar fills the compartment and smoke begins to pour out of the ventilation system. Hamda jumps out, then comes around to open my door. I have already made my decision. Clutching the sides of the seat and locking my legs against the front of the compartment I shake my head and say quietly:

"I'm not getting out."

They look at me as though I've lost my mind. Steam pours from the hood and Hamda starts making explosion noises. One of the fishermen grabs my shoulder and I shake him off and say with surprising authority, "*Ne touche pas.*" He holds up his hands in mock surrender, but at this point I'm having difficulty seeing. Spots dance in front of my eyes and my heart races so fast I have to swallow repeatedly to stay conscious. Saliva, rich and bitter with bile, fills my mouth, and I have to spit it out the open door.

I do not get out of the car. Hamda puts out the fire by

drenching the engine with all our available drinking water and the crisis seems averted. For the next thirty minutes I sit in the front seat while he curses and bangs away on the engine. Every once in a while he pulls down car parts from the luggage on the roof until he seems satisfied with the result. *We just need water,* he tells us. Beyond, an endless cold ocean pounds the long beach. Water, water everywhere and not a drop to drink. Not a drop suitable for the car, either.

About twenty minutes later a car drives by and mercifully comes to a stop. The Italians inside look like they've been fighting for hours and traveling for days. The woman is resting her bare and dirty feet on the dashboard and her hair is knotted and dry. When the man asks her to get a canister of water from the back seat she waves him away with one long hand, then rests it over her eyes.

Hamda's face rises in joy when he sees the car, then falls when the writing on the door indicates that they are Italian aid workers.

"I just need water," he mumbles under his breath. "Just give me water."

The Italian man seems to understand and goes into the back of his SUV to retrieve a plastic canister of water. Without a thank-you Hamda takes it and begins to pour it into the transmission. While everyone is peering under the hood, I bolt out of the car and run to the Italian woman.

"Look, can I get a ride with you guys back to Dakhla?" I ask.

She briefly removes the hand over her eyes, looks at me hard, then gestures to the half-empty back of the car.

"No room."

I suppose in that moment a sort of determination took over. No one was going to help me, not even aid workers who, I would have thought, might be sympathetic to a young woman stuck in the middle of the desert. I would have to sort this out on my own and I would need a plan. I had to stop the teasing and with it the mob mentality. Somehow I had to break Hamda's grip on the other fishermen's imaginations.

I did what comes naturally to me in moments of stress. I talked. I talked as though it were my wedding day and I the grandest hostess who ever lived. I held court, generously soliciting their opinions about subjects ranging from Islam to the movies. When their French ran out and my Arabic couldn't meet it, I talked about Florent, his job, how we hoped to have children. I talked about Paris in the winter, the stress of my job as a reporter. I showed pictures of my family and friends and the children of my friends. I talked about my father, my childhood church, my favorite deli in New York. When Hamda began to restart his antics, wheezing out the old *Neena* shriek, I just shouted over him. When he again reached for my leg I said *ne touche pas* very sternly, which led to a thirty-minute conversation on why European woman don't like to be touched despite their slutty behavior in the movies. When that topic petered out (I couldn't convince anyone that the movies didn't reflect real life) I talked about the books I had read in my teens and the difference between Christianity and Islam. I talked and talked until everyone looked like they wanted nothing more than to get away from me. And when we pulled in to the hotel on the Mauritanian border I went directly to the kiosk and bought Hamda a pack of cigarettes.

"You are my sister," he told me.

Hitchhiking at the Border

FLORENT AND I HAVE this old ritual. I ask him if he loves me and he says yes. Then I ask him if he loves me more than anyone he knows and he says yes. Then I ask him if he loves me more than everyone he loves combined and he says, "Well, that's a bit much."

I am, as one would expect, always a little disappointed by his response. He should be willing to give me anything, including being bossed around. I love the exchange, however, because I know he *does* love me more than everyone he knows combined. Or at least he did then.

It had been a long time since I played this old game with him, since before we had gotten married, and our relationship had become so distant and tense. There were so many things I needed the moment I arrived at the hotel on the Mauritanian border. I needed water. I needed to make a friend of the hotel proprietor to ensure that someone would help me find different transport out. I needed a new plan, but I needed nothing more than to ask Florent if he loved me and then to ask him if he loved me more than everyone combined.

After weeks of silence, of one-word emails that simply told

him my location and destination, I called him. It was about seven p.m. in Paris when he answered, and I could tell he'd had a rough day. His voice was scratchy and weak, as though he'd been smoking. I told him about Hamda and the teasing. I told him about the Peugeot's breaking down and the Italian aid workers. I told him I was at a hotel by the border that was populated almost exclusively by Mauritanian and Moroccan truck drivers. Then I told him I had no choice but to continue on with Hamda to Mauritania tomorrow since there was no public transport. I asked him if he loved me and my heart sank low when he ignored the question.

"You know, Nina, you cannot get back in that car tomorrow. Those men are spending the night together and they're coming up with a plan. They didn't know what to do today, but they'll figure it out tonight. Do whatever you need to do but don't get back in that car."

I'm still stunned that he ignored the question and try again for some emotional reassurance. "Will you come get me?" I ask. "I have five hundred dollars on me and this room costs ten dollars a night so I can stay here for a month or so. Longer if I prostitute myself." I laugh a little at the end, as though that were necessary, but I think it comes out sounding crazy because his tone softens.

"Of course I'll come get you. Just promise me that you won't get back in that car."

"I think you're overreacting . . . Do you love me?"

"Nina. You aren't thinking clearly. Promise me you won't get back in that car."

"No, we worked it out. Hamda called me his sister at the end."

"He didn't mean it. You need to trust me on this."

"What will I tell them?"

"Who cares? Who the hell cares?"

He shouts a little when he says it, except Florent doesn't

shout, hardly ever, and suddenly I'm very afraid. So afraid I consider walking downstairs to the gas station and asking one of the truck drivers to take me north right this minute.

"This is insane," I tell Florent. "I don't have a good sense of this anymore. I've lost my judgment."

"Yes, you have," he says.

The hotel shuts off its electricity at eleven p.m., but I can't sleep and around three a.m. I go outside to have a look. It's too cold to be balmy but the air is clean and the breeze is gentle and steady. In the courtyard, truck drivers are sitting around plastic tables playing backgammon by candlelight. It smells like wet cement and cold salt air. Above me a purple sky heavy with white and sparkling stars reveals the palest sheaf of Milky Way. It is a stunning sky, like nothing I have ever seen, and I stand there until I am too cold to bear it, imagining for just a moment that I could tip myself up into the air and fly.

The next morning I wake with a plan and this time, thank God, it's a good one. We are meant to leave at seven a.m. but I get up early and go find the hotel owner. He's grumpy and tired, but I tell him without elaborating that Hamda is a "bad man" and he nods as though this is common knowledge and tells me he'll take care of it. When he comes back he tells me that Hamda is deeply hurt and wants to know if the problem is money.

"He tells me if it is money, he will support you," says the hotel owner with a faint smile.

"Jesus. Tell him it's not money," I say. "Tell him I'm sick and want to rest here a few days."

That seems to satisfy Hamda, and he leaves in a great whirl of dust with the three fishermen pushing the Peugeot and jumping in the back seat once it's started. The hotel owner suggests several times that I ride on to Mauritania with his friends who are all truck drivers and I nod agreeably, biding my time. I'm looking for tourists, retired Europeans who take their campers down to Mauritania in the winter and go home in the spring. I'm looking for a woman, maybe someone round and grandmotherly from northern France or Holland, who will take care of me until we reach Dakhla.

Finally a couple from Belgium appears in a little white camper with their little white dog. I introduce myself without stating my purpose and the woman talks my ear off about the trials and tribulations of her vacation in Senegal. She marvels over the beauty of Mauritania's desert and the good fish on offer in the Western Sahara and when I think she really likes me I ask her if she could take me to Dakhla. Here she frowns and points to her white Winnebago. "You can see here, there is no room."

I plant myself in front of the gas station next to the hotel and decide that, just like reporting, this is a numbers game. If you talk to enough people, you will find someone with whom you will have a connection. Eventually, someone will give you what you need. I'll just ask all the tourists coming through here whether I can ride with them.

The problem, though, is that for hours, no one comes. The gas station is empty until late afternoon, when a silver van pulls up driven by two middle-aged men with ponytails and weathered faces. The plates say D for Deutschland. I hear my mother's voice in my head. *Visiting Germany was a big event in my day. You wouldn't get anything out of your system either if you spent all your summers picking strawberries in Germany.*

They have kind faces, however, weathered and tan with wrinkles around their eyes. I try very hard to see them clearly and decide that I think they are good men.

"Hi," I ask with my biggest Swedish smile. "Can I get a ride to Dakhla with you guys?" It sort of feels like *Brother, can you spare a dime,* but reporting also feels like that, so I remind myself this is no time for pride.

The first one gestures that he doesn't speak any English

by shrugging his shoulders but the other has a few words. He looks embarrassed and a brief conversation in German ensues. Then he gestures toward the back of his van and says, "This is all we have."

Inside are blankets and canned foods and Bunsen burners and more than enough room for me to sit.

I give them the thumbs-up and another goofy, full-toothed smile. "Yes, yes, good! Perfect!"

The ride back to Dakhla takes only three hours and passes in a dream. I'm so tired I feel stoned, and the Germans lend a distinctly surreal edge to the journey. They both work in a tool factory outside Düsseldorf and spend two months every winter traveling around Africa. Both are married, both were in the army, both eschew sweets, and both seem to really dislike West Africa. They are gentlemen, however, and every time we stop to stretch our legs, one of them comes round the back to help me out, gallantly holding out his hand in case I miss my step. They ask me to take lots of pictures of them standing with one foot propped on the side of their truck like great white hunters.

They are my saviors, and when I get to Dakhla I tell them as much. They are very embarrassed by that and awkwardly slap my back in camaraderie. Dakhla never looked so good, but before finding a hotel I ask a passerby for directions to the Air Maroc office.

Just as it are about to close for the night I walk right into the airport office. There is on the wall a picture of some Englishmen standing in front of a Land Rover. They wear beige pants and red shirts that say TIMBUKTU OR BUST! My heart falls, but I am comfortable with the sensation. Failure and I are old, good friends.

"I need a ticket to Paris. For tomorrow. And I don't care what it costs."

16

Death and Dying

MARY KINGSLEY NEVER MARRIED. She never fell in love but once. One winter evening in 1899, a wealthy Londoner invited her to a dinner party, where she met a young man named Matthew Nathan who worked for the colonial office and had served in Sierra Leone and Burma. He was handsome, self-effacing, focused, and romantic. He was also Jewish, which meant to Mary—always the servant's daughter fighting her Cockney accent—that he lived slightly apart from British upper-class society, as she did.

At the time, Kingsley was at the apex of her career—coveted by the London elite for her expertise on West African colonial policy, a frequent lecturer, and the author of two best-selling books. She was also a thirty-six-year-old spinster, however, who lived with her feckless brother and spent most nights alone in her overheated London apartment, studying fetishes and writing long letters or notes for her lectures. It is likely that even the tough, independent, and brilliant Mary Kingsley was a little lonely.

Nathan was charming but also a social climber, and Mary

represented opportunity. In her exhaustive biography of Mary Kingsley, *A Voyager Out*, Katherine Frank notes that Nathan wanted a prestigious position with the British government in Sierra Leone and courted Mary through correspondence. Although most of those letters concerned African politics, Nathan did occasionally stray into romantic territory. In response to a rather scattered letter she wrote, he said, "I want to understand you and I shall"—words I believe most women have wanted to hear from a man at one time or another.

She fell in love—hard, awkwardly, and unbeknownst to him. Soon he was on his way to Sierra Leone (having successfully secured the governorship) and she was pouring out her heart to him in long, emotional letters, written in a frantic scrawling hand. "My life has been a comic one. Dead tired and feeling no one had need of me any more when my mother and father died. . . . I went down to West Africa to die. West Africa amused me and was kind to me and was scientifically interesting and did not want to kill me just then—I am in no hurry."

In the course of her life, Mary gave many official reasons for going to Africa. She would finish her father's book. She would gather fish and fetish for her own scientific discoveries. She would go as a lark to burn a hole in her pocket and kill six empty months. She never mentioned dying, except in this one rambling letter.

Through the turbid waters of her humorous adventures and relentless search for specimens, this admission is the small bright diamond of truth beckoning below the surface. I believe Mary wanted to die in Africa, not because she was particularly suicidal or depressed (though after the life she lived she had a right to be) but because she valued herself just enough to believe she should go in a blaze of adventure and foreign glory. If the gods were going to give her a role to play in life, it would be Odysseus instead of Penelope. She wouldn't fester at home and she wouldn't give in to spinsterhood. It is both why I love Mary and feel such kinship with her, and why I also now think she was slightly naive.

Death, as Mary envisioned it, is both a terrible and an attractive thing. It can be the antidote to boredom, to apathy, and to the sense that no one really knows you. It is the concept that people play with when they are dangling their feet over the edge of a three-hundred-foot cliff in Western Sahara and contemplating "clean annihilation." It is the thrill, the anticipation, the sheer decisiveness of falling that appeals. It's the relief at knowing you will never have to make a hard decision again, but that everyone will remember you for that one dramatic gesture. This isn't dying at all, but a heightened version of living. In Mary's case, because it was so rare for a woman to go alone to Africa, it might even have been legacy-building: *Have you heard? Crazy spinster Mary Kingsley went to Africa to gather fishes and was drowned in a hippo attack on the Ogooué River.* My version, of course, a little more pathetic: *Have you heard, crazy Nina Sovich left that nice guy in Paris and threw herself off a cliff in Western Sahara . . .*

I reckon, now that I have had the flight back to Paris to think about it, that death and dying are two different things entirely. Dying, by being left on a land-mined beach near the border with Mauritania or cut to shreds by a band of fishermen, isn't clean at all. It's the total degradation of a human life—gutting fear, violence, blood, begging, humiliation. It's my body hitting the rocks below and the bones in my legs ripping through the skin and my hip bones jamming my heart into my shoulder. It is, even for the superheroes and martyrs, the feeling of sudden regret. A curse muttered through clenched teeth on the way down.

Mary knew dying better than I did. In agonizing detail, she saw both her parents succumb to terrible illness. Maybe that's why she craved death in all its majesty and glory over the sordid misery of dying. The two cannot be parsed, however. Gore and pain wait patiently for death to come, then rob it of its meaning. There is nothing noble about it, even when it's quick.

I wanted some kind of glory, and I occasionally yearned for some kind of extinction, but I didn't want anything to do with the business of dying. I knew that now. I didn't want to feel pain. I didn't want Florent to feel pain, and I didn't want him to have to call my parents and tell them that after thirty-plus years of their vigilant surveillance, *he* had managed to lose the subject.

The fact remained, however, that I wanted to walk up as closely as possible to the line that demarcated death and life. I wanted to live so broadly and expansively that I pushed against real danger and peeked into its darkness. Every day when I woke I wanted to feel just a little afraid so I could feel the tingle of excitement, the real and elemental notion of being a human being.

Much of my childhood had been spent in quiet confinement, cosseted and protected by parents afraid of losing their own child. Much of my adolescence had been spent in a type of emotional confinement with boys who broke my heart and friendships that flared, then faded away. My adult life promised no better with the duty of wifehood, soon to be followed by motherhood.

There was no physicality to this life, no glory to it, and I felt strongly that there should be. Like Kingsley, I wanted to shake off the emotional constraints that came from being a woman and walk through deserts, sleep under the stars, and meet people unlike any I had met before. I wanted my worries to come from the tangible world, rather than the imagined anxieties and phobias that seemed to infest my life in Paris. I reckoned there would always be time for making a home, making beds, tending to loved ones, doing the right thing. There had to be room for adventure too.

I also sensed that the hardship of travel would teach me patience and help me recognize the extraordinary privileges of my existence in the world. To have this knowledge at hand was important not just for me but also for Florent. It would be the thing that could turn our fragile union into a real marriage, in which I could say, *No, I don't want to make boeuf bourguignon.* Or, *Yes, I do want to have children, but I don't want to have them here in Paris.*

I'm not there yet though, and it is this sense of the unfinished that makes me feel uneasy when I come home to Paris. I don't belong in France, not right now, and I wouldn't be here if I was the woman I wanted to be, able to complete the relatively simple task of crossing the border into Mauritania without risking life and limb. I should be back in Africa. My journey is nowhere near finished.

Nevertheless, I am very grateful for the comforts of my life in a way I haven't been before. The apartment, once simply a showcase for my domestic failings, now appears a refuge. The walls are cream-colored and warm, the lights thoughtfully placed to aid reading. I look out the window at the falling rain and am startled by the smell of lemon. It's clean, meticulously cared for, and quiet. Not eerily so, but cozily, like a baby is sleeping in the next room. When I stand still in the living room, I can almost see the waves of warm and sumptuous stillness around me, bathing me in privilege. After weeks of cramped buses, tiny hotel rooms, shower stalls that doubled as toilets, I am impressed by the apartment's size alone. What decadence. This is the real wealth of first world nations, to be clean, to be safe, and to be at home alone.

Many of the people I met on the road in Africa would want to live in my apartment, at least for a little while. Thus I treat the place more kindly than I have before, hanging the painting that has been leaning against the wall for two years and doing laundry until there isn't a dirty sock in sight. I clean Florent's closet, emptying gold cuff links and blue striped shirts and silk neckties into a heap on the floor as the first step toward orga nizing it. I try to thank him for his wise counsel in Africa by cooking dinner and shopping for a new glass vase.

While I work on the apartment and arrange Florent's things, I drink wine. I don't feel bad about drinking alone, or drinking during the day for that matter. Daytime drinking energizes mundane projects (such as cleaning out closets) and helps me think. Sometimes it unlocks dormant bravery. To drink like this again signals a kind of getting back to basics, a return to a world that is formless, empty of routine, and propped up by faint promise. There is a sense that time and possibility are limitless, that in the end it ain't so bad, that I'm still young.

But inevitably, wine starts to take on a maudlin purpose. I start to look back instead of looking forward. As the thrill of my escape in Africa recedes, I catch myself lying on the sofa all afternoon, flipping through the images of my life—the red waffle house by the stony beach in Grisslehamn, the February snowbanks outside my college dorm room. I don't think about people, just places and times that are, as far as I can tell, random. I wallow in remembrance but neither in meaning nor reflection, and whole days pass without thought.

"So this is the new domesticity," Florent says, standing above me on the sofa.

"I'm giving it a shot," I say.

"Nothing much has changed," he says. "You should do what you have set out to do. Make this trip to Timbuktu, to Mali, but go wiser. No more cheap hotels. No more fifty-cent sandwiches." He is irritated just thinking about it. "No more martyrdom."

"I didn't mean it to go badly," I say, wounded but knowing I deserved it.

"It won't now," he says.

It is a little like talking to the oracle. All-knowing, all-powerful, mostly indecipherable. I fear we are going to slip back into our old ways. Fighting. Resentment. Then maybe we'll have a baby because we don't know how else to bridge the divide. I don't want that.

I am thinking about Africa again. I am going back, but will travel better this time, with less of an eye to racing to Timbuktu. I will move slowly. I will take more time to develop relationships with Africans. I will recognize that I have time on my hands and I should take advantage of it.

This time when I pack, I pack for the long haul. I bring three pairs of pants, two nice shirts, and a black dress just in case someone invites me somewhere. Then I go to the bank and take out a wad of cash, which I divide and stuff into all my extra pockets. For good measure I pack several packs of cigarettes for trading and many, many more books. Spy novels, romances, and, for the hell of it, Isak Dinesen's *Out of Africa*. I decide to fly right into Dakar, Senegal, then go up to Nouakchott in Mauritania. From there, it shouldn't be too hard to get to Timbuktu.

Part III

MAURITANIA

17

A Boy from Bordeaux

EVEN THE HARSHEST and driest Saharan countries have their dewy undersides. Algeria's waterless south is offset by fertile valleys in the north. Egypt is tempered by the Nile; Mali, the Niger River. Libya has thirteen hundred miles of palm-fringed Mediterranean coast, not to mention the Roman ruins at Leptis Magna.

Mauritania, however, is the undiluted Saharan country. No rivers or lakes transverse its core, few oases comfort travelers. It is desert from elbow to ankle, and the Sahara runs from the eastern border right up to the Atlantic.

Yet this desert is beloved. When the Moors who inhabit Mauritania built the capital, Nouakchott, they knew they needed to be close to the sea for shipping purposes. But Nouakchott is built on a sandy and humid depression five miles inland from the beach. No pleasant and airy spot by the shore for these desert people. Wake up in the morning, look around, and you could be on the moon itself.

It takes a special kind of soul to live here, and not many do. The country is almost twice the size of France but with only 5 percent of France's population. Every Mauritanian outside the capital gets three square miles all to himself, and from all appearances they seem to want it. Most are desert nomads who graze their animals across hundreds of miles of semiarid scrubland, seeing only their extended family for weeks on end. The cities that do exist are rambling, sprawling outposts, populated by nomads who migrated there because of the terrible droughts in the 1970s that killed all their livestock.

The isolation of Mauritania, the utter completeness with which it has been overlooked, has created a distinct, possibly odd, culture. Obesity is prized in women. Slavery still exists. Men and women consider themselves devout Muslims but take a decidedly non-Salafist view to the religion. Polygamy is relatively rare. Religious men called marabout, who rely on animism to heal, are prevalent.

If any outside people influence Mauritania it's probably the French, but they rarely bother. They took Mauritania in the 1800s as part of their colonial empire not because they really wanted to but because they saw no way of holding Morocco and Algeria without it. In 1960 they left, having invested little and with barely a word of good-bye. Since then the Mauritanian army has been running things, doing the kind of job you would expect an army to do. Unemployment hovers around 40 percent. Half the population can't read. Tensions are high between the Moors, who consider themselves white, and other ethnic populations such as the Pul who consider themselves black. Democracy flickers in and out; corruption is rife.

Still, Mauritania has a strong national identity and is not in danger of melting away like Somalia or Afghanistan. It is tied both geographically and historically to the trading culture of the Sahara and with that cities like Timbuktu, which sits in neighboring Mali. Mauritanians may be poor but they face the world in similar ways—women are respected, the family is everything, and the desert, even its most mysterious and hostile spaces, is a welcoming home.

I come to Mauritania knowing there are other ways for me to get to Timbuktu—across the desert from Libya, the eminently sensible option of approaching from the temperate south—but I decide, after spending a few weeks in Dakar, Senegal, to start in Nouakchott. This might not be the easiest route, but for historical reasons this country holds special allure. Here a twenty-nine-year-old man from Bordeaux began a journey that would take him across the desert through unimaginable horrors to become the first westerner to both see and escape from Timbuktu.

At the beginning of the nineteenth century little was known about the interior of Africa. The coast had been explored by Portuguese and Spanish traders, but no European had ventured inland beyond a hundred miles or so. Diseases like yellow fever and malaria usually killed Westerners within a few months of their arrival. The terrain itself was harsh—often waterless desert or thick jungle—and the rivers either tended to dissipate into mud and swamp at the ocean or throw up impassible rapids inland. Thus nineteenth-century maps of Africa still relied on the sixteenth-century observations of a traveler named Leo Africanus. According to Frank Kryza, the author of *The Race for Timbuktu,* Europeans knew more about the face of the moon in 1820 than they did about the interior of Africa.

This was the age of the great and mortal combat between England and France over the fate of the world. Having settled the Napoleonic Wars, the English were setting their sights on the riches of South Asia and East Africa. The French were beaten and disorganized but not about to give up on the great colonial prize. They turned their eyes to Algeria, and with it the northern interior of Africa.

There were, even then, whispers of Timbuktu. It was a trading town in the middle of the desert with a great king who ruled a vast kingdom. Its inhabitants wore ostrich plumes and brocade. The town hosted enormous caravans, some one hundred thousand men strong, which carried slaves and kola nuts from the southern reaches of Africa. Enormous libraries held rare medieval Islamic texts. Above all there was gold. The streets were paved in gold.

The promise of riches and the fear of the English spurred the French Société de Géographie to offer ten thousand francs in 1824 to any European who could get into Timbuktu and report on the city firsthand. The British promptly offered a similar amount to any Brit who could get into the city first. The race for the Sahara was on.

At a time when European society didn't offer working-class kids a chance of advancement, a prize like this represented a unique opportunity. Amateurs and professionals, doctors and journeymen, rich and poor could all try for glory. A guy working in a garment factory in Toulouse could think, without being crazy, *Perhaps I could walk there, and become rich and famous.*

The hunger for glory and riches and the sense that the prize was accessible produced for the next few years an almost universally tragic set of results. Daniel Houghton, an Irish major who started in Gambia, nearly made it to Timbuktu before being lured into the desert, robbed, and killed by his guides. Mungo Park, a Scottish doctor, got to the Niger River but lost so many of his men to fever and encountered such hostility among the local people that he turned around and went home before reaching Timbuktu. Gordon Laing got to Timbuktu by traveling several thousand miles across Libya and modern-day Algeria, but he was killed in the desert by his guides. The Swiss explorer Jean Louis Burckhardt spent two years in Syria learning Arabic—*two years!*—then died in Cairo of dysentery a week before he was scheduled to leave on his expedition. Captain James Tuckey was tasked by the British Navy to travel up the Congo to see if it joined the Niger but turned back after two hundred miles due to impassable rapids. On this aborted trip, he lost thirty-five men to disease and discovered nothing of scientific or military value.

All told, thirty-two European expedition leaders died trying to get to Timbuktu before René-Auguste Caillié, an orphan and shoe apprentice from Bordeaux, made it there and back to tell the tale.

Caillié was born in the wine-producing region of Mauzé-sur-le-Mignon and was orphaned when he was eleven. He became the apprentice to a shoemaker, but dreamed of riches and glory in Africa, and so shipped to Senegal at the age of sixteen with sixty francs in his pocket. There he joined a British expedition and saw firsthand how large, military expeditions could end in death and disaster, as bandits plundered supplies and progress was slowed by the sick and dying. After that he tried to convince French authorities to fund his own much more modest expedition to the interior, and when no one would, he prepared for the trip anyway. He went to live with the Brakna Moors north of the Senegal river, likely in modern-day Mauritania. Because he was poor and Christian they treated him horribly, alternately teasing, starving, and ignoring him for eight long months. In the end, however, he learned Arabic well enough to pass himself off as a native speaker.

Still, he was unable to get financing from the French government, so he decided that instead of leading an expedition he would travel to Timbuktu with the locals. He found a caravan of Arabs going northeast, and told them he was an Egyptian Muslim who had been enslaved in childhood by Europeans. He begged them to take him to Timbuktu, where he could catch another caravan to the north coast of Libya and then go home.

The Arabs took Caillié along, but they never really trusted him. His own guide and other members of the caravan pilfered his belongings, demanded random gifts, ate into his daily ration of food and water, rudely interrogated him, and teased

him for his poverty. He walked hundreds of miles in the burning sun without shoes or adequate water, fighting wild animals
and desert hornets. At one point, scurvy had so weakened his
bones he recounts dislodging sections of his upper palate with
his tongue.

Nevertheless, he reached the city in April 1828 and spent two
weeks there taking notes and drawing sketches from the top of
a minaret. When he finally returned home his account was so
straightforward and modest some members of the French and
British intelligentsia doubted his veracity. There was no way a
semiliterate kid from the countryside with no money and no
training could have completed such a journey, and in Arabic.
The salons were aghast. The critics were merciless, but his book
Travels through Central Africa to Timbuctoo became a bestseller.

In Paris, I had read half of Caillié's admirable, earnest, and
dead-dry nine-hundred-page account of his travels to Timbuktu. I admired his pluck, his drive, his absolute inability to
take no for an answer. As someone who had studied Arabic on
and off for a decade, I particularly admired his ability to learn
a language well enough to pass himself off as a native speaker
in a mere eight months. Like Mary Kingsley, who wrestled her
education from the jaws of an unwilling household and culture, Caillié proved himself a man whose intelligence and simple need to know pressed him to take greater and greater risks.

Mauritania was where it all began. So, like Caillié, I decide to start there. I fly into Nouakchott from Dakar with the
idea of going northeast into the Adrar Plateau and then perhaps across the desert to Timbuktu. It is an absurd route, across
swaths of desert that have no roads or water or transport, but
I reckon I will find a way. Here is a place of new beginnings
and unforeseen dangers and enormous unanswered questions.
I don't exactly know how I will get to Timbuktu, but I suspect
that when Caillié began, he didn't either.

18

Mood on the Streets

I AWAKE IN NOUAKCHOTT on election day. The hotel
lobby is bustling with journalists from the Middle East and
Africa thumping away on keyboards or doing stand-ups in
front of shoulder-held cameras. In the corner there is a circle of French newspaper reporters, wearing what seems to
be the uniform of all French reporters—Converse sneakers,
a blue blazer, and dirty blue jeans. They smoke cigarettes
and scowl, looking undernourished, exhausted, and utterly
French.

Today the military likely will step aside and hand power to
an elected civilian who will perhaps enact some economic reforms, allowing foreign investment. There is a sense of hope in
the air, rare in the Middle East, rarer still in Africa.

I am groggy from the flight, the short night of sleep.
Plus there is a heaviness to Nouakchott I didn't expect. It is
as though sand and sea have melted and created liquid atmosphere. I am, in seconds, grimy and sweating, dehydrated.

I am, however, enjoying the new ethos, which is to be comfortable while traveling. Despite the fact that I encountered a
dead white bird in the hallway this morning, the hotel is sur-

prisingly posh. There is a buffet breakfast—thick white bread, tomatoes, and Spam—and an espresso machine set like a work of art in the lobby. I understand you can even get a beer, although the waiter will pour it into a black glass so no devout Muslim will have to see what you are drinking.

I sit down next to a young Spanish woman who works for Oxfam and is gaping, mouth open, at the three-euro charge for her espresso. She seems stunned for someone on an expense account.

"How do you find your work here?" I ask brightly. A part of me always thinks I should have done some kind of aid work instead of journalism.

"Africa is very hard," she says, softening her r's with the tip of her tongue. "And in Mauritania there is nothing."

"Nothing?"

"Nothing," she whispers.

A young journalist comes and sits down next to her. He's tall and Egyptian and looks her up and down, head to toe, like she's a giant lollipop. My heart goes out to her.

"Are you covering the elections?" I ask.

He doesn't take his eyes off the Spanish girl.

"I don't have a story. These men could be the same man. You know, there were so many candidates eliminated in the first round I doubt voter turnout will be high."

In a great rush of words and with an exaggerated sense of the blasé he goes on to tell me, still looking at her, that both men seem intent on limited market reform, inviting foreign investment, and staying on the US's good side. Both are economists by training, in their late fifties and tied closely to the mechanics of power. One candidate is favored—Sidi Ould Cheikh Abdallahi, who was a minister for the former military dictator who ruled Mauritania in the 1980s. He's backed in mysterious and unseen ways by the twelve-man military junta. His opponent, Ahmed Ould Daddah, is equally well connected but not favored by the military.

The Egyptian is playing up the cool, cynical journalist thing to get the girl. Once I might have fallen for this. I was ever a sucker for the war reporters before I met Florent, but I'm not sure it's working on this serious Spanish girl. She keeps moving away from him until she is sitting right next to me and our legs are touching. I get up to go and she looks at me with inquisitive eyes. *You're leaving me all alone?*

"I'm going for a walk," I tell her. "Do you want to come?"

"A walk?" she asks again, pleading.

"A walk." I say patiently. Maybe not the sharpest knife in the drawer, this girl.

"Outside?"

"Yes."

"Oh no," she whispers, looking horrified.

I had planned to go out and take a walk alone around Nouakchott, but now I want to get a television crew or one of the reporters to take me along. It'll be more interesting to go with journalists, and maybe they can show me the hidden gems of Nouakchott. The TV guys look busy doing stand-ups, but maybe the French wire reporters are going out.

"Hi!" I say very loudly. All three jump. When I'm insecure speaking French, I sometimes yell in an attempt at confidence. "You guys going out soon? You know, to do a mood-on-the-streets type thing? Can I come along? I used to be a reporter in Paris. I'm really interested in the elections. I won't say a word, I promise."

They look at me heavily. One of them whispers to the other and he whispers back.

"What means *mood*?" one asks. Shit. I'm speaking English.

"*Ambiance . . . l'ambiance,*" his friend answers.

The third guy stands up and puts his hand on my shoulder. He looks at me with serious gray eyes. Oh, bless the French man. The smell of cigarettes, the comfort with intimacy, the utter, to-the-bones appreciation of women.

"*Ma cherie*," he says, smiling first at me, then over his shoulder to his friends. "You best stay here. There is no mood. There are no streets."

19

Nouakchott

IF LIFE WERE A SCIENCE fiction movie, Nouakchott would be the farthest-out and most brutal mining planet in the solar system. Colonists, dangerously isolated from earth, would be consumed with trying to survive the climate, and a perverse culture would have sprung up around skin color, body weight, and the state of your black Mercedes.

Humans were certainly never meant to live here. This is the land of sand. It hurtles down the avenues, eats up the sidewalks, strangles the trees, and settles into little dunes between my hotel and the concrete three-story houses that make up most of the city. It's in the air, hanging like daggers between atoms of oxygen and nitrogen, covering everything from sewage spills to the strong, leafy neem trees.

Yet I'm determined to explore, even without the help of the French reporters, so I set out. It's hot, maybe 105 degrees, and unbearably heavy, a mixture of ocean humidity and airborne sand. I walk a mile to the center of town, the axis on which two boulevards meet, and stand at the crossroads of two streets and wait for someone to pass by. Above me is a nine-story building with blue and yellow accents, but the rest of the city seems to be low and crumbling houses made of poured concrete. Some are pockmarked as though they had received gunfire. All have small fine white dunes gathered at the base. After ten minutes, a Moor, tall and thin with high cheekbones and a blue daraa bunched around his shoulders, walks by. He doesn't look at me, but keeps up his steady rhythmic pace until he disappears into the haze. Five minutes later a boy, probably thirteen, comes up and asks me if I would like to buy a phone card. I decline and he turns away quickly, embarrassed. Then a white-and-black jeep passes, full of soldiers in green fatigues carrying rifles. Then a black Mercedes driven by a woman in a bright melfha. Then nothing.

As I walk I find it easier to think about the city in terms of what it doesn't have rather than what it does. No streetlights, no traffic, no ATMs, no garbage (not enough people), no sewage. The edges of town are rows of wooden shanty slums stretching as far as the eye can see. The center is houses for the rich hidden behind fifteen-foot walls laced in concertina wire. When I walk up next to one large white wall and press my ear to it I can hear the splash of fountain and rustle of acacia trees.

I make my way to a polling station. People are standing around outside joking while two policemen sleep in the sun, cradling their AK-47s. After ten minutes the doors open and we are allowed inside. Five well-nourished men and women sit behind a table. They are election observers from Senegal. One woman wearing huge diamond earrings rises to greet me.

"Can I help you?" she asks me kindly.

"I want to take a look around," I say.

"Of course," she says, plainly thrilled. She takes me to the corner of the concrete hall where there is a little plastic chair and table with a big clear box on top. Inside are election chits. She invites me to sit down and pulls down a cloth that is pinned to the wall.

I'm bathed in green light, cut off from the hall. "Very impressive," I say from behind the curtain.

"Isn't it?" she says brightly, whisking away the curtain.

Outside the polling station a couple arrive to vote. The woman is tall and beautiful and wears a tightly wrapped melfha and sunglasses with big gold c's on the side. Her smaller, rounder husband is in jeans and checked button-down shirt. After voting, they meet a friend and speak joyfully in French with lots of Arabic thrown in.

"Who did you vote for?" the friend asks the man.

"Daddah," the man says proudly. "But you know the funny part?"—cocking his thumb toward his wife—"she voted for Sidi!"

All three dissolve into hysterics, rocking back and forth on their feet and holding on to each other for support. The beautiful wife gathers the edge of her melfha to dab the tears away and so does her husband, who has turned purplish with merriment. The friend laughs so hard snot actually comes out of his nose.

"Oh, but Sidi is going to win, everyone knows that. Who votes for Daddah?" She laughs again so hard this time she looks set to throw her back out. Then they suddenly see me, watching them. I smile and they smile back, joyful, friendly, a little curious. My outsider status isn't threatening or annoying. So few tourists come to Mauritania I'm an oddity, perhaps a little sad, but not an irritant.

I walk all day through the town. Down to the beach to watch women shell crabs, across to the embassy district where diplomats live behind high white walls. Gradually I become accustomed to the heat and my legs relax into an easy pace. Before I've even noticed it I find myself on the outskirts of the city and the edge of the desert.

There everything is white—the sky, the land, even the

dusty road. The sun reflects brightly off the highway, and when that is behind me it bounces off the sand in blinding sheets of unwavering light. I walk up dunes, some as tall as a two-story building, with sand that slips out from under my feet on the way up and slides down my back on the way down.

As the sun sets, steel gray clouds roll in from the west and streams of sunlight bounce off the distant desert, turning it gold. Suddenly the wind shifts and it's cold and humid and the air smells strongly of salt. Storms are preparing themselves to strike the Mauritanian coast. In an hour to two this harsh, dry desert could be hit by rain.

I sit at the highest point I can find and look at the desert that rolls almost without interruption toward the Red Sea. Before me lie desert towns and underground aquifers and slate plateaus so hot no bacteria can survive. There are mountain ranges and dried-out wadis and oases surrounded by supple date trees. It is harsh and beautiful and gently numbing, promising the reassuring notion of annihilation, the peaceful easing into another place.

I've never been alone in a desert before. Not like this. I always went with people, afraid that the heat, dirt, and dust, the sheer emptiness could somehow swallow me. This place doesn't feel dangerous though; it feels warm and protected, almost godly. In a desert like this, religions were founded, the stars were mapped, dangerous spirits named and codified. It was here that we knew, as a people, that everyone was ultimately vulnerable to the same wants—shelter, water, a measure of privacy—and the only real greatness was divine. It was in the desert that both hope and despair were born, as fortunes changed so quickly every nomad could become a king, every king become a nomad.

I had spent so much of the past years in cities, running around, dodging rainstorms, ducking into cafés, that I forgot the leveling aspect of nature. I had forgotten how the bare earth evens out the hierarchies of the world by making us vulnerable to the same needs. Here toughness, wit, and luck mattered more than birth or money. Here everyone was humble below the faint white winter moon. And while one's fortune as rich man, poor man, soldier, or spy seemed written in stone at home, especially inviolate in these paralyzed times, that wasn't true here or anywhere else. Strip away the comforts of Paris or New York and there was just desert, where everything could change faster than we imagined and in ways for which we had not prepared. This notion was a little scary, but not, by definition, bad. The essential message was one of liberation.

20

Slate Mountains

TWO DAYS AFTER THE election every single person staying in my hotel clears out. I walk down to the lobby and there is no bellman, no bartender, and not even a concierge behind the counter. Abdallahi is declared the winner, Daddah graciously concedes. With violence kept to a minimum, and no initial sign of a military coup, everyone has gone home. I suppose it is time for me to leave too.

The next morning I rise at five thirty and head for the bus station. I plan to go northeast, to Atar, then to a village called Chinguetti that was once a station on the caravan routes from Morocco to Mali. It's a crumbling medieval town, half-swallowed by sand dunes but also home to a library that holds thirteenth-century Qur'ans. It is said that Chinguetti was once one of the most important towns in the Sahara, a place with a population of twenty thousand and mosques and libraries to rival Timbuktu's. The climate here in the Middle Ages was also relatively wet, and when caravans came across the desert there were rivers and lakes and date palms enough to feed thousands of starving, thirsty men. Due to natural climate changes the town became progressively drier and dunes began to overtake the scrubland. The oases dried up, now only fifteen hundred people live there, and I'm told that there are no roads or electricity. Tourism has recently made a modest rebound and the Moors who live there make some money bringing French trekkers out into the desert. Some local inhabitants still hold on to their traditions, however, keeping in chests locked away from the sand thousand-year-old-books in Arabic that have been in their families for generations.

Atar is high and cool, set above the dunes of the coastal plain but not quite in the mountains. I spend the night in yet another empty hotel and it rains, and I wake to a muddy desert town full of Bedouin who have arrived for market day. I walk into town and stop at a stand on the street where a man has nailed together boards into benches and serves Nescafé and french bread that is white and chewy and filling. It is already April, the beginning of the hot season here, but it feels like an early spring day.

He tells me to go down to the central square to find the cars leaving for Chinguetti but by the time I arrive all the seats in the Land Rover have been taken. What's left is a beat-up white Toyota pickup truck that is mostly taking food and other necessities to towns east of Atar. I'm told I can ride in the back on top of a crate of bottled water as long as I hold a canister of gasoline between my legs.

"Whatever happens, don't let that fall," says the driver, wagging his finger in my face.

I climb up in back and find a seat right behind the passenger compartment, which I hope will shield me from the wind. With one foot I can secure the gas can against the side of the railing while resting the other comfortably on a bag of sorghum. The driver even comes around and throws up a trunk-size package of sanitary napkins for me to use as a cushion.

Then he offers me a small cup of sweet coffee, I believe to compensate for the indignity of sitting on a pillow of sanitary napkins. Gallantry in the Sahara is not dead.

At around seven thirty we pull out of town. High atop the Toyota, I am lord of all I survey—men drinking milky tea and eating loaves of French bread, sheep picking their way through mud from last night's brief rain. The air smells fresh—like wet earth and henna trees and warm yeast. I wrap my turban around my head and over my face hoping that people on the ground can't tell whether I am a man or woman, Mauritanian or French.

We drive slowly, as the dirt road has turned to mud, and stop on the outskirts for gas. As the driver fills up, a teenage boy rolls a drum of gasoline the size of a redwood tree trunk toward us. He reaches the edge of our truck and looks up at us expectantly.

The driver comes back and starts yelling.

"Move, move," he says in Arabic, and then, for my benefit, *"Bouge!"*

The three of us push back toward the passenger compartment until we are nearly sitting on top of it. Four men lift the barrel of gasoline onto the truck and jam it into place by punching it with two-by-fours. My bag of sanitary napkins goes flying off the side of the truck and is chucked back up to me by the driver who again wags his finger at me. Two more men climb on board, one of whom is carrying a wedge of butter as big as a briefcase. It ends up under my arm as does the other young man, who is in his early twenties. I throw myself up a little higher in the carriage and manage to put the butter between us. All six of us have now found seats and the oil drum seems secure. But I am perilously, dangerously high up. My hand stretches to hold the rusty, greasy side of the oil drum.

Outside town, we pick up speed. My turban rapidly comes

unraveled, and the noise of rushing wind is deafening. With every jolt in the road I'm thrown half a foot in the air and land on the soft butter or the sanitary napkins. I hold on to the gas drum for dear life with one hand and use the other to protect my face from the wind.

The desert around me is stark and stunning. Black slate mountains rise thousands of feet, out of flat desert, surrounded on all sides by peach-colored sand dunes. Some waves of sand are several stories high and shedding their peaks under a hard and steady wind.

The Toyota slows and begins to climb up a series of small mountains to the plateau. The temperature drops. We ascend slowly, arduously, and sometimes at such a stark angle I fear the gas drum will breach the back door of the pickup and we will all be lost. When finally we reach the top of the mountain, the driver takes the truck out of gear and we careen down the side. My stomach drops, and I am lifted, for one perfect still-life second, into midair. I land painfully on the oil drum, which begins dripping gasoline through a rusty crease onto a bag of rice.

We drive like that for two hours, up and down mountains that become smaller and smaller toward the plateau. My hands, bloodless and stiff, become fixed to the gas can. I lose my long green turban cloth into the wind and the cold wind batters my cheeks into dry patches. The noise is so loud, so awful and consistent, I start humming songs to myself to try to block it out.

Finally the road flattens into a grassy plain flecked with shrubs that glow a bright, almost neon green under last night's rain. The driver slows again, and we come to a stop. Out in the distance a woman is standing on a small mound facing the road. Everyone in the back stands up, flicking the outside of their hands up in the Arabic signal of "What's up?"

People start appearing from behind the mound—two children, a man, and finally the woman, who's holding a baby wrapped in a brown blanket. They carry with them two large jerry cans of water, two tin cans of gasoline, and a forty-pound bag of rice. They look at us. We look at them. It was ever thus.

If I sit up any higher in the carriage I'm going to fly off the truck like one of those rolls of Styrofoam I'd seen so many times on the New Jersey Turnpike. These are the dangers we live with. And this is how Africans live. Danger is everywhere and the burden is shared. We must simply trust the driver.

Like an old river shifting course, we make room for the newcomers. The family settles in at the far end of the truck, safely tucked between the bag of rice and the oil can. No one can find room for a young girl in a pink party dress so they pass her around until her father agrees to let her sit on his lap. We set off again and the woman covers her baby's face with a blanket. The wind picks up and becomes brutal, flying at us sideways now, but she yells over it, cracking jokes and telling stories for the whole crowd. When something is particularly hilarious she slaps the top of her head. Everyone around her laughs and claps, entranced. Another hour passes and we are in Chinguetti.

When the truck comes to a stop on the outskirts of town, I jump to the ground and my legs collapse under my weight. People clap each other on the back and grasp hands to help each other out. They are merry, happy to be alive. To my surprise the woman in the back of the truck hands me her baby as she climbs down. Sitting in the sand, trying to gather my breath, I sneak a look at his tiny sleeping face. He thrusts his hands over his eyes to avoid the sunshine and opens his mouth to mew like a tiny lost kitten. It is perhaps the sweetest thing I have ever seen, and for a moment I enjoy holding the child. If I am very still I can almost feel his heartbeat through the thick cloth.

I'm not quite ready to let him go, but his mother comes and whisks him away. She and all the other passengers disappear into the new town of Chinguetti, a bunch of one-story flat-topped concrete houses that lie at the muddy bottom of sand dunes. In the distance, across what looks like an old river-bed, I see the vague outlines of the medieval city. Its mud brick buildings are crumbling on themselves, and half the town is consumed by sand dunes.

Two slender black women walk down the hill to greet me. Emissaries for the town, they take my hand and stroke it solemnly as though I were an anxious child. I ask in French for an auberge and they take me to a small walled compound filled with clean sand and goatskin water bottles. Around the edges are four square tents, each large enough to hold a family, and in the back is a squat house with a blue door. A young girl in a torn calico dress tells me that I can rest in one of the tents until the owner, Cheikhranny, arrives. Exhausted, I wash my face and choose a tent in the far corner that's light green with red flowers. Inside it's roomy and hot and smells faintly of freshly washed fabric. I try to unpack my bag but my hands are still shaking from the strain of holding on to the side of the truck for so many hours. I put one hand over the other to still them and try to take deep breaths. I feel exhausted and dreadfully alone. I lie down. The sounds of Chinguetti are stifled by the yards of fabric around me. It is hot and quiet and close and soon I want to sleep. Only a short wind blows through the seams, and the tent settles around me, like a softly breathing animal.

21

The Lothario of Chinguetti

IT ONLY TAKES ME a couple of hours to fall deeply, pro-tectively in love with Chinguetti. My infatuation centers around the auberge, which is run by a young Moor named Cheikhranny who is, to be honest, disturbingly handsome. He is tall with black eyes, high cheekbones, and even, white teeth. His nose cuts such a sharp angle, he looks cruel when he doesn't smile, but he smiles often. Under his blue daraa he wears Western shorts and no shirt, which reveals much of his muscled torso and arms. When we meet for the first time he very lightly touches my arm and directs me toward his tent for tea, a young alpha male, plumping his lair.

"You are here alone?" he asks.

"Yes, but I am married," I say.

"I see," he says soberly.

As he goes about lighting the Bunsen burner to boil water, a Frenchwoman with black frizzy hair pokes her head in.

"Qu'est ce tu fais, Cheikhranny? Tu dragues, tu dragues?"

What are you doing? Picking her up?

She disappears as quickly as she comes, and Cheikhranny

continues making tea with careful unhurried movements. He casually asks me about my travels but doesn't try to make conversation. While I talk he studies me through a half smile that reveals all his sharp white teeth. I remember, as though from another life, how many men regard courtship as a game to be won, like horseshoes or backgammon. Though I know I shouldn't, his gaze makes me feel ever so slightly coquettish.

He is a cad, a flirt, and clearly used to sleeping with Western women who pass through here. But he's no villain and when I explain that I am not here for that, he backs off. He even seems relieved to be freed from the obligation to court me, and quite quickly he turns from lothario into thoughtful hotel concierge. He recommends particularly lovely dunes, tells me not to miss the museum, and takes me on a tour of his tiny establishment.

When people come into his auberge, a rare occurrence as we are far from the tourist season and only locals are around, he stands and bows with hand to heart. His gaze is steady and his manners slow and impeccable. I always worry about traveling alone as a woman and here I am sleeping in a tent that anyone can walk into, day or night. But somehow I feel safe. The hotel that he runs mostly caters to a group of camel drivers who take both tourists and goods between the small towns on the Adrar Plateau. They come in that afternoon and are a rough bunch—dirty hands, grunting speech, and the faintest whiff of contraband whiskey, but he treats them with respect and great care. Most important, when they catch sight of me, he guides them firmly away. *She is my sister,* he whispers to them. *Not a Frenchwoman.*

I sleep well and soundly in my softly breathing tent, and in the morning Cheikhranny is up sweeping the sand into small fanlike arches. He nods curtly to me, then arranges the broken-glass mirrors above the outdoor sinks—which I find out are not shards at all but purposefully cut into interesting shapes—and waters the base of his four small trees. After that he arranges the decorative goatskin water bottles and Tuareg jewelry and takes a damp cloth and wipes down every still object in the auberge. It takes all morning. He does it every day. And it's touching. For under the great noble Moor, the casual seducer, is a man who seems to love order and beauty above all things.

I spend the first couple of days with Cheikhranny, mostly because I like him and he is smart and seems to enjoy my company. I do laundry and take long naps and read all afternoon. In the evening, I'm put to sleep by the sound of children next door singing verses from the Qur'an. In the middle of the night when I'm thirsty I run barefoot to the pump for water. The entire town is without electricity at night, and I find my way to the pump by the light of the huge gold moon that illuminates the entire sky. In the morning I wake to the sound of Cheikhranny unrolling his prayer mat and lighting the portable gas stove to make tea.

"The tourists are good for us," he says. "But the town has changed. Now it is all money, money, money."

"I'm sorry to hear that," I say.

"People, they used to really talk," he says. "Now there is no time. We are all working very hard."

"I can see that," I say. I mean it as a compliment, for I admire his work ethic and sense of ownership over the hotel, but he takes it as a slap in the face. His look hardens and I want to correct myself, although I'm not sure how.

"There is not even time to make a decent cup of tea," he sighs, letting go of the insult. I can't help but look slightly surprised. He looks at me blankly.

"Truly?" I say.

Cheikhranny seems to spend the better part of his leisure time thinking about or making tea. From start to finish he can take just about thirty minutes pouring mysterious concoctions of hot water, tea water, and sugar water between pots until a tiny cup of frothy sweetness is finished. It seems incredibly labor-intensive but he says he's taking shortcuts.

"Done correctly, tea takes three hours to produce and ideally women should do it," he tells me apologetically. "I just don't have that kind of time."

He hands me the small cup of tea. Lovingly prepared. Perfect. The green tea leaves stick with sugar to the side and we scrape them out and chew them contemplatively. We drink and chat, slowly, almost languidly, as the temperature outside rises first to eighty, then ninety, and finally one hundred degrees. Eventually he excuses himself to pray, but he doesn't go outside, just moves to a corner of the tent, washes his hands and face, and unfolds his prayer mat. He turns east toward the qibla and raises his hands to his ears. *Allahu Akbar.* Fine sand drifts in with the breeze and settles across his face like a shroud. He places his right hand over the left on his stomach and intones the opening verses of the Qur'an, *Bismillah irrahman irraheem.* When he finishes al-Fatiha he wipes his brow. At the end of the sura his hands go up to his ears again. *Allahu Akbar.* He moves his hands to his knees. *Subhana rabbiyal adheem* (Glory be to my Lord Almighty) three times. Then he is standing, a small smile on his lips. *Sami'a Allahu liman hamidah. Rabbana wa lakal hamd.* (God hears those who call upon Him. Our Lord, praise be to You.) He goes down to the ground. *Subhana rabbiyal a'ala* (Glory be to my Lord, the Most High). There is sand on his forehead but he is too deep into prayer to notice. Then he is reciting the Tashahhud, then he is sitting—*Allahu Akbar.* And now prostrate. *Subhana rabbiyal a'ala.*

When he is finished he sighs contentedly, rests comfortably on his haunches, and stands.

"More tea?" he asks.

As he lights burners and cleans teapots and shifts tea leaves from one canister to the next, I close my eyes and think about time. It's longer here, more substantial, and sweeter. It makes me think, with half a sigh, about the coffee machine in the news bureau where I worked in Paris. I wish I could explain that coffee machine to him, but I doubt he would believe me. I barely believe it anymore.

I still remember the numbers, etched in my memory like trauma. It was 22 seconds for a cup of decaf with milk, no sugar; 23 seconds for coffee with sugar and just 20 for regular caffeinated coffee. Decaffeinated, no milk, no sugar coffee (really the closest approximation to water) took a split-second more than regular coffee—about 20.2 seconds. This extra beat used to confound and infuriate me. There were some mornings when my body didn't need more caffeine but I went for the regular coffee because that extra moment could very well have sent me into hysteria, or even gotten me fired.

Given that I didn't speak French when I started, I should have been grateful to have any job at all. But this position was less about journalism (or French, for that matter) than about speed—how fast you could get out a headline, whether you could beat Reuters or Bloomberg by a second or two. The story had to be fast and the update faster. Then someone had to quickly insert pictures and graphs and you had to move on to the next story, the next deadline. Getting coffee in the midst of this chaos was an unimaginable luxury and a total terror.

I would do it anyway because I was brought up to believe in the redemptive powers of coffee. My mother drank on average nineteen cups a day. She began and ended each day with coffee in bed and found seventeen more opportunities throughout the day to enjoy a cup. She drank so much coffee that her skin smelled vaguely roasted and she was always warm from the effort of processing caffeine.

Most important, though, my coffee break was a small act of rebellion. I would leap up from my desk, speed walk across the newsroom, and leave the early-morning slot desk unmanned. This was heresy in the ethos of the newsroom, *where the desk was never to be unmanned.* On winter mornings, when the streetlights had gone off in anticipation of a sunrise that was still several hours away, and the office was lit only by emergency signs, the coffee machine would glow and hum and tower above me, sending coded messages. *Stay away.* Or sometimes, *You should have gotten more sleep.* By the time the plastic cup dropped and the coffee arrived I knew I had been away from my desk too long. My bitterness toward the machine expanded all out of proportion with its role in the world, and sometimes I would hiss at it in fury and frustration: *Why, why, after twenty years of doing the exact same task, does it still take you twenty seconds to make a cup of coffee? Can't you see that you should prepare the hot water ahead of time? Can't you see that we have no time?*

Then I would sprint back to my desk, hips snapping like an Olympic speed walker, holding the hot little plastic cup that I believed was gradually melting off my fingerprints. The coffee was horrible but I drank it anyway because coffee was life and bad coffee was better than none at all. Then I would slouch very low in my chair and wait for the news. EADS's new A380 superjet was behind schedule and over budget—French consumer confidence had fallen to a yearly low. Press releases would come in so fast there wasn't even time to write about them. I would send out one-line headlines, one after the other, fingers shaking as the clock in the lower right-hand side of the computer mocked my slowness. Two minutes and thirty-three seconds to turn that press release around. Three minutes and four seconds for that one. I was failing.

By the time people started coming in for work, I was covered in a thin layer of gleaming sweat. I had probably sent out ten headlines but I could not have told you what any of the stories were about. I smelled like burnt coffee and fear. The dark circles under my eyes had turned into purple puffy half-moons, and my throat was sore from the bile that had risen and fallen within it countless times. Worst of all, my hands were shaking and I was starting to make mistakes. An editor in London called to scold. The bureau chief walked by and gave me a cold stare. By the time my shift ended at four p.m., I was as splintered and shaky as a recovering alcoholic.

Inevitably, when I left it would be raining outside. It was always raining in Paris, as though some postapocalyptic weather pattern had settled on the city and wouldn't move until the world had regained its proper axis. In the elevator on the way down I took stock of my thirty-three-year-old face. A year ago a glowing bride. Now puffy neck, dark eyes, thin skin, possibly the beginning of jowls. Poor Florent.

Then I would step out the door of the newsroom and the reality would hit me. Ahead lay a lifetime of working at the wire, my world confined to the small alleys and small fears of my own mind. For many more years I would feel splintered and haggard. The sheer monotony of my life, the indistinguishability of one day to the next, would make me feel like I didn't exist. Dread would greet me every morning and sit like a heavy weight on my chest until I dislodged it with wine and food and other distractions that would shatter my sleep and in turn invite more dread. Grandeur and God were entirely gone. Adventure and solitude were relics of the past. I would never wake up to the sound of the muezzin calling the prayer in Jerusalem, or sun streaming through the window on a blustering day in Baku, or the smell of pakoras being fried in the old city of Lahore. I would never again see the broad, clean, bright desert outside Cairo. I would never again wonder what new wonder the world would bring me today. And then, in my head, I would write the most painful headline of the day: *Well, Nina, this is life.*

The memory is still so vivid and acute that my eyes fly

open. I actually hold my hand to my heart, which has begun to beat faster from the adrenaline surge of a daydream. As I focus I see that all is as it was, or as it should be. Cheikhranny is making tea. The tent breathes softly in the midday heat. A Qur'an is on the table. He has opened some crackers, and their talcum powder smell adds to the earthy closeness of his home, where he has so kindly welcomed me. He smiles.

"You don't want yours too sweet," he says, practicing his English. "I am remembering."

"No, not too sweet," I say.

"Yes, it will be good," he confirms. "I have gotten new leaves just now."

"Cheikhranny, you should never go to New York or Paris."

He blanches and rubs his eyes. But then thinks about it a moment, like a man who has never had this thought before. "God willing," he finally says, "I never will."

22

Fortune Tellers

I AM A HOMEBODY in Chinguetti. Not in Paris, of course, where my apartment makes me feel as though I should be cooking boeuf bourguignon, but in Africa, where I seem to thoroughly enjoy making myself comfortable in other people's houses. For days I hang around Cheikhranny's tent enjoying his tea, chatting about the scourges of tourism, feeling snug and cozy.

Finally, Cheikhranny kicks me out. I think he's beginning to feel as though it's unseemly to spend this much time with a woman he's not sleeping with. (In this respect, he could be French.) He finds me a guide named Hadrami, who takes me on a whirlwind tour of the town. I see manuscripts from the twelfth century depicting the constellations in precise format with dancing horses riding behind the moon. I see a Qur'an from that period, with tough old pages made of leather and careful gold-leafed geometrical designs on the side. These are beautiful, wondrous things, but in the end I am hot, irritated, and breathless from walking up and down slippery dunes. I complain to Cheikhranny when I arrive home.

"Too much sand. Too hot," I say.

Finally, exasperated, he just sends me next door.

"Get your feet hennaed," he says. "It's very beautiful. You should be spending time with women."

This is true and so I am passed, like three-day-old fish, from one house to the next. There, Ayesha takes one look at my feet and one look at my hair and decides that much should be done to improve me.

Ayesha is a very dark Moor, probably of the slave class called *haratin*. She lives alone on a compound with her four-teen-year-old daughter Miriam, and they have a happy though precarious existence. Ayesha makes necklaces, sells vegetables, and sometimes works for Cheikhranny. To her credit, she has not yet married off Miriam.

She and Cheikhranny are close, but I can't quite sort out the nature of their relationship. He sort of flits between his house and hers, but they aren't related. Her house is next to his, which in the geography of Chinguetti means you have to climb up a dune and down one to get to her compound. That dune will engulf her house, if not this year then next, and every morning Ayesha has to dig out a path to her front door, like people do after snowstorms. But once you get inside, the compound is tidy and well decorated, with wooden trunks holding ancient manuscripts. Although she reads poorly, she says she will never give away her books.

When I arrive at her door, she doesn't know I am coming, but she smiles and bows and takes me up seven enormous stairs to a small room with thick walls that is cool and carpeted. There is a small window across which one can sit and see a dry riverbed known as wadi. Like everyone in Chinguetti, she doesn't have a television or a computer and gets electricity for only three hours at night. Thus, she spends her days looking out across the wadi and gossiping with her friends about who is coming and going.

"Did you see me walking across the wadi the first day I arrived?" I ask her.

"Oh yes," she says. "We hadn't seen a white in many months. You glowed!"

She motions for me to sit down and fires up the gas burner for some tea. A gray mouse scurries across the carpet but she doesn't notice, because she is concentrating on the tea and tea is so important. She pours it from small blue kettle to red cup to kettle to cup until it is frothy and not too hot. I notice she does this in a short fifteen minutes and looks stricken when she hands me the cup.

"It's delicious," I tell her.

"I didn't have time to make a new pot," she mumbles, ashamed.

Then, with the comfort of a woman who spends all her days with women, she places her hand on my thigh and squeezes a little.

"Miriam," she calls. "Come in. Let's henna her feet."

Miriam comes bounding in, as fine and light as a fox. She brings with her pots of henna and motions for me to lie down on my back. The ceiling is lined in beams and the carpet is clean and soft. Flies buzz in the corner by the tea and Miriam sings to herself a little. Then she proceeds to drip cold, wet henna on my feet and ankles, which feels like some kind of massage or ancient healing practice. Each drip of thick red dye seems directed to a nerve or pressure center that needs soothing.

Cheikhranny bounds in, cell phone in hand, and takes the seat by the window.

"I could write a book about all the things I see on that wadi," he says.

Ayesha fires off something in Arabic I don't understand, and he sort of snaps back. He's a man and a white Moor and clearly used to being in charge. He turns back to the window and plays a video game on his cell phone, casual and confident in his power.

Miriam moves me to my hip so she can paint the inside of my ankles. Another woman comes in carrying a cistern of rotting vegetables on her head. She puts it down with a heavy sigh and looks at me.

"Does she want a fortune?" she asks Cheikhranny.

"Oh yes!" he says, putting down the phone. "I'd love to see this."

With me sequestered on my side, I can't even really see her face, but I can see the small white shells she pulls from her change purse. She chops the side of her hand across the inside of her wrist and they scatter on the ground. Cheikhranny comes over to look. Everyone groans a little.

She throws the shells again. Ah, that's better. Everyone smiles, and little Miriam squeezes my big toe in encouragement. It appears that good news is just around the corner. The vegetable seller tells me that my husband is thinking of me. I will find new work. My husband will call in two days and—here everyone holds their breaths with suppressed pleasure—someone *besides* my husband is thinking of me.

They all look at me with knowing looks and I disengage my foot from Miriam's grip.

"I don't know who that is," I say, feeling unusually indignant.

Ayesha nods sagely and Cheikhranny smirks a little. "Everyone has someone else," Ayesha says.

"I don't."

Ayesha smiles and Miriam gets hold of my feet again. Cheikhranny bounds back into the window. They don't believe me. I can't believe they don't believe me.

I refuse to defend myself and we fall into silence. Then the vegetable-selling fortune teller turns a plastic can over and starts lightly drumming on the top. She finds a rhythm she likes, and in a low voice starts to sing. Her drumming is inexpert but her voice clear and strong, as though she learned to sing reciting the Qur'an.

Hey yeah ya-aay. Allah. Allaaah. Hey yeah ya-aay. Allah.

She brings the note very high and Miriam closes her eyes. I rest my head against the carpet and watch the dust dance in the sunlight streaming in through the window. I try to picture Florent's face in Paris. I love that face, but all I can conjure is from the first time we met. The image comes back to me in fragments.

He shook my hand firmly like an American but said his name too softly for the noisy room. He was tall and hunched over, like a man uncomfortable with his height, but he held his hips at an angle and with grace. In the taxi on the way home he wrote down his phone number on a business card and blew gently on the ink so it wouldn't smudge. It was a small gesture but one that seemed so significant. He was trying to show me something, but I didn't know what it was.

Once, before we were married, when life was slower and we didn't live in Paris and I didn't work at the wire and he didn't work twelve-hour days, I started to learn to read the signs. I knew that he showed love through small acts of tenderness—my house keys left on the door handle so I wouldn't forget them, his hand held protectively on my hip as I slept. Then life in Paris got hard. The wire drained me and left me scattered. I lost what little ability I had to read his love, and even in the moments that mattered, like the night before I was to leave for Africa, I had lost my sense of him.

I think now of that night. It was dark again in Paris. January. It had rained for days and the sun couldn't pierce the clouds to light the city. The streetlights on our block had stayed on that morning until nine thirty, but they should never have gone off.

I had quit my job at Dow Jones, telling myself I would

never regret leaving the long hours, poor pay, and utter joyless-
ness. My little backpack was packed with just a few things. In a
few hours I would be alone, in Africa. I hoped that I would feel
like I was living my life for the first time since I married.

But in the days before my departure, doubt had crept in. I
remember wandering the apartment while Florent was at work,
trying to order my thoughts and arrive at a justification for
leaving my husband for such a long time. In the dark hours, a
knot had formed in my stomach that wouldn't go away. Anxiety, which I usually kept at bay by working hard and pushing
off the big questions, raised its head. I was afraid, I thought
grimly. I had forgotten how to be alone.

I had kept these fears from Florent, not out of malice but
from a sense of protectiveness. After all I'd put him through he
didn't need to hear about my doubts. He wanted to see confidence. He wanted a glimpse of the warrior.

"A little alone time for both of us would be good," he said as
I gathered my belongings around me. "And you will see wonderful things. I'm jealous."

It was a bland, almost meaningless statement, but he was
also so easygoing, my husband. Maybe this wasn't the time
when he should tell me what he honestly thought. He leaned
back in his chair and took a long drag of a small cigar. He didn't
think that cigars were as bad for you as cigarettes, so he had
started to smoke them. He also thought that ice cream head-
aches were an American myth, something dreamed up to stop
children from eating too quickly. His quirks made me miss him
a little, preemptively.

"When I come home we'll take a romantic weekend somewhere," I said lightly.

"Maybe," he said. "Do you have your passport? Enough
money?"

I rolled my eyes and didn't answer the question. Florent had
never acted like my father. I didn't expect him to start now.

Then he leaned forward and looked at me with steady eyes. He seemed strangled at the edges, as though he wanted to release himself from something heavy sitting on his chest. I walked by and he reached for my hand, but I drew it up before he could take it, and kept walking.

"You just need to remember," he called after me. "You come back if something goes wrong. If it's not the right place for you, and if you doubt . . . you just come home. No one will think less of you."

I came back toward him, puzzled. Was he doubting me? Was he questioning my courage or ability or resilience? Perhaps he had the right, but it still made me angry. I came to stand right in front of him.

"I'm good at this," I said, spreading my arms wide, "traveling alone in the world. You don't need to worry about me. Here I won't fail. This won't be like the wire. I won't carry the misery and dread. I won't be such a mess again . . . such a failure." There was some bravado in this statement, even obvious evasion after my disastrous interlude in Western Sahara, but to relinquish the notion that I traveled well alone was just too much for me.

His face fell a little. He reached up to clasp my hand as though willing the meaning to flow from his body into mine. But he didn't say anything, because he didn't have the words. In their absence I filled in the spaces. I felt in that moment that he judged me. Maybe that he even hated me on some level because I was his wife and I was leaving him. So I shook my hand free from his and went on with the packing. I was going to Africa. I wasn't changing my mind now.

If I could go back now to that night I might ask him more directly what he meant. He, who was so careful with words, relied on signals but these too were difficult to read. They flew by me and, even though I saw them, I was in such a rush that I never got the chance to interpret.

Now I think I know what he meant. It's okay to think of yourself one way, fight hard to get back to yourself, and then wake up in that place feeling lost. It's okay to go away looking for a grand purpose and come back with fragments that don't add up. Life isn't clean, but we'll muddle through, together. There is love here. Don't be afraid to come home.

Ayesha nestles up next to me, with her big, hard black feet scratching the back of my legs. She senses my sadness but doesn't know the source. So she turns back to fortune telling, the reassurance of a future with a present that is wholly known and accounted for.

"This someone who is thinking of you. It could also be someone you haven't met yet," she whispers into my ear in surprisingly good French. "Someone who is just sensing you."

23

The Good Doctor

THE WAY I HAD UNDERSTOOD love before I met Florent was as a hyperarticulate Anglo-Saxon affair. I was drawn to difficult men, with complex backgrounds and messiah complexes. There was the academic who lost his father and could never finish his PhD. He would talk about Heidegger for hours and I would listen, enraptured, as he martyred himself to the inscrutable thinking of brilliant men. Needless to say, he never finished that PhD, but he probably still wows coeds with his take on German philosophy. Then there was the Anglo-Indian human rights lawyer who grew up in poverty and violence in East London but managed to scratch his way to respectability through sheer charm and the ability to sound sane on the Israeli-Palestinian conflict. He never felt loved and so had to get love from as many women as possible. That, too, ended badly. Then there was the English writer I loved who didn't love me back. I can't even talk about him. Still too mortifyingly painful.

These were verbal, dynamic men who invited adoration and then love. They could light up a dinner party. They could make you feel special because you liked the right books or music or furniture. Most important, they draped themselves in higher purpose. They were artists, or at least artisans, drawn to the cause of education or saving Palestinians in refugee camps or reading Nabokov translated into German. They made even failure sound fruitful and lofty.

Needless to say, these relationships were exhausting, time consuming, and ultimately empty. They worked as long as I felt ever so slightly inferior and blew up the moment I realized that behind their intellectualism and bravado they had very little of real substance and a total absence of character. For a while I would try to hold on, but my love would slide from adoration to acceptance and then finally a kind of morbid fatality. The relationships became an irritation for me as I slowly became their mother, pushing them to finish the PhD or get that great job at the UN. When I realized they couldn't, that their dispositions precluded the taking of real chances, I would eventually leave them, only to be drawn in by another morally bankrupt man filled with intellect and potential and promises.

Every single day I'm grateful I didn't marry a man like that. It's safe to say those men are probably also grateful they didn't marry me. But I do think it's funny that a man *exactly* like that should appear suddenly in Mauritania, just as I am beginning to get a clearer picture of my husband.

The first time I see the Venezuelan doctor he is bending over a little girl and placing drops in her ears. As she quakes in fear, he rubs his hand over the top of her head and hums a song in Spanish.

"*Bonjour,*" I say, "I'm just passing through and would love to see the hospital."

He looks over the little girl and extends his hand. He has black curly hair, hazel eyes, and a broken nose that looks like it never healed correctly.

"English is better for me than French," he says. Then, "My name is Casper Ramirez."

"Like Casper the friendly ghost?" I ask.

"Yes," he says, not laughing, "like the ghost."

This is what I know about the doctor in Chinguetti. He's lived here two years and has only called in sick once. He sees about thirty-five patients a day and will often drive his Toyota out to neighboring villages on the weekends. He never leaves Chinguetti except to buy medicine in Nouakchott and hasn't seen his family in Venezuela for four years. He has never accepted a bribe, never slept with a local girl, never refused a middle-of-the-night emergency. He lives in a small house in the old town and always walks to work in the morning, crossing the wadi at six a.m. and coming home again at seven p.m. Sometimes at night he takes his brand-new truck and drives across the wadi into the desert, playing Spanish music loudly with the windows open.

He's overseen the construction of the clinic and the flow of funds from unnamed, wealthy benefactors in Spain. Two months after opening, the electricity bills suddenly tripled and some government officials from Atar arrived demanding his truck, his generator, and his X-ray machine. When he told them to leave, they cut the power to the hospital, and diesel for the generator stopped arriving. For weeks he worked in the dark until the son of a prominent local needed to have his leg set. Suddenly the lights went on and he hasn't paid a power bill since.

Now he is something akin to a shaman and a hero—a strange man who turns down dinner invitations to spend every night alone, who looks between a woman's legs even before the baby arrives, who counsels people to bathe with water instead of sand and eat plants instead of couscous. *He's crazy,* people whisper, but they camp outside the hospital anyway, pressing their heads to his hand when he arrives, teary with hope and prayer. After witch doctors and Islamic rites, he is their last defense against death and disease.

This is a man who both knows Chinguetti and is apart from

it. He's probably the only person in town who I can ask, in English, about the inhabitants without looking like a clown. So I tell him I'm hanging around Mauritania for a few weeks and we arrange to meet near the water tower at noon. It's gotten hot in Chinguetti, suddenly, stupendously hot, and by the time I make it to the water tower I am sweating and foulmouthed. In all those romantic musings on the desert in rainy Paris somehow I had forgotten that it could get this hot.

"These fucking dunes. I'm so tired of walking over these fucking dunes," I say.

His laugh is full and immediate—unfettered and proud, and seeming to come all the way from his toes. The laugh of a tall man. He hands me a piece of bread he'd bought that is still warm from the oven. Then he pulls out a cigarette and lights it while he's still chewing. He looks like a South American soccer player, with his curls tied back in a black bandana.

"Ballsy, to smoke as a doctor," I say.

"Yeah, well, you don't want to live forever. You end up peeing on yourself."

He offers me a cigarette and I take it. Marvelous. Smoking and eating at the same time. We get into the truck and he offers to take me with him on a trip to a nearby village where he will check in on some children and pick up fresh vegetables. When we arrive, though, most of the lettuce has gone to seed and the carrots are wrinkled and dried. The doctor sighs heavily and gathers what he can.

"I'm still trying to explain the whole concept of vegetables," he says. "I think they just grow them for me and don't really understand when they are ready. One day I am going to have to make a salad for them so they see what it should look like."

The village itself is perched on top of a hill without either water or vegetation. The villagers are black Moors, the freed slaves of nomads who have been pushed toward Chinguetti by diminished grazing land. Most live in tents or brick huts.

It's the first dirty place I've seen in Mauritania, with garbage, animal waste, plastic bottles, and rotting chicken carcasses lying around between the houses. Children run to us in rags and grab at the doctor with snotty hands. Some wheeze from the effort. They live with the animals and suffer from every kind of infection—skin, lungs, urinary tracts, and eyes. Tuberculosis is also rampant here and often progresses until death.

"The biggest health problems in Mauritania are diabetes and hypertension," the doctor says. "But as you can see, in this village they are so poor they just suffer from infection and malnutrition."

As he looks in the ears of a little girl, so sick she is glassy-eyed and listless, I watch a woman remove a tray of human feces from the latrine. She balances it carefully, just a little slopping onto the front of her melfha, and places it carefully on the ground. Three sheep come running over. They lap it up gleefully, licking the sides of the tin tray, nosing the underside for more.

"Want to stay for dinner?" the doctor asks lightly. But the sight of this kind of poverty makes me crumble. I feel sick and ashamed. The doctor comes over quickly and guides me by the elbow to the truck. He turns on the air conditioning and puts on some Spanish guitar music.

"I feel stupid," I say.

"Let me finish here and we'll go somewhere nice for lunch."

I don't know why we get along, but we do. I feel like I have known him all my life, but perhaps it's just a function of being lonely. We have a lunch of boiled eggs and tomatoes in a little auberge I've never heard of before on the outskirts of Chinguetti. The doctor says he comes here on Saturday afternoons because no one bothers him. There is even a tiny pool where he bathes in the summer when afternoon temperatures jump up above 110 degrees.

It's been a long time since he sat and talked to an American, he says. The hospital has nurses who come through for two- or three-month stints, but he doesn't much like them, as they are Spaniards and all Spanish hate South Americans.

"They treat me like a fool."

"I bet they think you are a hick," I say.

"What is a hick?"

"Someone from the countryside, like a farmer, who doesn't have much education."

"This is good! This is good!" he enthuses. "You know lots of great phrases. God, I miss Americans."

He's like the boys I met when I used to travel, but lighter, easier to get along with, and less narcissistic. He's in Mauritania for the good cause, but he doesn't wear that fact on his sleeve and he doesn't do it as a means of seduction. He is articulate and caring and manly and terribly handsome. It's hard to escape the fact that if I were unmarried I might develop a crush on him and think, breathlessly, hopelessly, that he was different from all the others.

We meet for dinner. Everywhere we go, he is treated like a king, offered tea and bread, and I am treated as his queen. Suddenly I go from a strange single woman to a big shot, a kind of local celebrity. I wake up in the morning now not feeling blue and lonely, but instead wondering when the doctor will come and pick me up that day. Everyone in Chinguetti is talking about us, but I don't care. We are innocent. Let them wag their village tongues.

"I never go around with Europeans, you see, or tourists. They are so happy I have finally found a woman. It answers a lot of questions for them."

I don't talk much during our dinners. Casper, who is clearly thrilled to have an American to talk to, unloads two years of frustration and cabin fever. *People don't eat right. They don't look after their children. They don't bathe and they put entirely too much emphasis on sand.*

"Do you see a lot of folk medicine?" I ask.

"Ah, this is a good question," he says. "I can tell you are a journalist."

This of course makes me feel good. We are on the same team, and the team is good and I am a reporter after all, not just a lone soul walking around a continent, hunting fruitlessly for Timbuktu.

He says people use sand for everything—to bring the baby sooner, to wash in. Once he saw an old woman who jammed sand up her vagina in order to restore her fertility. Finally when she got sick she came to the hospital and was horrified when the Spanish nurse cleaned her out.

"You can't imagine what she smelled like," he says.

He talks and talks, but because he is passionate I don't mind. Women come into the clinic weighing one hundred kilos and asking for medicine for their knees, and when the doctor suggests they lose weight they ignore him and come back the next week. No one has ever doubted his care, he says, though it is a much bigger deal when an adult dies than when a child does.

"The mother is more valued than the child, even a son," he says.

We talk late into the evening, and after the electricity has gone out we sit in moonlight. Casper unloads story after story about Mauritania. Freed slaves he hired out of mercy who returned to their former masters after a week. People who stole from him, lied to him, mocked him. He has given so much to Chinguetti. As it gets late he turns tragic. While here, his wife left him and his girlfriend, a nurse in Spain, seems poised to do the same. His father is ill and Hugo Chávez has inexplicably taken power in his lovely, fair-minded country.

This man needs to be taken care of, I think.

"Sometimes I think about coming home, loosening my tie,

pouring a glass of wine, and putting on Carla Bruni," he says. "Wouldn't that be great?"

"This is a very attainable goal. You just need to leave Africa or at least go somewhere where there is alcohol and electricity . . . and neckties," I say, laughing.

"Yes," he says, overriding my last words. "But I'm all alone in the world. I've been alone so long."

"I'm sorry. That sounds terrible," I say.

"And you are alone too," he adds.

This isn't true, not by a long shot, but for some reason I don't say anything, don't try to correct the impression. I think to do so would seem rude and put a wedge between us when, after all these weeks traveling, it is so nice to feel close to someone.

Over the next days, I reassure myself that all is aboveboard. We like each other and have a spark but that's it. Absolutely no romance lingers on the horizon. And I look for evidence of this. On our way home from dinner one night he stops at the big dune on the edge of town, where guides take Western women in order to seduce them.

"This is the dune of love," he says.

"Really? Do they call it that?"

"Can you imagine taking someone someplace so far away, so *uncivilized*, in order to seduce them?"

This joking makes me feel safe.

"Generally speaking I'm not in the business of seduction," I say. "But I think not."

He smiles and runs his hands through his curly black hair.

"In Venezuela we dance with women and that is seduction. Do you dance?"

"No. Not really. No."

"You would learn," he says.

It's bright tonight under a full moon and the sand is as soft as talcum powder. We sit on the edge of the dune, digging our fingers into the warm sand to reach the buttery parts underneath, and look out at thousands of other dunes glowing under the dark blue sky.

"You know this is therapy for me, talking to you," Casper says.

He lies down and puts his hands behind his head as though he's looking for stars. I glance back at him and point out that the Toyota on the big dune looks positioned for a car commercial. He smiles but doesn't sit up. He's so casual, like an American man would be.

Suddenly Casper sits up. He looks at me intently and then, as though unable to stop himself, his eyes dance across the dunes. He's thought so long and hard about this desert and been alone for so many years that he's distracted by it now.

"Sometimes there are desert foxes out here. Have you ever seen one? They are beautiful, like small deer really."

"I haven't seen any foxes, how interesting . . ."

But he interrupts. "You have the eyes of a fox."

I look at him sideways. I don't believe it. He smiles back confidently and winks mischievously. The joke is on me, I think. Or not. But now he's looking at me with thick, heavy eyes. I stand up abruptly. I am suddenly out in the middle of nowhere, really nowhere, with a man. I step back again and look at him. Am I imagining it? I start shaking sand off my bottom, but he doesn't move. I conjure the hard maternal voice of my mother, the voice that seems to come to all women over the age of thirty who have had enough of foolish, narcissistic men.

"Come, Casper," I say, walking toward his car. "Time to go home."

He follows. Takes me home and chats on the way about Spanish music like nothing at all had happened. I arrive in the auberge as Cheikhranny is dousing the candlelight and getting ready to go to bed. I sleep fitfully, almost guiltily, but wake the next morning to a bright blue sky and the sound of Cheikhranny making an omelet. The girls next door are singing verses from the Qur'an and the camel drivers are rolling up their tents after their morning prayer. All is well with the world, ordered by Islam and tea. I spend the morning chatting with Cheikhranny and doing my laundry in a big steel tub with a rock in the middle where I beat the clothes. It is, as it sounds, tremendously peaceful.

Around noon Ayesha and her friends stop by. I can tell that they've gotten wind of the fact that Casper and I have spent time together and want to know the dirty details. They assume we are sleeping together and want to know whether we are doing it at his place or out in the desert. It's an entirely surreal conversation, had in Hassinaya and French and English, with me scrubbing my trousers and them making many gruesome gestures to mime the act of consummation.

Their assumption that I am sleeping with someone isn't entirely out of sync with the logic of Chinguetti. For a tiny community, anchored by adherence to traditional Islam, the village is a hot pot of licit and illicit affairs. The most conspicuous coupling involves Nicole, the Frenchwoman who came into Cheikhranny's tent the day I arrived and asked him if he was hitting on me. She hangs around Mauritania for undetermined reasons, and is sleeping with her driver, Ahmed, a tall thin Moor.

Every morning they emerge from their tent like some kind of old married couple, she fussing over his tea and he tearing into the bread, and every evening they duck into their tent with squeezes and smirks. I'm not even sure they speak a common language, but they spend all their nights together and never try to hide their passion. Cheikhranny is particularly upset by their affair, saying that Ahmed has a lovely wife and two children in Atar. Like many Lotharios, Cheikhranny is traditional when it comes to marriage. He tells me that he is set shortly to marry himself. When I express surprise over this he blushes and buries his chin in his chest like a small, shy boy. She is very nice, he says. *Refined.*

But I notice that beyond the sexual nomadism of Mauritanian men (Nicole's phrase, not mine) Mauritanian women seem to radiate a near-universal sexual energy. Their sensuality arises from a supreme confidence in their own beauty and a community-wide consensus on the definition of beauty. To be blunt, that definition is fat.

Many cultures appreciate a woman with a little meat on her bones—I think often of a singer popular in Pakistan when I was there who was known fondly by the locals as "thunder thighs"—but Moorish women are obese. Here a woman with three rolls of fat on the stomach, calves as broad as her thighs, a bottom that protrudes from under the melfha, and stretch marks on her upper arms (no easy feat, stretch marks on your upper arms) is sexy and intensely feminine.

Cheikhranny says that no man would want to be with a skinny woman any more than he would theoretically want to be with another man. Fat turns a girl into a woman and signals that she is sexually mature and desirable. This was why the doctor sometimes saw very poor women from the desert who weighed over two hundred pounds. Their desirability, their survival, rested on their ability to fatten up. Even facing diabetes and weak knees and gallstones, they refused to lose the weight.

The tragedy was that fattening little girls could be a grisly business. From the time she lost her baby teeth, a little girl could be forced to drink a mix of sorghum and water to the point of illness. Sometimes she would be separated from her mother, who might stop when her child was ill, and given over to a less emotionally attached adult, like an aunt or grandmother, who would see to it that she was properly fed. Little girls who resisted were sometimes beaten or pinched with metal tongs into submission.

Fattening was also the reason some Moors didn't want to give up their slaves. Officially, Mauritania emancipated its slaves twenty years ago, but I was told that it wasn't hard to find families in the desert who maintained loose work relationships with the members of the haratin class. These slaves did domestic chores so that Moorish women could stay in their tents, eating and drinking and conserving calories.

The tradition was so entrenched that little had changed for the last thousand years. When the Arab traveler Ibn Battuta came in the thirteenth century he wrote that Mauritanian women ate cow's milk and raw sorghum washed down with water. Today, girls eat the same thing, with maybe some oily meat, couscous, and sugary tea thrown in. Overall, the diet was almost entirely made up of carbohydrates, dairy, and sugar — pretty much the same foods that make people fat in the West.

The underpinnings to obesity were not especially appetizing, but the effect, once a woman reached maturity, was to create a society of women who felt pretty damn good about themselves. At least in Chinguetti, they spent all day eating and drinking and lying around in the shade. They enjoyed the unabashed appreciation of their men but never their harassment. I admit that I was a little bit envious. Never in my life would I attain the Western ideal of beauty, especially if it remained a 120-pound runway model. For Moors, their ideal state of beauty was always within reach. This made for a group of self-confident, sexual women.

Ayesha, being of the slave class, is not fattening Miriam. She needs to be slender to work, unless she becomes exceptionally lucky and catches the eye of a Moor. Nonetheless, both Miriam and her mother have the same vision of physical satisfaction, which is through the lens of obesity. When they stopped by the auberge that morning to ask me about the doctor, they thought I didn't know what they were talking about so they imitated a man grabbing fistfuls of fat around a woman's waist and thrusting into her. That's how they conceive of sex, as a raw and hilarious thing.

I am naturally prudish about sex. Unwilling to discuss it with intimates and downright closemouthed around people I don't know. Several times in the Middle East I had been present during Arab women's frank discussions about their husbands and was shocked into silence by the harshness and honesty with which they judge them. Something about Islam's leniency toward sex (had within the confines of marriage) and the habitual separation of men and women creates a fertile atmosphere for these discussions.

I feel awkward again in the company of Ayesha's light-hearted teasing, but I keep my discomfort as quiet as I can. I smile and laugh along. They are enjoying themselves so much and I am lucky to be a party to these conversations. So much separates me from Ayesha and her friends. I'm an outsider, white and Christian and relatively rich. I am also far from my family and without the bonds of kinship that hold this society together. I am essentially an awkward presence for them, as I am for myself. Very little binds us. For a few moments, though, we hold a common ground. We are women in a world where a woman's burden is the heaviest of all and can only be lightened by laughter.

24

The Good Doctor — Part II

CASPER IGNORES ME the next day and the next so I begin to sniff around for transport to Timbuktu. I ask a couple of the guys down at the market whether they have heard of camel drivers taking people across the desert in that direction. They shake their heads. *No, we've never heard that.* I ask some of the women who sell beads to tourists near the museum. *No, no one goes east from here.* I even try to ask the camel drivers who stay at Cheikhranny's place, but they, it turns out, have never even heard of Timbuktu. Eventually Cheikhranny takes me aside.

"It's a stupid idea," he says. "Why do you want to do something stupid?"

"People said climbing Mount Everest was a stupid idea," I say. "But look, they did it . . ."

"This is not Mount Everest," he says. "But that was probably a stupid idea too."

This I find hard to argue with since I have always thought mountaineering a foolish endeavor. Even Mary Kingsley, who took great pleasure in adventure for adventure's sake, seemed to think her ascent of the 14,000-foot Mount Cameroon a vague waste of time. She conceded that it was "none of my business to go up mountains. There is next to no fish on them in West Africa, and precious little good rank fetish," but went anyway for the glory of being the first European woman to the top and the promise of gorgeous views. When she got to the summit after a week of excruciating conditions—rain and cold and enough sunburn to remove a chunk of skin from her cheek—her view of the terrain and the Atlantic below was obscured by fog. She didn't take it well, and she never bothered to climb a mountain again, sticking to the lowlands, where not just fish and fetish dwelt but also actual real live Africans from whom she could learn.

"*Someone* has to be going to Timbuktu," I say again.

"Someone is," he says. "Smugglers and Tuareg. Bad men." He lowers his voice, conjuring the worst of the worst. "Algerians . . . you can't go."

This sends me into a funk. It's not exactly depression, but a kind of despondency. I know that all through the desert, caravans of wealthy and well-equipped Westerners are making incredible journeys in their Land Rovers. This seems a dishonest and vaguely exploitative way of seeing the hidden oasis towns of the Sahara, not unlike the great caravans that were sent out from Paris and London in the nineteenth century, but the fact that there seems to be no other way is troubling.

I could ask Casper, I suppose. This is a preposterous idea, but I bang it around in my head for a little while anyway. He has a truck, and a new one. If we got a guide we could make the trip together.

Casper hasn't stopped by in a couple of days, however, and when he does he's in the sort of mood that makes me grateful we aren't traveling across the Sahara together. He arrives just as Ayesha is retouching the henna on my feet, and he walks right into my tent as though he owns it.

"Henna's disgusting."

"What's wrong?" I ask.

He looks short-tempered and intense and his eyes are puffy. "This town is wrong," he mutters.

"Well, I can't find anyone who will take me to Timbuktu and I'm pretty sure Cheikhranny is telling people not to take me. So I'm stuck here."

René Caillié eventually made it to Timbuktu but only when he left Mauritania and caught a caravan in Guinea traveling from the south. It's not easy to find folks who are going where you are going and are willing to take you. Plus there are probably fewer caravans traveling through the Sahara these days. I feel like mentioning this to Casper, who has taken very little interest in my trip, but he interrupts me, as though reading my mind.

"I'll take you to Ouadane," he says.

Ouadane is a town a couple of hours north of Chinguetti that's even older and more consumed by dunes. I actually do want to see it, but it isn't in any way closer to Timbuktu. I also am wary of him now. I mull it over. He seems too irritable and exhausted now to be in much of a seduction mode. As if on cue, he apologizes for his bad mood.

"I'll be better as soon as I get some coffee and am on the road," he says.

His mood does improve perceptibly once we get out into the desert. There is no road but he drives between the dunes like a professional, allowing the truck to skid when it needs to or following the tracks of previous drivers. We pass through small encampments of nomads, sending goats and people fleeing in every direction and stirring up a cloud of dust. With HÔPITAL DE LA FRATERNIDAD written on the truck, we are like local gods. Soldiers wave us through checkpoints and Bedouin hold their hands to their hearts in a gesture of thanks. A few old men actually salute us as we drive by. Casper salutes back, in a slick move that makes me wonder if he was in the military.

Then he puts on some music—cheesy James Blunt, then Andrea Bocelli—and sings along. He seems much better now, and I'm relieved. I sing along too. When those CDs are done he puts on a Spanish record by a group called Mano and translates all the lyrics for me. They are about betrayed love and he winks at me, conspiratorially.

I may have come to the Sahara to test myself, to find solitude and adventure, but instead my life seems to have developed into that of a teenage girl—driving around in his pickup, smoking cigarettes, dirtying the dashboard with my sandy boots. But it is, if nothing else, a relief. To be out of melancholy for a moment, to be free and flying through the desert, to feel bathed in the romance of the place and the man.

We arrive at Ouadane around noon. Its caramel brick houses all seem to be tumbling down the side of the mountain and into the date palms below. We leave the truck on the outskirts and walk up a hill. The town is bigger than Chinguetti, with narrow streets and two-story houses made of sandstone and fired brick. When we reach the top, it is cool and breezy. There are a few kiosks selling soap, oil, bread, cigarettes, and sardines, but hardly anyone else is around. As we wander the narrow alleys, climbing in and out of deserted houses, an old man comes out and introduces himself.

"I am the mayor and would the good doctor come out and take a look at my brother's foot?" he says. "We think it may be broken."

Casper becomes unaccountably irritated and tells him to go to Atar, nearly six hours away, to have it checked.

"The hell with these people," he mutters.

I slap my hand on his shoulder in support and camaraderie.

"Thirty-five patients a day for four years would burn out Mother Teresa," I say, but he flinches when I touch him.

"American women are so masculine," he says cruelly.

• • •

There's not much to do in Ouadane, except to visit the local museum run by a retired high school teacher named Sidi Abidine Sidi. He's so happy to have us he waives the entrance fee.

"I have very good prizes for you to see."

The museum is like a crazy aunt's attic. Priceless fourteenth-century Qur'ans are thrown in with Dutch clogs, tortoise shells, old telephones, and blue plates made in India. It's so crammed with stuff that you can't see floor or ceiling.

After we poke around a bit Sidi invites us into the backroom, where he lives, for tea. His house is also stuffed with junk, such as loose bits of paper and stray peanuts, leading me to believe that he's less a museum curator than a pack rat who happened on some nice things. We take a seat on the floor and Casper leans back, almost lying down. As Sidi and I talk, Casper fishes through my handbag for cigarettes and water. Even Florent doesn't go through my purse.

"Tourism has been good for us because there is such desperate unemployment," Sidi says, as Casper empties the contents of my purse onto the floor with a loud clatter. "It's just difficult to keep the children in school because they prefer to beg from the tourists all day."

The curator talks for a long time. Casper smokes and drifts in and out of sleep. He's the big man here in this small town, the doctor everyone knows, and he can be rude or childish when he wants. I sense that his mood is fluctuating today. One moment he offers to look at Sidi's aching elbow, the next he tells him that he thinks the pain is in his head. Sidi merely nods and says that he may indeed have spirits in his head, which makes Casper go purplish with fury.

"Spirits!" he hisses at me. "Spirits!"

A young man comes in bringing tea and some peanuts. Sidi slaps him on the back and says, "This here, this is my slave!"

The young man smiles and scuttles out backwards.

"Ah bon?" I say. Casper snorts.

"He is a voluntary slave. He prefers to stay here because there is no work in Mauritania. Besides, someone who isn't your *patron* will be very hard on you. The government knows there are still slaves. It's no problem. The NGOs are the ones who don't understand," Sidi says.

"Do you pay him?" I ask.

"I feed him," he says.

"Yes, that is more than enough," Casper says bitterly.

His mood that afternoon gets more and more dark. He is hungry, he says, and irritated. He starts walking to the bottom of the hill, where there is an auberge. Suddenly he becomes helpful, telling me that the proprietor is an amazing woman.

"Her name is Zaida and she runs the auberge all by herself. She divorced at the age of twenty-three and started this inn alone," he says enthusiastically.

For lunch we have shredded cabbage, tomatoes, lettuce, and pasta with a kind of tomato sauce, a veritable feast that lifts both our spirits. Zaida takes us into a small room on the edge of her compound that has two windows looking out on a garden of red flowers. We take the floor and eat our lunch while Zaida sits in the corner smoking and not saying much. When oil transport trucks arrive, she goes out to see the drivers, most of whom are French. They have stopped to call home before going out into the desert and out of contact for weeks on end. One man with a long beard and long hair simply says, *"Oui, je suis arrivé."* And hangs up.

I stare out the window while Casper eats in uncharacteristic silence. I'm conscious for the first time that many of my experiences in Mauritania are looking through small windows. Outside I can see a red flower, a green plant that must be watered twice a day, a white tent, and a stone wall. Above is that blue sky that never flinches, never dies. The mud walls of our room are cool, and it's pleasantly dark inside. As the drivers settle down to lunch on the other side of the compound their voices become far away and muffled.

Casper lies down on his back, while I take out my notebook.

"So how do you know nothing will happen to you out here?" he asks. His voice is harsh, angry even. My heart falls. He's really in a bad mood. It wasn't just low blood sugar.

"I'm with you. I'm not worried," I say, trying to make my voice light.

"No, how do you know I won't do anything to you?" He seems insistent on picking a fight, on getting some kind of reaction out of me.

"I have good instincts about people. I can tell who is a danger, who is not. Besides, you are a thirty-year-old doctor living out in the desert with a bunch of nomads. How bad could you be?" I try to laugh.

"If I tried to hurt you what would you do to stop me? I could have pulled the car over and done anything I wanted to you."

"I would shame you. I would use words that shamed you."

"I don't know if that would work."

"Why, are you planning on taking me out into the desert?" This guy really isn't like my other boyfriends, I think miserably. He's beyond a bloodsucker. He's crazy.

"No . . . But sometimes I think I am sick. Really sick in the head."

He turns over on his side and looks at me, but his eyes dart around as though he can't find what he's looking for. He is gray in the face, and his breath is heavy with cigarette smoke. All this time I spent worrying about my safety with Africans, and the good doctor turns out to be the threat. Serves me right for making assumptions.

Then he sits up, quite suddenly, and startles me. He looks me in the eyes as though he's finally landed on the great idea.

"You know sometimes, sometimes I think about coming home, loosening my tie, pouring a glass of wine, and putting on Carla Bruni. Wouldn't that be great?" he says, repeating what he had told me a few days ago.

I reach vaguely toward him in a gesture of friendship. What I have is my warmth, my humanity. It's why he likes me and he's got to see it in me right now.

"Oh, Casper. You really need to go home. You really need to get out of here."

I don't say anything else because it'll make it worse if he knows he's crazy. He has to think he's still the good doctor, still in control. He's been the big man in a small village for so long that he needs to feel like he can help everyone he meets in the same way. I've irritated him by not needing him to do anything for me—set my broken leg or deliver a baby. I don't need him at all, and he's forgotten that he can meet people like that.

"Yes, Nina. You are right. You are a good girl, and I like you."

Quickly and seamlessly, we drive back to Chinguetti. He tells me that my husband is lucky. I tell him that the people of Chinguetti are lucky, but he has given them quite enough. The next day I wake up at five thirty a.m. and look for the last time at Cheikhranny's ordered, clean commune. I leave a wad of cash under his door and a note. *Thank you for your hospitality. I am sorry that I won't be able to say good-bye.*

Then I catch the first bus for Nouakchott. I do the entire nine-hour trip in one day, sitting for much of it on top of a truck amid a high pile of bags. By the time I arrive in the capital I'm shaking and dehydrated. I have a temperature of 102 and can't keep down food or water. I am so sick that the enormity of what happened with Casper skates off me. Casper calls me on my cell phone fourteen times in a row and finally I pick up. I ask him if I need to go to the hospital. He tells me to drink, even if I want to vomit, and stay in bed.

"You left for Nouakchott so quickly," he says, slurring a little. It sounds like he's gotten his hands on whiskey, the most common alcoholic contraband in the Sahara. "I was going to come there tomorrow and pick up some medicine. I could buy some seafood and make paella for us at the beach. You know, the way real Spaniards do it."

"If that doesn't happen," I say, "promise me you'll leave Chinguetti soon. Promise me you will have left for Spain."

"Spain." He says the word like he doesn't know the place, and the sound sits there on the telephone line. He doesn't say anything else, and it seems as though he has fallen asleep. I hang up, drink as much Fanta as my body can take, and around one a.m. fall into a heavy, dreamless sleep.

25

Gnostic Life

I HAD NEVER READ *Out of Africa* before I came to Africa. The book seemed dated and irrelevant—important to a subsection of scholars and intellectuals who found, in Isak Dinesen's memoirs, a reflection of Africa that no longer applied. What meaning could I possibly find in the story of a Danish woman running a colonial farm and her love affair with a British big game hunter named, rather loftily, Denys Finch Hatton?

I read *Out of Africa* during my travels through Senegal, before I came to Mauritania. I found that I had been very wrong to ignore it. Here was a book that transcended both time and place and spoke directly to the dangers that arise from too much solitude. Dinesen's life in Africa, rendered in sparse Scandinavian prose, recalls not just Casper's struggle, but my own and my mother's. This became more evident as I lay in bed in Nouakchott and considered my strange brush with the doctor.

Dinesen, whose real name was Karen Blixen, was a wealthy Danish merchant's daughter who married a ne'er-do-well Swedish baron named Bror. In 1914 they came to Africa and started a coffee plantation on the highlands above Nairobi. Like Mary Kingsley, Dinesen had an absent and traveling father, and like

Kingsley is never completely clear on why she came to Africa. It is likely that she simply wanted to get away from the expectations and constraints of upper-class Danish life.

Unlike the movie, which is all wrenching love scenes and beautiful shots of the Serengeti, Dinesen's book is a lyrical and anecdotal recollection of her time in Africa. It is less a love story, or a story at all, than a series of scenes depicting the difficulties of being alone, the pain of trying to run a farm in a capricious climate, and the small insanities that arise from spending years on end living in a foreign land. Like all the other Scandinavian women I know (I include here not just my mother but my grandmother, aunt, and cousin), Dinesen doesn't have much time for either self-revelation or emotional hand-wringing.

She is, despite her chosen residence, Scandinavian to the core: beneath her outer reserve and resolute good manners lies a deep well of conflict and complex emotion. Thus, for all the poetry of her writing, the book maintains a down-to-earth, practical center. Dinesen is a hard-eyed frontier woman, hiking up her skirt to fight drought and British colonial officials who want to cart off beloved servants. To her immense credit, she puts Africans at the center of her life and writing. She is worrying about Kamante, one of the Africans who live on her land, who comes to her with a sore on his leg for which he resists hospitalization. She is conferring with her bodyman Farah on the protocol for hiring servants and running a farm. She is begging the stars for December rains and caring for wounded gazelles. Denys may have been her lover but it is Africa and the Africans she loves.

For all the richness of her life, however, she is also very lonely and strangely unlucky. In the first year of marriage her husband, a chronic womanizer, gives her syphilis and disappears with another woman. Denys, with whom she shares a great emotional and intellectual connection, is gone for weeks on end and she is alone with her thoughts on the farm. Work saves her during the day, but at night you sense her solitude is much harder to bear.

Dinesen writes in *Out of Africa:*

> At times, life on the farm was very lonely, and in the stillness of the evenings when the minutes dripped from the clock, life seemed to be dripping out of you with them, just for want of white people to talk to. But all the time I felt the silent overshadowed existence of the Natives running parallel with my own, on a different plane. Echoes went from the one to the other.

She is comforted by the echoes in her house—what I imagine to be the whisper of servants on the stair, the reflection of a face in the mirror—for she relies on the people who run her house and farm, not just for food and work and water, but emotional sustenance. In the silent days and weeks between visits from friends and word from Nairobi, her interaction with Africans, although essentially muffled and fleeting, may have been the only human communication she had at all—an incredibly important external link to the world beyond her writing and ruminations.

The analogy is imperfect but Dinesen's situation was similar to my mother's. She eschewed the easy chatter of Connecticut women but spent much time among the rose bushes with the gardener, sharing the pride and common purpose of creating an entire English garden from scratch. Often when I came home from school she was in the attic with the carpenter discussing the Sheetrock over the dormer window. Eventually she had more in common with these men than she did with the people who lived under her roof, her own countrymen as it were. Even at the end of the day, when they were gone and she could turn her attention to husband and child, you could tell she was still thinking of the work she had done with them. She was uncomfortable in the social circles prescribed for her—country clubs and tennis matches—but very mindful of the people with whom she worked with every day. She had no snobbism in her. *You must get dirt on your hands,* she often told me. She worked with her hands and admired others who did so as well.

Lying in bed in Nouakchott, drinking my Fanta, I am haunted now by the notion of the echoes of people who inhabit our lives reaching us in our loneliness. Whether they were Africans or not hardly mattered. The Africans who lived around Dinesen brought her comfort in times of loneliness and also demanded she act responsibly. The doctor would have been a better man had he heard the echoes of the Mauritanians in his own house in Chinguetti, if he had acknowledged how much of his worth and self-respect came from interacting with the people around him. Instead, he allowed the loneliness to infest him. He pushed the people in the village out of his life, becoming detached and violent, more like an overlord along the lines of Joseph Conrad's Kurtz. He became the great white doctor instead of the humble white farmer. He let the loneliness drip out of him and refused to hear the echoes bouncing between his world and the world of the people who lived around him.

He became a cautionary tale for me. Had I chosen a different life and turned away from love, as I supposed I had planned to before I met Florent, I could easily have had a life like the doctor's. I could have joined an NGO and gone to Africa alone. My search for solitude could have become a quest, the pivot of my life, rather than the pleasure of it, and in the end I could have just as easily missed the important influence that the people with whom I lived had on me. Perhaps I wouldn't have been able to muster Dinesen's strength of character.

I confess that until I met the doctor a part of me had begun valorizing the kind of solitary life he lived. Not just traveling alone through Africa, but really being alone in the desert for months on end. I imagined the peace and comfort that came from moments with nature. I could see the appeal of living in the desert, perched on my dune, like some kind of Gnostic, eschewing the comforts of modern city life. I would pare everything down until no material things would be left. This, I imagined, was how I liked to live and how I had lived before I moved to Paris.

The doctor cured me of that particular romantic notion. It seemed evident that on one side of the equation lay adventure and solitude and on the other lay security and love. Too much solitude and adventure and one became self-deluded, even crazy. Too much security and one became restless like my mother, escaping to the Shetlands or Cairo just to keep her sanity. In either scenario people ended up getting hurt. The balance wasn't easy, but it had to be found. There would be no Gnostic life for me.

Part IV

MALI

26

Bamako

I'M GOOD AT THIS NOW. I lie there a moment, in my small mud-wattled room, and feel neither lonely nor afraid. I am on the cusp of something—a state of mind that is solid yet includes light and joy. I'm becoming outward gazing, which has turned my world from a small gray place with infinite alleys of the mind into a large and light one with broad avenues.

I listen to the quiet. This quiet will never get tiresome for me. It is the center point of my life, around which I base all my emotions. After a few moments of relishing the peace, I start looking for my boot. I must have kicked it under the bed when I got in at three a.m. last night. I get down on my hands and knees to search. The thick mud floor of my room seems moist, which is strange. I find the boot, and while I put it on the air conditioner starts to steam a little. I go to the tap. The water that comes out is warmish. I splash some on my face and try to pinpoint the source of a growing unease.

I walk out of my room into the hotel courtyard and stand there a moment under an enormous gao tree. Its thick rubbery leaves filter the morning sunshine. The air is rich with cooking fire, soot, and floating red dust. It smells like foliage and earth, and for a moment I feel like I am floating, high above the courtyard into a deep purple sky. My spine tickles and the soles of my feet itch. None of this is particularly unpleasant, but it is odd.

I walk out into open sunshine and for a moment it's as though I am frozen in time. I tilt my head just a little toward the sun and wonder at its early morning size. *It takes up the whole sky,* I think foolishly, *the whole sky!* but then, confusingly, bright green and silver spots dance before my eyes. My skin tightens and contracts. Every breath of air singes the back of my throat. My lungs feel heavy and compressed as though they are pressing down into my stomach to get away from the sun. My light-headedness turns to a wrenching nausea and I clutch the side of a chair because I think I am going to faint.

This is heat. This is Mad Max, Swedish sauna, end of the world, pack-it-up-and-go-home Sahara in the summer . . . heat. I knew it was the dry season. I thought I could handle it. No big deal. I've been to the Sahara before. I lived in Cairo, albeit in the winter and spring. This, however, is an entirely different deal. It is 110 degrees, in the shade, at nine a.m. Later today, the temperature will go up, if that is at all possible. I am horrified. What's worse is that I only have a small window of time in which to travel because the monsoons are coming, and when they arrive they will wash out the roads and make the country impassable.

I tick through all the issues I will now face.

Transport: While everyone else stays inside to avoid heat stroke, I'll be crossing the country in a un-air-conditioned bus. To get to Timbuktu I'll have to leave Mali's one paved highway and take a bush taxi through desert and savanna without water sources.

People: If everyone stays in bed all day to avoid heat stroke, how am I going to ever meet anyone? They will close up shop during the day and come out at night when it's cool. This means trudging out alone after sunset to talk to people in small towns in Mali, where I know no one and no one knows me. I will be wandering the streets of Timbuktu at eleven p.m., looking for a friend. This will be misconstrued.

Dehydration. Water will fly out my pores before converting into sweat. I'll need to drink constantly, but the bottled water is called Tombouctou. Timbuktu is one of the driest towns on earth, leading me to wonder *where exactly they are getting this water.*

I retreat back to my room, where the air conditioner is heaving and sweating under a great strain. I turn it off and listen, try to feel the place around me. It was so lovely last night when I arrived in Mali. At five a.m. Bamako was not yet awake but the air smelled pleasantly of baking bread and smoldering cooking fires. The main road into town was sleek and black, under fully functioning highway lights. This alone was impressive, which I guess was the idea.

To the left and right, the city broke off along little red dirt lanes, barely visible under long neon lightbulbs tacked above shop doors. Most houses were squat one- or two-story concrete jobs with small courtyards and a nim or eucalyptus tree for shade. Delivery trucks idled on the side streets, dumping crates of Coca-Cola and bags of white rice from Thailand outside shops, while sheep prowled under mango trees, waiting for fruit to drop. The only other people awake were young boys watching soccer on televisions jerry-rigged to overhead power lines. It was warm and humid, and people were sleeping outside their front doors on flowered mattresses, the bottoms of their feet red from walking in the dust. I didn't suspect that in just a few hours it would be this intolerable.

On the plus side, there are no tourists. My hotel is empty save a few eccentric souls—a Mauritanian who keeps to himself, a blowsy American woman named Lorna who lives in Los Angeles, and a Frenchman named Pierre dressed all in black with a big laminated Native American chief on his shirt. We look at each other like soldiers thrown together in a ditch.

"Pret-ty hot," Lorna says to me. She has a weird Mae West accent. "Ta-morrow . . . it'll be . . . ev-an hot-ta."

"Really? How are we supposed to get around?" I nervously pat the back of my neck. I'm not sweating. That's what freaks me out most of all. And I don't know how long between drinks of water it will take to desiccate me if I don't sweat. It wasn't this hot in Mauritania. It wasn't this hot in Senegal either, where I stayed a month before coming to Mauritania, then Mali. How it suddenly got like this is beyond me.

"It-sa good qwes-tion. Hire a cab and leave ta-night. 'Round three a.m. it goes down to ninety dah-grees."

"I'm not leaving tonight," I say. "I just got here."

"Ta-morrow then. We'll go togettha. I'm going to Ségou. Dusty little desert town. You'll love it."

"Uh-huh." I don't want to travel with other people.

"You are gonna love traveling with me," she continues. "I drove from Barcelona to Cape Town and wrote a book. The publisher loved, *loved* my notes but didn't want to run with it because it didn't take a woman's perspective."

This is making me feel weaker.

"I'm notta feminist," she says triumphantly.

She's that uniquely American mixture of right-wing Republican and West Coast free spirit. On one hand, she clearly has money and isn't afraid to spend it on things like a face-lift, breast implants, and collagen injections for her lips. On the other hand, she's floated around for years, visiting every country in the world, even Sierra Leone and Tajikistan. I reassure myself that she is nothing like me. Yet she does and says things that strike home. I could see myself striving to visit every country in the world. That would feel like a kind of success to me. I'm probably a couple of trips, a couple of decades, and a stern talking-to from my mother from becoming Lorna. I shouldn't be so judgmental.

Pierre, on the other hand, is completely bonkers.

"I spent the last six months with my balls freezing in water and my head burning in the sun," he offers.

"What?" I ask.

"Gold!" he crows. "I was looking for gold! In Guinea. Locals threw me out."

"Did you find any?" I ask.

"No, but I lost fifteen pounds and lost my appetite for love."

I don't ask, but Lorna can't help herself.

"What do ya mean?"

"You imagine, *ma cherie*," he says, raising his thick eyebrows at her. "Not even my guide could help me."

She shoots him a stern look anyway. "I never ever deal with African guides. Horrible."

Isak Dinesen had a good line about the people in Africa who come in and out with their own agendas and strange set of preconceived notions. In *Out of Africa* she writes, "Sometimes visitors from Europe drifted into the farm like wrecked timber into still waters, turned and rotated, till in the end they were washed out again, or dissolved and sank."

In the end, I hope I'm the kind that gets washed out again rather than sinking, but one never knows. I think Pierre stands a poorer chance of survival. Over the next few days he holds court under the gao tree of the hotel, speaking often and violently about the Guinean chieftain who cheated him of his gold, while sits a young Malian prostitute on his lap.

I give both Pierre and Lorna a wide berth, as do the Malian hotel staff, who clearly think we're all a little nuts. They spend their afternoons sleeping in chairs, watching TV, and talking about the rains, which are still a month away. They look utterly exhausted, and despite the fact that they live in this heat, and it comes every year, they never stop talking about it.

"It's so hot," the cook says. "Too hot to sleep, to eat, to walk. It's terrible."

"You must be used to this," I say, laughing. "It comes every spring."

"Oh no," the cook says. "Have you seen how hot it is? Would you ever get used to it?"

No, and their worry about the heat compounds my own. I am itching to hit the road but end up spending a couple of days hanging around the hotel trying to figure out how I will see Mali without getting heat stroke or dying of dehydration. On my third morning I'm having coffee with Lorna when a guy shows up at the hotel looking for me.

"Your husband sent me to protect you," he says.

For a second, my heart sinks at the idea of Florent's actually sending people to look out for me. Then I register the acid-washed jeans hanging low around his hips, the tight red T-shirt, his sleepy, overworked eyes and nervous intensity. He's a hustler and a guide who's done a little research and come up with a good line. I applaud the effort and invite him to sit down.

He declines, hand over heart, full of apology and modesty.

"My name is Bakori. If you like I can show you the town. For maybe ten dollars? If this is okay with you we can work together over a few days."

He speaks French with careful grammatical correctness. He bows a little as he speaks to me and backs away nervously when I stand up. Not much of a hustler.

"I accept," I say.

Not much of a hustler and, to be honest, not much of a guide at first. He doesn't talk much but just walks next to me, offering, I suppose, protection. He'll answer questions when directly asked, but that is about it. The presidential elections are coming up this weekend and Malians will have to decide whether they will reelect President Amadou Toumani Touré, nicknamed ATT, or one of the other minor candidates. He talks openly about the elections, telling me he's going to vote for ATT because he worked with Jimmy Carter to eradicate guinea worm, a parasite that infects drinking water.

When I visited Mali in 2007, it was one of the only countries in the world with a majority Muslim population that were deemed totally "free" by the democracy advocacy organization Freedom House. This didn't necessarily put it in the same league as Norway, but it was among the best you could get in the Muslim world and not bad on a global scale. People in Mali voted for their president, political opponents were not severely repressed, and the press was uncensored. Considering Mali sat in one of the toughest neighborhoods in the world, with Algeria, Côte d'Ivoire, and Sierra Leone all next door or close, these statistics were impressive. Mali had managed to stay intact and peaceful despite all that conspired against it—the constant meddling of Libya's leader, Muammar Qaddafi, the rebellion of light-skinned nomadic Tuareg against the black central government in Bamako, and the rumored infiltration of Islamic radicals from across the border in Algeria.

Mali's own paucity of natural resources helped to keep the peace. It has no diamond mines like Sierra Leone, no oil like Nigeria. Its one export, cotton, is enough to feed government coffers but not enough to excite much interest from the hordes of undereducated and unemployed young men who find themselves in African armies.

It does, however, have a long-standing, simmering conflict with the Tuareg. Sadly, in March 2012, well after I visited, soldiers overthrew the democratically elected government of Amadou Toumani Touré in part because it wasn't doing enough to control separatist Tuareg. However, the coup created such disarray in Bamako that the Tuareg seized the opportunity to realize their dream of creating an independent state. Working with Ansar Dine, a group whose name means "defenders of the faith" and that takes a Salafist interpretation of Islam, they overtook the northern half of the country, including Timbuktu and Gao, and declared an independent state called Azawad. Today these towns live under a strict interpretation of Shariah law and there have been reports of shrines being desecrated and hands being cut off by local militants for minor infractions. It is a nearly unimaginable turn of events in a country that prizes its inclusiveness and its tolerant brand of Islam.

At the time of my visit, however, there are few indications in the capital that the country could face civil war. As we walk, the city wakes. The tree-lined avenues become packed with men and women on scooters, overcrowded green buses, blind beggars, and fat market women. Clouds of diesel fumes swish up and down the avenues, covering everything with the taste of gasoline, even the expensive pears from South Africa. By the side of the road Fulani women sell piles of yellow and orange mangoes from Guinea and bananas from Côte d'Ivoire. They swap stories and gossip with one another, sometimes chuckling so heartily they fall off their plastic stools. The din of conversation and traffic is overwhelming.

Still, Bamako is in good shape for an African city. Like Cairo, its hard commercialism is tempered by the river flowing through its heart and a favorable ratio of chaos to tranquility. For every street choked with traffic and beggars, there are three ruled by naked running babies and softly bleating goats.

We walk and walk. It feels good to walk this much. My sore back straightens and loosens. As the morning wears into a blistering hot midday, a small breeze blows red dust into tornadoes around our feet. Sheep migrate to the shade under the nim trees and kids in brown uniforms hide under the awnings of their schools before going home for lunch. Women in tightly wrapped workday skirts pound millet in wooden mortars, locking their knees and bending at the hips. Several times we see that families have moved their entire bedroom into the street—lamps, night tables, wardrobe, carved oak bed—to catch the breeze running off the river at night.

Like many cities in West Africa, Bamako's population swelled after the droughts in the 1970s and 1980s drove pastoralists out of the savanna into the city. Today, 1.6 million people live in Bamako, some under atrocious conditions. Yet the social fabric of the city feels remarkably intact.

I tell Bakori that the overall sense of peace is impressive, especially amid such poverty.

"We call it cousinage," Bakori explains. All of West Africa is made of overlapping tribes—Bamana, Fulani, Mandinka, Wolof, Moor. "We intermarry. We adopt each other's traditions. Only the Tuareg care about tribe and refuse to marry out of it. But for the rest of us tribe is insignificant."

Then he asks me if I mind coming with him to the market because he needs to pick up medicine for his cousin. We turn off the dirt paths onto a busy two-way street. Young men have peeled the concrete slabs off the sidewalks, revealing the running sewers beneath. Several men are swimming under the water, so black and thick it looks like oil, to pull free leaves and sticks that block the passage. The women shout words of encouragement, and one man covered head to toe in sewage gives a thumbs-up.

"If the sewers are clogged when the rains come the city will flood and we will get many diseases," he says. "They do important work."

I shudder and he nods, understanding.

"It is necessary. We are all grateful to them."

"I suppose a job is a job," I say vaguely.

"Oh no," he says. "They don't work for the government. They are just local boys," he says, gesturing left and right, "who know it needs to be done."

He guides me away, proud of the work people do on the sewers but knowing I shouldn't spend too long near them or it will be my main memory of Bamako. He directs me to start climbing a small hill that slopes up toward a table-topped mountain. We reach the plateau and I see a sea of waist-high corrugated roofs running up the side of the slope. In the distance I can see the president's palace, lying across the crest of a mountain like a long white snake.

"Come," says Bakori. "You will see how much fun a market is."

This is a prosperous market for a country that according to the United Nations is among the third- or fourth-poorest in the world. Under each small shelter sits a woman and her wares—everything from eggplant to perfumed herbs meant to attract a husband. One section sells automotive parts, another wicker baskets, fish straight from the river, dried goat. One woman is selling digital cameras in cardboard boxes while she roasts peanuts in a small wok. Bakori stops to chat with people he knows, often speaking in French so I'll understand and using the formal *vous* when speaking to people he doesn't know.

"That your second breakfast?" he jokes with a particularly round lady who is sucking on a fish bone. She laughs and throws the bone at him.

True joy is evident in this market—uproarious laughter, backslapping, teasing, and little giggles. A child falls into a bucket of fish heads and everyone smiles. A husband takes a verbal beating from his wife for forgetting to prepare the midday meal and it provokes hilarity. Laughter doesn't lurk around the mouth or get swallowed in deference to the narrative. It starts in the belly and comes gushing out in wet snorting waves, submerging everyone around it. The sheer noise of humans constantly interacting with each other is deafening. It makes me feel that I have wasted too much of my life in formal dinners or cocktail parties, clinging to irony and knowledge.

I want some of their joy, but it isn't for me today. Few women meet my eye and several conversations stop dead in their tracks as I pass. This market isn't used to foreigners, and I wish I had worn a skirt instead of my provocative trousers. I wish I was black so I blended in at least a little. Children run up and touch my hands, but their affection is false. They beg and scowl. Bakori throws his empty coke can at them, calling them bandits.

We climb the hill and reach an area devoted to beauty products—a concrete floor sloping a little with the hill and shaded by rubber-leaved trees. Bakori motions for me to sit. I am used to African men bringing me into the women's section and welcome the rest. I have begun to believe, like many African women, that beauty is a necessity of life. A nice hairstyle, an application of henna to the feet, and a clean, well-pressed boubou make all the other trials and tribulations infinitely easier. Poverty is no excuse for sloppiness.

In the women's section, people are friendlier, and a woman pats the seat next to her. I sit and watch her plait another woman's hair into a thick mat of intertwined braids that falls like a sheet down the back of her head. Another woman mixes thick green henna and another rubs cocoa butter on her legs. Bakori comes in, nodding and deferential, hand to heart, and he is welcomed with smiles. He finds the woman he's looking for and hands her the medicine he just bought. She has two black tattoo marks just under her eyes and a stone talisman around her neck. She is very beautiful, and Bakori looks at her for a long moment.

I feel dazed, and hot. The sensory overload of the market, the heat, and the short night of sleep have sent me into a pleasant stupor. I am malleable and good-natured, a little dumb.

The concrete under us is cool and dry, and the voices around us are muted by the murmur of water trickling down the mountain. I am reminded of how Kingsley wrote of moments like these: "I just lose all sense of human individuality, all memory of human life with its grief and worry and doubt, and become part of the atmosphere. If I have a heaven that will be mine." I close my eyes and sway to the far-off sound of stringed Fulani music playing from someone's radio. It is so peaceful here. If the rest of my life is spent in a terrifying interchange of tedium and panic; if I never visit Africa again; if I never have a moment to myself or feel whole as I do now, then I will forever remember this moment of peace in the market in Bamako.

When I open my eyes, the woman next to me is looking at me curiously. I smile and she says something sharp to her friend, who laughs. I feel the need to explain, but am caught off guard by a naked baby who crawls out from under her skirt. He positions himself in front of me, then comes to a rather abrupt stop, landing on his bottom and swaying. He looks up at me and his eyes grow very wide for a moment and his lips part. Amused, Bakori strolls over, picks him up, and puts him on my lap. A woman behind me chuckles, warm and deep. The baby sways on my knees, and I put my arms around him and he nestles into my chest.

He is eight months old. No, maybe four. I know nothing about children. He smells like dust and milk and his skin is soft. Around his waist three leather laces with silver amulets protect him against evil. Again he looks up at me, mute and serious, revealing four perfect white teeth, set impudently in the front of his mouth. I run my nose along the top of his head and he gurgles.

His mother smiles in approval and asks Bakori, "Where are her children?"

"She has none," he says, shrugging off the mystery of Westerners.

She nods and asks no more, discreet enough not to pursue the line of questioning since I must be barren.

Again, I feel the need to explain, but then I have no explanation. I'm not sure any of these women would believe the fact that I had been married for over a year and consciously decided not to get pregnant. They would think it an elaborate ruse but that in truth my husband didn't really love me or wouldn't sleep with me. Many would think that I had been cursed by a rival but was too stupid to go to a witch doctor or a marabout to have the effects of the spell reversed.

I thought often of children in Paris while my friends and neighbors got about the business of making families. Florent and I never really managed to understand each other on the subject, however. We tried several times to broach it, but it always felt as if we were talking at cross-purposes.

ME: Harper had a baby.

FLORENT: Harper is great.

ME: People have babies. Even Harper.

FLORENT: My brother has babies.

ME (*alarmed*): They have three children.

FLORENT: That's too many.

ME: Yes.

FLORENT: We should get some dinner.

Sometimes it felt like I left Paris to get away from these dysfunctional conversations. I hated how these talks revealed how poorly Florent and I communicated. I hated that they revealed how little either of us actually knew about children. But in truth my discomfort went much deeper. I didn't really know *why* people had children.

There was such a wonderful life to be lived without babies. A life with travel and sex and long Sunday mornings lying in bed reading the *New York Times*. It didn't take much thought to decide that it was more fun to spend forty-five thousand dollars on a really wonderful year in Thailand than on a year of my child's college education. I didn't think it really mattered if I didn't have children to look after me in old age. Why should I plan for old age anyway? What a terrible way to live a life.

The idea of bringing children into this world seemed so fraught with obvious risk. Here we would bring something into being, something that didn't ask to be born, only to potentially make it miserable. What were the chances that I would produce or could nurture a child into well-being? Even if I were generous about my own ability to love, I placed those odds at one in two. So there was still a 50 percent chance that the child would be unhappy. That seemed a great risk to take.

People had children, I thought, because they thought they would make them happy. That they would give meaning to life. They had them because they wanted someone to look after them in old age or to have a slightly bigger crowd around the Christmas table. Maybe they thought only very selfish people didn't have children. But even if all the conditions were right—you were happily married with a stable income, a healthy sense of self-worth, and a support network of friends and family—having a child seemed to speak to our selfish, narcissistic natures. People had kids to fit in, to get along, to not be left behind by others in their group who were having children. People had children because they didn't have a better plan.

Unless you believed that bearing children was essentially good for society (specious because of all the resources First-World babies consume) or decreed by God, there was no intellectual way to arrive at procreation. It was all instinct and animalism and I want, I want, I want.

What Florent thought remained fuzzy to me, but if his family was any indication, he held a pretty standard French Catholic view. Children, in this context, were good because propagating the species was good. Specifically, bringing more French babies into the world was good. Florent valued himself enough to believe that any child he fathered would by definition be a benefit to the world. Needless to say, I thought this line of thinking was total rubbish, though I suspected a lot of men thought that way.

The baby on my lap makes a sharp little gurgling noise that makes me think he has swallowed something. I hold him up and inspect him swiftly. He looks back at me with black liquid eyes, smiles, and opens his mouth. I look inside at four little teeth and a wet pink tongue. He seems okay. His mother, who is now plaiting a customer's hair, lets out a long peel of laughter. She motions for me to set the baby on my lap and stop swinging him through the air. I smile. She goes back to her task, contented, chatting, her baby in the hands of a total stranger.

These are happy people, and by my standards they have absolutely nothing. Certainly no financial stability and no sense of what the future will bring. Who knows if this woman is happily married? I would wager she spends most of her days in the company of other women and barely thinks about her husband.

There were still very good reasons for not having children, but the practical rationale—I wasn't settled, happy, stable, or rich enough to bring a child into the world—was very weak. This woman had had a child under much more difficult circumstances. This child was not a burden but a joy. That joy spread and multiplied through the market and made it into a place where mothers fell off their buckets in laughter and Bakori gazed with love and longing at the young mother plaiting hair and grandmothers fried fish for children who didn't belong to them. Joy, in its most elemental form, seemed born in these children, and they brought it to us as a gift, which made the world a kinder place. It was this laughter and optimism, embodied in a baby, which all these people relied upon to compensate for the deficiencies in their life.

I had love at home in the form of my gentlemanly husband,

but what if there were more? More people, more noise, more love. What if I could make my apartment in Paris feel, even if just for a moment, like a hot and sleepy afternoon in the Bamako market? The quiet din of far-off voices, the laughter of women, the soft gurgle of a black-eyed baby. What if I could re-create the feeling, the reassurance, and the hope of unfettered joy?

27

Boubous

FOR TOO LONG I have been wandering around Africa in trousers and ratty skirts, an unpardonable offense in a culture where beauty and cleanliness are so prized. I need new clothes. Before I board a bus east in search of transport to Timbuktu I will buy new dresses. Maybe if I look more African people will deign to take me along to the city that remains *impossible* to get to.

The boubou is the West African uniform, worn by men and women alike, and an ode to modest practicality. Men wear loose trousers with a long smock over it, while women wear a long tight skirt and a bodice that can be sleeveless and simple or coated in frilly collars and sleeves. Nice boubous are handmade in West Africa and made of stiff fabric with lots of wax so they shine in the sunlight. Casual working ones are made from soft cotton and act more or less as wraparound skirts and tops.

Boubous make everyone look good, covering up a man's paunch and flattering a women's waist and bottom. Since the skirts are usually too tight to allow squatting, I imagine the boubou helped create the typical West African image of a woman bending down over a cooking pot, legs straight, bum straight up in the air.

I've learned that breasts are no big deal in West Africa, and down by the river girls will bathe topless, but showing off the contour of one's legs in Mali is pretty risqué. Even in Bamako I can feel young men sizing me up and old women shaking their heads at my provocative clothing.

Every day I think about visiting a tailor and every day I put it off. The heat has made me strangely lethargic. I had intended on staying on Bamako for three days but now it's been five. I dread the idea of suffering through a bus ride through the scorching desert, and the Tamana, where I am staying, is such a lovely hotel. Soon I find my rhythm, and it's a good one. Wake at eight a.m., go for a walk around town, stop in at one of the super air-conditioned Lebanese restaurants for lunch and eat my main meal, usually tabbouleh and roasted chicken. After lunch, go home to the Tamana and read or write until five p.m., after which I emerge for cocktail hour by the pool with Pierre. I'm always in bed by ten or midnight.

I could live here, I think. It has something to do with the way people interact with the heat. The heat slows everyone down and makes action deliberate, even thoughtful. Greetings are long and languorous; storytelling and small jokes deeply valued. Everyone is forced onto more or less the same schedule—a siesta in the afternoon and an outing in the late evening when the worst of the day has finally worn off. Because midday is so brutal, nature's other small gifts become precious, like the morning mist rising off the Niger and the cool breeze that arrives suddenly around three a.m. and invites sleep.

I also like Bamako because I can get a drink without judgment, the live music scene is great, and some supermarkets stock Oreos and HP Sauce. It's a lot easier to live in Bamako than either Dakar or Nouakchott, which fall on the opposite ends of the spectrum in terms of habitability, with Dakar a madhouse of traffic and pollution and Nouakchott akin to a colony on Mars. Bamako is big enough to be a real city but not so big that it swallows me whole.

I stay a few days longer than I should, sleeping late into the morning, telling myself that I need a good tailor, and then not doing anything about it.

But one morning Bakori stops by the Tamana, looking like hell ("Big party last night," he tells me) and asking me whether I need any help.

"I need a boubou, a couple actually. Do you know any good tailors?" I ask.

His face brightens immediately. "You will look very lovely in a boubou. Have you thought of a pattern?"

I'm delighted to be taken so seriously. I thought this would be a solitary enterprise, but I have found a companion in my need to beautify my life. Bakori wants to go shopping with me, and even though I am paying him, I am touched.

While it was nearly impossible to get him to talk politics or religion, he is very happy to talk clothes. He discusses design options, and encourages me to get a quality fabric with a lot of wax. "Sometimes that fabric is less than comfortable, it is very stiff, but it is also very beautiful," he opines.

I buy blue cloth shot with bright yellow suns, and maroon cloth cut in geometric patterns. The shopkeeper gives me a long, mournful look when I try to bargain, so I don't and spend the outrageous sum of thirty dollars. Throughout, Bakori sucks on mangoes in the corner, and proffers his opinion. "White girls should wear blue," he says gravely. "They should not wear lilac." He shudders at the thought.

The tailor lives in a poor neighborhood on the outskirts of Bamako that consists only of one-story red mud houses with flat roofs. If wealthy Bamako has been dirt paths shaded in nim trees, poor Bamako is barren and blasted out. Barely a tree has survived the firewood gatherers, and this makes the quarter unbearably hot. A few dark heads peak out at us from behind wooden doors, but otherwise we are alone and the streets are empty. After a few moments of walking in the sun, I feel disoriented and sleepy. My French comes out in thick, dripping phrases, and Bakori looks at me sympathetically. "We'll go home soon," he says.

We round a corner and come to a house with two men standing in the doorway. We go into a dark room dominated by an old-fashioned Singer sewing machine and a large wooden table. Behind the sewing machine sits a man in glasses who is carefully feeding fabric to the needle while pumping the treadle with his foot. Four men sit around on wooden benches, drinking tea and chatting. The walls are covered with magazine photos of women in boubous looking seductive and voluptuous, and a great, messy pile of cloth sits in one corner, while in the other new boubous are neatly folded. The room is cool and smells of pipe smoke.

The tailor pulls up a wooden chair glued together like the ones in elementary schools and invites me to sit. He takes my cloth, inspects it closely, then passes it around to everyone else, who fingers it and asks me where I bought it. The tailor comes out from behind the sewing machine and takes a tape measure off the wall. With the concentration of a surgeon, he measures the width of my shoulders and the length of my legs from hip to floor. When he gets to my chest Bakori barks out "*Fait attention!*" in a policeman's voice, which makes everyone laugh and whistle. After taking the measurement for my hips and bottom, the tailor inspects the numbers and says approvingly "a body like a Coca-Cola bottle." I manage a coquettish smile.

This is the mellow nature of Mali, the tolerance and generosity toward women. In a small room with six men on the outskirts of Mali I feel safe but still appreciated for my natural assets. It's a hell of a lot more fun than buying a dress in Paris from a scorchingly indifferent salesgirl.

Measurements taken, we settle down to the business of choosing a pattern, which draws everyone around the sewing machine. The tailor hands me a piece of chalk and invites me to draw my design on the wooden table, but after seeing my scribbles, he pulls out a huge laminated book filled with hundreds of Polaroids of women in boubous of every shape and color. Everyone gathers around, flipping pages and offering suggestions. *Maybe a little squarer in the back? How about a zipper? A little longer to cover your ankles? Would you like extra cloth in the back for freedom?*

Bakori tells me that sewing and weaving are male pursuits in Mali and jealously guarded against female interference. Until very recently, clothing also represented a significant portion of household wealth in West Africa and often acted as a woman's dowry. In Sembène Ousmane's book *God's Bits of Wood,* about the Dakar–Bamako railroad strike of 1947, women nearly starved before selling their boubous. Bakori told me that for me to enter a tailor's shop with high-quality fabric and ask for a boubou was a big investment, which was met with care and consideration.

Eventually I settle on two styles, both rather simple, with skirts that flare a little at the bottom and square-cut neck and back lines. At the last minute and under intense pressure I agree to have the backs cut deep so the cloth just clears my bra strap.

When the boubous are finished a few days later, Bakori brings them to the hotel and I wear one for dinner. Lorna snorts derisively, but everyone who works there comes out to see me. The cook walks around me two times and pronounces me *trés belle, une vraie Malienne,* and even the French owner pats me on the shoulder and chuckles. Perhaps in Mali the boubou represents all sorts of important things—pride, dowries, income for semiskilled men, and the last defense against fundamentalist Islam—but it's also just a tight-fitting, high-waisted skirt that flatters the hips. I feel pretty and feminine for the first time in a long time, and also just a touch African.

28

Campari by the River

WITH BOUBOUS IN HAND, I decide to head for Ségou, a small city by the Niger River, which is known as Mali's rice and sorghum bowl. I'll spend the night there, then head east to Mopti, then on to Timbuktu.

Before I leave I call Florent. I think that once I get into the heart of Mali my cell phone won't work and it will be several weeks again before we talk. He sounds so happy to hear from me, I'm a little surprised. His voice is warm and rich and he says my name twice as though he was cherishing the memory of a long-lost love. *Nina, Nina,* he murmurs. He usually says my name so little.

"I'm on my way to Ségou, then to Timbuktu." Usually he has no time to talk at the office so it's also better that I tell him the logistics right away.

"Finally," he says warmly. "And then what are you going to do?"

"I'm going to go to Niger and then I am going to come home."

"That's Paris, right?"

"Yes," I say, a little startled. "But before the rains come and it gets too wet to travel I want to go east into Niger . . ."

He takes in a deep, audible breath and exhales in what sounds like relief. It is the first time he has hinted at any kind of opinion either way on whether I should travel or stay at home. This was strategically brilliant, for with each passing day I felt my loyalty toward him grow. Now it seems like he has been feeling abandoned, and I get the sinking feeling that I have been wrong all this time.

"God, are you angry at me?" I ask. "You never said anything. Now you say something?"

It's difficult enough in real life to get Florent to tell me what's on his mind, but over the phone I know it will be impossible. And the heavy sigh really could mean anything. I should just let it go, but instead I plow right on and consider the options. Maybe he has worked alone these many months, woken up every day to an empty apartment, watched sports alone on Saturdays, and read the paper on the balcony, and now no longer sees a *need* for me. Maybe in my absence he has thought, *Well, she was kind of a pain in the ass and a lousy cook to boot. Good riddance.* Maybe his life is just fine without me. They say a good marriage is like icing on the already tasty cake that is your life. Maybe he doesn't like icing anymore. Perhaps the cake tastes just fine alone and the icing is fatty and cloying and gives him a headache.

"Do you not like icing anymore? Is that it?" I whisper.

"Icing? What, no. I will just say that . . ." He pauses, worried. "Are you eating a lot of icing in Mali?" I could have sworn we'd talked about the analogy before, but maybe not. Or maybe he forgot. "Is that an African thing?"

"No, no, never mind. Tell me what you were going to say."

"Well, I was going to say that it will be good to have you home."

"Why?" I ask, suspicious.

"Because I miss you," he says slowly.

I can see him leaning back in his chair at the office, studying the ceiling and throwing up his hands. It's what he does when he negotiates. And then the chair comes down and he is pointing at the wall.

"I miss you too," I say.

"Okay then," he says, chair creaking. "I have a meeting. Safe travels." And he hangs up the phone.

He has made his point. He'd like me to come home. I think that is what that means, though talking to him is still like talking to the oracle. I understand the words, but I really have no idea what is going on.

When I board the bus for Ségou at five a.m., I find that, mercifully, the radio is broken. Music in Mali is good, soulful blues and instrumentals played with a harplike lute called the kora, but no music is good cranked out over a blown-out sound system before sunrise. I say a little prayer in thanks and get on board, hoping I might be able to sleep for a few hours.

The trip is made in dreamy, swaying silence. Women and children sit up front with men in the back, arms and legs splayed across each other in reckless sleep. Little yellow curtains above the windows rock in time from the loose suspension, and the city submits to a countryside of baobab trees, weak-looking eucalyptus, and the occasional mango. Everything has been garnished by dew, which deepens the dirt to a purplish red and the mango trees to rain forest green. In an hour, the sun will bake out this morning freshness, hardening and lightening the colors and releasing a fine red dust.

I sit next to a pretty young woman who turns her eyes down to the ground and whispers her name when I introduce myself so no one wakes up. Her boubou is made of cloth that has the picture and slogan of a smiling ATT woven into it. She is returning to her hometown of Ségou to vote in the elections on Sunday. "I will vote for ATT for he has done many good things," she says, lightly touching my hand to hold my attention as she searches out a word in French. "He is *normal.*"

I doze and am woken by a woman thrusting a greasy plastic bag of brown cakes in my face. Our morning snooze has been interrupted by hoardes of smiling, sweaty women selling eggs, mangoes, apples, and breakfast cakes. They are deeply competitive, elbowing each other to get on board, jumping on and off the moving vehicle while balancing huge silver bowls on their heads. They bring noise and life to the bus. People order breakfast and the driver turns on the radio, not broken after all, just turned off in the morning in a show of consideration.

The woman sitting next to me asks me if I have ever had manioc root and buys what looks like a long white carrot that is covered in clumps of dirt. She offers me half and, thankful for the kindness, I begin chomping on it confidently. It tastes exactly as I imagined Malian dirt would taste, creamy, rich, and pungent with the influence of sheep. Gently the woman draws down my hand and shows me how to remove the pliant outer layer of the root with my thumbnail. Apparently manioc is meant to be peeled, even in Mali.

I get off the bus expecting another dusty African town with concrete houses and running sewage and children underfoot. I expect a toned-down version of Africa, with the great sights diminished by semimodern intrusions like eighteen-wheel trucks and phone lines hanging between houses and the occasional television blasting from behind mud brick walls.

But the sight of the Niger River in Ségou is so beautiful I thrust my hands into my pockets and chuckle in protective cynicism. Like the moment I fell in love but made a stupid joke, the perfection makes me uncomfortable. I'm better with the flaws, the seascape that smells of low tide, the circles under Florent's brown eyes. The flaw gives me something to latch on to so I can absorb the splendor around it, but just pure beauty, like pure love, blasts right through me without waiting for a response. I think I'm just supposed to take it, but I find that hard.

The Niger here is clean and light, empty of industry and people, stretching nearly a third of a mile across. Brown grass sways in a light wind and mango trees cluster by the river like old women at a well. A fisherman in a faded green pirogue paddles by, barely disturbing the surface. A white crane swoops near the water, loses sight of its prey, and pulls up into a high arch before cutting out over the savanna. For half an hour I stand by the banks with my little backpack in the sand, watching the huge red sun head for the horizon, emptying the river of light and ushering in an evening of blacks and blues.

By the time the sun sets, I'm drenched in sweat and sunburned. I've found nothing to make this place less ideal—no plastic bags, no motorboats, no smelly fish guts on the side of the river. There is nothing but golden savanna and swaying trees as far as I can see. This isn't Eden. This is the world after humans have passed on and God has returned to earth.

I thought the Niger would be like the Nile, a working river that through irrigation and tourism feeds the moral and economic muscles of the country. I thought it would be loud with farms and motorboats, and tour guides trying to sell me sex and hashish from their rickety feluccas. Where are the angry buffalo and million unsupervised children? Where's the chaos of a river town with a hundred thousand inhabitants? This river seems profoundly unambitious.

I check into a hotel by the river run by gregarious Lebanese brothers (*Come drink! We have English TV!*) and search out dinner. Down by the river, I find a bar and restaurant with outdoor tables where I order a luxurious Campari on ice. I drink so rarely in Africa. And when I do, it is with no panic or abandon, but almost with a sense of contemplation or reflection. It is better to drink that way. I settle into my chair. It is still so hot. Over ninety degrees. But I am getting used to it. The heat feels like an opiate, shaving the edges off my neurosis and making me kinder. The moon rises soft and huge, sending shimmering light over the river. A young man with an unusually large lip approaches my table.

"My name," he says, hand on heart, "is Biton . . . Mamadi . . . Coulibaly. May I join you?"

Anyone who says his name with such aplomb deserves a seat. I motion for him to join me.

"That drink there is very beautiful," he says, nodding to my Campari.

"Oh, would you like a sip?" I ask.

"Okay."

He takes a tiny sip of the Campari and looks up at me in alarm.

"*C'est trés* . . . bitter," he says.

"You don't like it?"

"No, not so much," he says miserably.

"Well, why did you drink it?"

"You know, I didn't want to be impolite."

It takes about a minute and a half to realize that Biton Mamadi Coulibaly is paralyzed by politeness. He shields his mouth with his hand when he talks, barely makes eye contact, and nearly faints when I ask him where the ladies' room is.

"In Mali we say we're going to make a telephone call when we go . . . there," he says nervously. "Just so you don't make the same mistake again."

He is also an aristocrat and deeply conscious of that fact. His name, Coulibaly, which he presented with such gravitas, indicates that he sits comfortably on top of Mali's complex caste system of nobles, hunters, blacksmiths, and storytellers. He is also from the Bambara ethnic group, as are most people with names like Traore, Diarra, Coulibaly, and Diabate. Among these clans the Coulibalys are nobles, for example, while the Diabates are griots, traditional storytellers and singers.

Coulibaly, who calls himself Amadou, is in an especially tight spot because he isn't just local gentry, he's from one of *the* noble families of Mali. He's descended from the great Ségou king Biton Mamary Coulibaly, who founded the Bambara Empire in 1712. It is not the most noble family in Mali, but pretty close, and Coulibaly is surprised that I don't immediately recognize his heritage. Quickly, as though embarrassed by his own greatness, he explains that the King Coulibaly put together a riverboat armada so impressive that his small group of loyalists controlled the Niger to Timbuktu for nearly fifty years. Though they fell from power, they remained the prominent family of Ségou.

Sadly, aristocracy doesn't come with a bank account any more in Mali than it does in England or France, so Amadou has become a guide. He wears the role miserably, talking about the genus of the nearby foliage (he knows the scientific name of every tree and shrub in Ségou) for hours without mustering the courage to make a pitch.

He's also embarrassed by a bum lip that makes him nearly impossible to understand. When he was nine, his brother hit him in the face with a clay pot, permanently inflating his upper lip and turning the tooth beneath a gray-green. His upper lip is so much larger than the lower one that all his *v*'s come out as *b*'s. *C'est b-rai, c'est b-rai* is his constant and confusing refrain when I question an assumption. He exacerbates the problem by speaking with his hand in front of his mouth, and when he laughs, which is often, his hand flies up to hide his funny lopsided smile, and he becomes as modest and refined as a geisha.

We sit by the river for hours discussing nature in Mali and swatting away mosquitoes. Around the time he launches a disquisition of Ségou's birdlife, I stop the torture and ask him if he could possibly show me the sites of Ségou tomorrow. *I would be so much obliged. Imagine a Coulibaly taking around a simple girl like me. I'll feel so safe.*

Flattered. Magnificent in his largesse. Mindful of the hospitality his family must always show, he obliges and promises to pick me up the next morning at seven.

29

The Talisman

I SLEEP WELL IN Ségou. I have no dreams. I get up and take a shower, using a little hose at the bottom of the bathroom that spits out cool, dark water. I dry off with my hand towel and put on my boubou and put sunscreen on my face. Then I go sit outside the hotel and wait for Amadou. Mist rises off the river and birds dive for fish. A very old Malian man in a straw hat peddles by on an even older bicycle. He has an ancient rifle on his back, and he rides very slowly. It is utterly quiet.

At seven on the dot Amadou arrives in front of my auberge, pushing a small red scooter. He seems to share my contentment.

"It is beautiful in the morning," he says.

He offers me a seat on the back of his scooter and we do about ten miles an hour on a road that hosts eighteen-wheelers and buses. Every time a big truck comes, he pulls over to the side of the road and we wait. It takes quite a while to make it down the road, but soon scrubby little eucalyptus trees give way to soaring eucalyptus and balanzan trees that block out the sun and create havens of cool, almost dry air. Then we enter the old colonial quarter. The houses are beautiful, pale yellow bungalows with terra-cotta roofs, floor-to-ceiling windows, and wooden shutters to keep out the heat.

Most are falling apart, which adds to the melancholy air. Sheep wander among the ruins, and creeping vines burst through fallen roofs. Squatters have pitched burlap tents and planted vegetable gardens in the front lawns of formerly grand houses, and children chip away at the plaster walls with metal sticks. A few properties have been put to good use and turned into nurseries run by women who sell tomato and melon vines, but few, if any, of the houses are still inhabited. By the river, French expats have restored some bungalows and those are truly lovely. I'm about to mention this when Amadou makes an angry motion toward one of the houses and says with bitterness, "The French. They control everything in this country.".

We get back on the bike and head for Ségou Toro, an old town beaten into submission by freak rains, which is a labyrinth of one-story mud houses. Not many Malians live here but people come to pray in the saints' tombs and the mosque by the river. Here I see for the first time the archetypal West African mosque with crenulated walls and the trunks of palm trees sticking out the sides so that laborers can climb up the sides after the rains and replace the mud.

Amadou parks the bike near an old man who agrees to watch it, and we walk down to the river. A few men fix brown pirogues, and the ground is scattered with conical fish traps that work like lobster pots to trap river fish called capitaine with a bit of bait. Women in bright blue-and-red skirts stand in clusters of three around enormous mortar and pestles, pounding millet into dust for the animals to eat. After one woman brings the pestle down with all her might she lifts it into the air, then lets it go, and it is grabbed by another woman who brings it down with similar force. They hum a little and chat as they do the work, never missing a beat or allowing the pestle to miss its mark. I know it's hard work, but it looks like fun and I smile at them as though we are sharing a joke.

One of them beckons me over. She hands me a pestle and urges me to try. I lift it high and bring it down awkwardly, hitting more wood than millet. I try again, using my back muscles to get some height, but don't get the satisfying thump and crackle they do. I try for the third time, but then my arms are so tired I'm barely able to lift the pestle above my head. I understand why the work is often done in threes and why they can't lose the rhythm of the flying pestle. I hand it back, and they smile in encouragement. The smallest and most impish among them holds out her hand for money. I give her some coins and she seems thrilled, pocketing it quickly and flashing me a huge smile. But then we don't know what to do and we look at each other a few moments before wandering off in our own directions. She speaks no French and I speak no Bambara. I walk away, wanting more from them even as they get back to work.

I half listen to Amadou as we wander through the village. He ploughs through his speech impediment and talks excitedly about the history of Ségou. I stop asking him to repeat things and just catch bits of history here and there.

This is our most holy mosque. See how it sits by the river guarding against evil spirits? It is made of mud with bits of wood sticking out of it so we can reapply mud after the rainy season. You cannot go inside.

This is where women come to pray to this saint for babies. Many women come here from all over Mali. Would you like to say a few words? You should just make a quick prayer. Your Jesus will not mind.

On he goes, interspersing history with his own set of beliefs. He's Muslim, but also keeps some talismans around for safety. He pulls down his T-shirt and underneath are no less than three stones encased in leather and tied around his neck. Each is designed to keep away evil spirits and protect him from witchcraft. We sit down under the tree by the river and watch the fishermen bait their fish traps.

"When I am really worried about something I go ask the river for help. I don't really go to the mosque," he says.

"Don't the imams hate that you still believe in fetishes?"

Amadou searches the ground and finds a small gray stone, evenly ridged on one side as though it were part of a fossil. He presses it into my hand and explains.

"This is just a rock. A normal rock. But we take it to a man in Keyes I know and he will *egorge un poulet* and say some prayers. You could take it to a marabout, he could do the job, but a fetishist is much faster."

His voice becomes reverent.

"This stone will be inhabited by a spirit from the river that can protect you or harm you, depending on how you treat it. But it is no longer just a rock, you understand? You can never just treat it like a rock. It is a spirit."

He releases his finger from the rock in my palm and we both look at it intently. It's still a rock, no chickens have been slaughtered in its name, but we seem to both agree that it should be treated with respect. I pocket it and Amadou nods approvingly, touching the talismans around his own neck.

I suppose it's easy to dismiss his beliefs as unsophisticated and pagan; both Christians and Muslims often do. But I cannot because I've been brought up with fairies as well.

In early December each year my mother unpacks a really impressive array of Christmas decorations, including straw tree ornaments, candlestick holders of moss, and embroidered red table runners that go under the smorgasbord. But the one I love most is the large bearded *tomte* who sits on the mantel above the fireplace. Clothed in gray wool, his face hidden by a white beard and a red cap, he distributes presents on Christ-

mas Eve in return for a bowl of porridge with a pat of butter on top. If he's treated well, he protects the house, shoo-
ing away trolls and watching over livestock (I guess for us that
would have been our Lhasa apso, Chippy; our cat, Fluffy; and
of course the chickens) from predators. If he's treated badly,
he'll ruin your life. An angry tomte will kill the cow or start a
fire in the barn. He'll jump out of nowhere, box your ears, and
then break everything in the house. Inflated with the importance of his Christmas tasks, he's Santa Claus gone haywire, a
prima donna gnome who demands certain considerations, like
the finest salty butter on his porridge.

My mother hems and haws about the existence of God,
but she's clear about the power of tomte. When she takes him
out of his wrapping in December she murmurs to him gently
like a small child, stroking his beard, straightening his coat and
apologizing for the long confinement. If she buys a new tomte
in Sweden she packs him in her hand luggage so he won't be
smushed in with clothes and shampoo and emerge irate. One
Christmas she moved him from one side of the mantelpiece to
the other so he wouldn't get too hot. *Sorry about that. If I had
known the heat rose straight up here . . .*

The myths of my childhood never hardened into beliefs,
but I retain superstitions about the pagan world. If a glass of
milk has turned over or suddenly gone sour, I'm sure I annoyed
a nonhuman. Mist in the morning still reminds me of fairies
dancing on the lake, and I can't stand walking through the dark
pine forests of Sweden at night because I know the trolls are
watching me. Thus Amadou's unseen world of river spirits sits
easy in my brain. Both Connecticut and Sweden are a world
away, but we have our fetishes and superstitions too.

30

Patience

I STAY IN SÉGOU a couple of days. Then a couple more. I start to feel like I live there, in the Lebanese hotel, that this place is my home. It is all so lovely and hot and comfortable. The Lebanese brothers make such good couscous and Amadou is easy company. Just walking out of my room and taking a look at the river in the morning or at sunset feels like a kind of religious epiphany. The beauty is healing. Plus I *sleep* there in a way I haven't slept anywhere in years—a dark dreamless sleep that makes me feel smug with refreshment each morning.

Just two months ago, I would have been shocked by the conditions of my existence. I am reasonably certain that the "lamb" being served with my meals is some kind of bushmeat. It tastes too gamey to be domesticated and is likely rodent or lizard. My possessions have been pared down to only the most essential. I have only two sets of clothing, both African boubous, one that I wear to bed and one that I wear when going out, depending on their cleanliness. I take my showers with a rubber hose that hangs from the side of the bathroom right above the toilet and live with all manner of animals, from lizards to medium-size mice who chirp away all through the night and eat through a corner of my backpack to get to the crackers inside. In the evening, I wander the town alone, sometimes barefoot, because Africans don't wear shoes and all I have are boots anyway.

I'm not lonely, but I must do something to pass the time so I start to read thrillers that people have left behind. When I finish those, I go through the old British newspapers the cook sometimes uses to wrap onions. If you had come to my hotel one evening in late May you would have seen a white woman in a dirty blue boubou, with bare feet dyed red with dust, reading an *Evening Standard* from 1999 and drinking a healthy tumbler of Campari. What's more, I probably would have jumped up when I saw you and asked a thousand questions about the weather in Paris and if the rains had started in Bamako.

It all starts to look a little strange. A little too British in Kenya in the 1930s, without the society, the parties, or the cross-dressing. One day I go down to the local store to buy a Fanta and, upon finding the store closed, sit down outside and wait. I watch a mama goat gnaw at its tether while the baby runs around nosing mangoes. I doze a little. I consider the undersoles of my feet and how hard and leathery they have gotten. A mother comes and sits down next to me with her baby and begins to plait her hair and I watch them for a while. Two hours pass before I consider leaving, and then it's only because I really have to go to the bathroom. When I go everyone else sitting around the store looks at me like I'm crazy to give up so soon.

I have always been slightly impatient and I am grateful for my newfound tolerance of waiting, but the process of living alone for this long has thrust me into a kind of monastic pose. I want less, but I also do less. My ability to find entertainment in the smallest things, to soak up the heat and quiet around me without feeling the need to produce anything but my own observations is becoming firmly, perhaps dangerously, embedded in my personality. I am floating through the world attached to nothing and no one. In a few more weeks there will be no tether.

Mary Kingsley would not approve, and I feel the weight of her opinion keenly. She rarely lingered anywhere, unless she was waiting for the river conditions to improve or for supplies to arrive. "It is one of my disastrous habits well known to my friends on the Coast that whenever I am happy, comfortable and content, I lose all knowledge of the date, the time of day, and my hairpins," she wrote of her stay in Kangwe, one of the few places in her travels that seemed actually pleasant. Ashamed of her indolence, she resolved the situation by traveling ninety miles down the river, learning how to paddle an Ogooué canoe and spending her afternoons hacking through the dense, pathless forest with a machete. These challenges and hardships brought her in the end greater satisfaction.

Still, I can't help but think that the ability to live as slowly and simply as I am will help me when I get back to Paris. I am patient now in a way that I never was before and good-natured about inconvenience. Since I know how to live with so little, the small everyday riches of Europe will seem stunningly grand. Imagine what joy I will feel with a decent book in hand or watching a riveting television program. Imagine sitting down to coffee with a good friend who knows me and loves me and with whom I can talk for hours. Imagine driving freely through the countryside in a safe and sound car. Imagine taking a hot bubble bath. The luxuries of home have been unseen and unimagined until now. All my privileges taken for granted. Now when I think about them, lying in my bed in Ségou, they come into startling and clear relief.

Yet I don't want these pleasures, not really, and I don't believe that even they will make me happy. It is in a small way a relief to think like this because it feels a little like I have mastered fear. Fear of discomfort. Fear of getting lost in Africa. Fear of waking up every day in Paris with dread. The only thing that really makes me afraid now, really makes my eyes water, is the thought of losing Florent. Sentimental woman, I think, how silly. What has Mali got to do with a man. What has any of this to do with a man. Yet it is true. This is where I have ended up. I don't need his presence. I don't even really miss him much. Yet he is the only thing, it turns out, I really want.

I am ready to move on, and so I leave beautiful, mystical Ségou, believing that the rest of Mali, and by extension Timbuktu, will be as beautiful as this little town by the Niger River. I have mastered want and pared my life down to its most essential, and after many days on the road I believe I know something of simplicity and solitude, even hardship.

I do not.

31

Tyranny and the Mosque

DJENNÉ HOLDS THE WORLD'S largest mud building, a multistory mosque that is a hundred years old and a marvel unto itself. It is why I am here, why I have deviated from the road to Mopti that runs to Timbuktu. Of all the towns in the Sahara this is one of the holiest.

The bus drops me on the outskirts of town just after midday. I wander into town, looking for the mosque. In the back alleys, rivers of raw sewage have created canyons that force people to cling to the sides of houses as they walk. Persistent nasty little flies crawl into my ears and attach themselves to my eyelids. Sheep and goats wander in and out of houses, bleating miserably in the heat and coughing with disease. Children in rags, their thin arms covered in red bumps, come out of their houses to stare at me and yell *touba,* the slang word in Bambara for white person, as I walk into town. The whole town reeks of swampland, garbage, and the diesel fumes thrown off by a generator near the market.

As soon as I left Ségou life got immediately, palpably hard. It was as though the gods wanted to pull me back down to earth. The landscape dried out, the baobabs disappeared, and people became religious. Food, which was plentiful in Bamako and Ségou, became scarce, all except pasta and fried onions and mangoes. People were hot, cranky, and unwashed. They had dark circles under their eyes, and for the first time I saw ill-looking children with distended bellies and listless eyes. The heat, the bad food, the heavy air, and restless sweat-soaked nights created a kind of stress in me that limited my ability to reason well. I saw this same stress in the faces of the Malians around me. They seemed listless and exhausted. Tempers flared. Patience, which I had come to think of as a national trait, began to run short. On the bus one market woman accused the other of theft. They screamed at each other, and when the bus driver tried to interfere they turned on him.

"You, why were you four hours late today? Why? Why?"

"There was a problem with the engine," the driver said.

"No, you were taking tea! You were taking tea!" they yelled, nearly hysterical with fury.

"No no no," he said, holding his hands over his head in protection. One of the women batted him over the head with her handbag anyway. I'd wager a month earlier, before the heat came, people would have laughed at this. Now they are stony silent.

Djenné should have been a refuge, but as I look around for a hotel, even a place to get a cup of tea, I can't find anything open, much less catering to tourists. I search out the mosque, which is impressive. It has crenulated towers and irregular palm branches sticking out the sides in rows.

I approach to take a closer look and a man wearing a T-shirt with Osama bin Laden on it waves me away.

"Interdite pour le touba," he says.

When Djenné was a great trading town of the Songhai Empire in the fifteenth century it sat right on the Bani River, an offshoot of the Niger, and drew money and commerce from all the surrounding villages. Since then the river has moved several miles north, leaving Djenné alone on a plane of mud flats for much of the year. Many of Djenné's men make their living by digging up sand and mud on these flats and fashioning bricks. Done in 120 degree heat and nearly 90 percent humidity, it's the kind of work that kills the healthy and turns those who remain toward religion.

Conservative Islam is strong here. Women wear veils rather than the loose cloth turban of most Malian women. Shopkeepers play verses from the Qur'an on boom boxes outside their front doors and sell Salafist sermons on CD. The little green Saudi flag flies everywhere, over new wells and Qur'anic schools, indicating that education and aid have fallen beyond Bamako's orbit. Foreigners are not welcome. Two years ago a riot ensued when several Italians were spotted on the roof of the Great Mosque. Thinking that Westerners had taken over the mosque, the townspeople tried to storm the building. The Italians, engineers called in to fix the roof, barely escaped with their lives. Djenné still feels tense to me, like a town aching for a fight.

I find a shop with a nice view of the central square, order a Fanta, take a seat in a plastic chair, and try to make myself as innocuous as possible. I play a game to see if anyone walking into the shop will say hello to me first, but no one even looks at me, much less says hello.

Just as I am about to leave, a black Mercedes with four men in it races through town, throwing up white dust. It circles slowly back toward me and stops in front of the shop. Hip-hop thunders out of the stereo and a man no older than twenty gets out. He and all his friends are wearing identical black T-shirts and black sunglasses.

"You need a ride? You need any help at all . . . *cheeerrie?*" he says, placing his hands on his hips and rotating them in a circle like a dance move. "This is my dad's Mercedes. You like it? You come for ride with us."

I nod vaguely, half smile, and don't say anything. People don't stop to stare—Malians are too polite for that—but I can tell they are watching. I'm embarrassed.

"I'm talking to you. Mademoiselle. I am talking to you."

He comes around the front of the car. The store owner disappears into his shop.

I just look back, as neutrally as I can. "I am very tired, very hot, and would like to enjoy my Fanta," I say in English slowly and hold up the bottle. "I don't want a ride. I don't want any help from you at all. I just want to sit here, by myself, for as long as I like and look at the mosque and the town. "

Often if I want a situation to end quickly I speak English because most people don't. Today is not my lucky day. The young man repeats his funny dance move.

"So, you like Fifty Cent?" he asks in perfect English.

He's a fan of hip-hop, a musical genre I know absolutely nothing about, but I lie. I lie like a kid offered pot by the cool kids her first day of high school. I lie because I am a guest in this country. I should try to get along.

"Um, I do like Fifty Cent."

"Oh yeah? What's your favorite song?"

"I forget."

"Can you sing it?" he asks, now genuinely curious.

"No, not really. I have a very bad voice."

At this point the rest of the guys in the Mercedes get out of the car to see what we're talking about. They stand against the hood, arms crossed. A quick conversation in Bambara ensues and someone turns up the car radio. Hip-hop thunders over the mud houses of Djenné, drowning out the Qur'an, the electric generator, and even the siesta time radios.

"Is it this one?" he shouts.

In all the hours I spent preparing for my trip to Africa—reading the nine-hundred-page travel logs, pouring over topographical maps, reflecting on Mary Kingsley's travels—it never occurred to me that I should actually be brushing up on American culture.

"No, it's another song," I shout. "I like another song, but this one is good too."

They seem to accept this and all the guys standing against the car bob their head in unison with the beat. I begin to bob my head a little too. It's good, actually.

"You want to come to a party tonight?" one of them asks me.

"No, I'm okay," I say. "I'm pretty tired."

"It's hot," he says sympathetically.

"I know. I'm not prepared for it."

"Sleep on the roof, it's better," he says over the din.

"I will tonight."

He nods. Then, because they are essentially good boys and there is nothing more to say, they get back into their car. The atmosphere of the entire town seems to relax. The storekeeper comes out of his shop. The market women in front of the mosque begin to sell. The kids playing in the dust resume their game of tag. Everyone breathes again and my presence, once so conspicuous and irritating, no longer seems to grate. The boys drive off and the great mosque begins to broadcast the evening call to prayer. I finish my Fanta and search out, yet again, a place to sleep for the night.

32

The Road to Timbuktu

THE FIRST LAND ROVER for Timbuktu leaves at seven a.m. from a small dusty field behind the proper bus station in Mopti. Experience tells me we won't leave for several hours so I show up that morning at nine.

"*Il est parti.* It's gone," the scheduling man says. "It left at seven fifteen."

"Well, when is the next one?"

"Any minute, any minute. *Installes toi.*"

At eleven a.m. we start to load the truck. I stuff my small black backpack and six bottles of mineral water at my feet. A woman helps me wrap my thirteen-foot-long green scarf around my head like a Tuareg warrior. She doesn't speak French but clucks and pats my cheek when finished, as though I look lovely for a white woman pretending to be a Saharan man.

I'm not that far from Timbuktu now. It is very likely that René Caillié's caravan passed through Mopti before making the final push to the trading town. From there they would have traded again in Timbuktu, then gone north into the deserts of Libya, heading for the Mediterranean coast. It is a trip that is unimaginable in its discomforts.

For then, as now, there was no road to Timbuktu. From Mopti, it is just driving across the savanna in the dry season or taking a pirogue up the Niger in the wet. The track is dangerous and unpredictable and often people end up spending the night in the desert. Hence all the water. Who knows for how long we will be out in the desert?

Our driver is named Moussa, and I introduce myself forcefully, hoping I can assess his mettle by the look in his eye and handshake. Moussa, resplendent in a brown leisure suit and a Phoenix Suns baseball cap, has to be able to drive twelve to fourteen hours over rutted, rocky, sandy terrain without puncturing a tire or breaking an axle. If our truck splits in two he has to be able to fix it, because no one else is coming along to help us. He has to find Timbuktu without maps or marked roads and protect us from the unlikely but not impossible eventuality of banditry. In short, he has to perform duties closer to that of a fighter pilot than a taxi driver.

Thankfully he's about six feet five and bangs away at the engine with supreme confidence. He's also bringing along an apprentice who will sit on the roof, keeping an eye on all the bags and helping if there's a serious disaster.

I buy the two front seats of the truck and consider the money well spent. I have enough room to move a little if I need to and my leg is safe from the truck's huge drive shaft. The windshield has innumerable cracks and small spider tears but has never been fully broken. This is all a good sign.

Three women and a girl, all in identical calico melfhas, get into the seat behind the driver, four men in the next seat and four teenage boys who squeeze into the jump seats in the way back. We're loaded. It's noon. It's already well over a hundred degrees.

We leave Mopti quickly, casting out into low, flat savanna marked by shoulder-high green bushes and clay earth. We're cutting northeast, away from the Niger River for a while, but will rejoin it in a few hours when it bends back toward Timbuktu.

It's rained recently and the landscape is riddled with puddles and small ponds of muddy water that throw cool air into the cabin. Moussa never takes his eyes off the road and never takes anything for granted, sometimes stopping altogether to look around before choosing one of five or six different paths.

"How often do you make this trip?" I ask.

"Every day," he says. "It's just changed since it rained."

Several times he backtracks after arriving at a gully too wide to cross, a fallen tree, or a stretch of mud that could swallow the Land Rover. Everyone, even the guys in the back, are watching the road in respectful silence. This is an art, and I begin to appreciate the series of tough choices Moussa has to make. Go around the sandy patch of road or accelerate over it, hoping the wheels never have time to dig in. Take the straight hard path that brings us off course or stick with the infuriatingly muddy winding road he already knows. We snake through shrubs and the occasional termite mound and never make it much above twenty miles an hour. Sometimes the road will surprise him and he'll throw on the brakes or drive too quickly over a bump, eliciting groans from the guys in the back. When he does, he curses quietly and looks at the ground out the window to make sure he can still see the shadow of his apprentice, who is clinging to the roof.

The land is flat and shimmers in the midday heat, the sky cloudless and light blue. Occasionally we pass mud villages perched on small mounds, the remnants of previous villages that melted during the rainy season. A light wind blows dust across the savanna but it's quiet, empty. We don't see a soul. The men are out with their herds, the women inside working or pounding millet under shady eucalyptus trees. Even the small mud houses seem like natural features and the shoulder-high termite mounds like frozen sentinels.

The road doesn't get better. My neck is sore and my stomach queasy. I force down some Tombouctou water, which is now the temperature of hot tea. We come upon a village and then another with new two-story wood-and-wattle buildings painted red, blue, and green. They look like forts to me.

"What's that?" I ask Moussa.

"*La Mosquée*. The Saudis build them all over, all over." He smiles. "People ask for wells, for animals, for schools. We get mosques. Nothing but mosques."

"So no one wants them."

"We are not stupid."

We rejoin the Niger at a small village of Bozo fishermen and prepare to cross. We wait an hour by the banks, luxuriating in the slight coolness running off the green water. The river is so low we could probably drive across if the bottom weren't so muddy. The boys in the back get out and start smoking. "Are you married? Do you have children?" they ask me.

We cross the river on a broad flat-bottom scow that has been painted sky blue. The engine is broken, so two men stand at the square bow and punt us across with long sticks like Venetian gondoliers. One of them offers to show me how to punt, but I demur out of respect for Moussa and our general timetable. Down the river, fishermen up to their thighs in water throw out round fishing nets while women lay freshly washed clothes on the bank to dry.

From now on we will follow the dry riverbank to Timbuktu, an easier road along a flat riverbed. Moussa relaxes, leaning back in his seat for the first time and taking a swig of water from a yellow can at his feet. The afternoon hangs low and heavy, with the dust stirred up during the morning holding and intensifying the midday heat.

We fly over sand, some hard and some soft. Moussa now drives with loose controls, letting the truck fishtail or run off course when it wants to. He's having fun scaring the zebu cows that have come down to the river to drink or graze on thin strips of grass. The women behind me come to life, chatting and arranging their own veils and helping me retie my green turban. Mango trees line the outer bank of the river and cows nibble at their bottom edges. Girls bathing topless in the river smile and wave at us, and I am reminded of Ibn Battuta's shock and dismay that the good Muslim women of Mali did not veil and went topless "despite their perseverance to their prayers."

It's beautiful, but fragile. Each village has to sustain itself with no help from the outside. No electricity and no irrigation to soften the blow if the once-a-year rains should fail. Already it feels like there are too many cows for the tiny strips of grass by the river, and out beyond the mango trees the huge herds of zebu cows so prized by the Fulani herdsmen have beaten the savanna into dust and scattered straw.

The rains are everything in this part of Africa. In Senegal they rely on the river and sea, in Mauritania they live in an oasis or ship in water, but Mali lives on that fragile line between desert and fertile land. In the south they grow cotton for export, and here in the north they rely on animals. If the rains don't come in a few weeks the landscape will change and the people driving their cattle out there on the plain might not survive. Isak Dinesen wrote:

> But one year the long rains failed. It was, then, as if the Universe were turning away from you. It grew cooler, on some days it would be cold, but there was no sign of moisture in the atmosphere. Everything became drier and harder, and it was as if all force and gracefulness had withdrawn from the world.

She writes an entire chapter about the rains and what they do to her farm. And this from a woman who had the resources to leave if the land dried out. Imagine if you had to stay and everything that sustained you disappeared.

After nine hours of driving, we arrive in Niafunké. There aren't even mangoes to eat. Women sell peanuts and dried fish with gelatinous edges and nothing else. No Fanta here. I catch a glimpse of myself in the mirror of our truck and realize with alarm that my face, neck, and shoulders are beet red. I rinse my face with water but realize the color is not dust but sunburn or windburn, possibly heat exhaustion. I walk around behind the truck and drink a few sips of water but my stomach cramps in protest. I force more down, gagging and in pain. A group of children come out to watch me, the littlest, snottiest ones touching my wrists and ankles. I try to shake them off but can't. Eventually they are scared away by a toothless man wearing three sweaters. He stares at me, wild-eyed and filthy, vaguely rubbing his crotch.

Moussa pulls in to Timbuktu at midnight. He's tired and grim because tomorrow he will do exactly the same thing, and the day after and the day after that. His apprentice bounds off the roof, his eyelashes glowing with red dust under the fluorescent lights. Moussa shakes my hand in a professional way and invites me to ride back with him to Mopti the day after tomorrow.

I stumble to my hotel both sick and sore. I rush to the bathroom, dry heave into the toilet bowl, then lie down with my head against the bathtub. Shaking with heat and dehydration and the exertion of keeping myself together over all those bumpy roads, I lie there on the bathroom floor, where my tender body seems to fall apart and splinter into a million pieces.

What's in a Name?

IT SHOULD BE NOTED that René Caillié, after surviving scurvy and near starvation, not to mention almost nine months of walking barefoot in sand, arrived in Timbuktu, spent two weeks there, and hitched the first ride out. Even then, when the city was closer to its medieval glory, Timbuktu couldn't quite muster the majesty that its name demanded. "A mass of ill-looking houses, built of earth," Caillié said, undoubtedly with the sad, slightly hangdog look of the chronically disappointed Frenchman.

I knew not to expect much. Timbuktu reached the height of its power in the sixteenth century, when no trade routes existed on seas and traders had to pass through the Sahara to carry goods from Africa to Europe. Caravans, some with tens of thousands of camels, would arrive in town from Ghana and Côte d'Ivoire, trading slaves, precious metals, and even peacocks in the great open-air bazaar. Around the wealth grew up lavish mosques and libraries. It became the commercial and cultural center of the Sahara. A place to go in its own right.

Once sturdy oceangoing ships had been developed in Europe, however, the necessity of this terrible trip across the desert diminished. The land-based trade routes dried up and with them Timbuktu's wealth. Caillié found a defeated place, struggling to prosper in the face of an unpredictable desert and the Tuareg, who raided the poor inhabitants with dismaying regularity.

By the time I arrive, a good two hundred years after Caillié, Timbuktu has not had a bout of prosperity in five hundred years. It has been neglected by the central government, picked over by the Tuareg, and victimized by the increased drying out of the Sahel and the shift of the Niger River southward.

This town is down-at-heel, caught in a permanent dust bowl, and it shows. The next morning I wake up still shaky and dehydrated, and look out on the desert from the doorstep of my hotel. It rolls on into a fog of softly moving sand that blocks the sun and turns the daytime moon into a haunted, hollowed crescent. Timbuktu, such as it is, is far-off and blurry, low-slung to the earth and constructed of hardened mud. It seems small and more piteous than other Malian villages, which at least have the Niger to ennoble them. Without that great river there is no definitive outline to either the town or the landscape that surrounds it. All in all, Timbuktu seems not unlike a mirage.

I try to imagine what I would say or think of this vision if I were home, healthy and rested, but that woman is very far from me now. In her place is a sense of hesitation. I am somehow slow to respond, crippled in some way by the exhaustion of seeing new things every day and having to weigh and evaluate them for some further consumption. Years from now, when my soul needs healing and only the memory of Africa can do it, I will ask myself, How was Timbuktu? How did you feel when you finally made it? A definitive answer will surely present itself in time—for no one's mind likes a vacuum—but none does now. *I just don't know,* I whisper to myself, *what I think.*

This could be construed as a kind of failure, but I see it as a small triumph. I have lost any ability to judge for the reassuring sake of judgment itself. Like many things on this trip, my first encounter with Timbuktu seems to present no obvious solution, no epiphany or even eureka moment. Yet the ambiguity of the place—the floating sand, the rising heat, the blurred outline of a town—throws me off, just a little. I need to return to the earth, I think, get my bearings again and shake off yesterday's ride. I go back up to my room and take my shoes off. The sand is so soft that I will walk.

There was a time when I wore boots to protect myself from some imagined danger lurking in the sands of Africa, when I socked away money in all the pockets of my boubou, when I gave the hotel owner my passport to lock up. No more. I am deeply trusting now and cognizant of the fact that passports and money don't really help you in moments of real danger. They are an imagined security like handguns and life jackets. I leave money in my room and my passport on the bed. My boots I haven't seen since Ségou.

And so, in the midst of some confusion and inordinate exhaustion, I walk. I do the thing I always do when I arrive in a new town. I try to see what sets this place apart from others; I stay as close as I can to women; I make sure neutrality is etched into my face.

Soon the women appear. They walk along the paved road in soft white caverns of sand, and I come in just a little behind them. This is habit and a practicality, for the road by midday will be hot enough to blow out the tires of a jeep. They wear brightly colored boubous of pink, yellow, and green, some emblazoned with the name of the presidential candidate Amadou Toumani Touré. The women are fresh and bright, some still wet from the bath, and they carry big silver saucers on their head that hold mangoes and rice. Small children run alongside brandishing sticks torn from the hard desert shrubs. Some wear T-shirts and underwear, some acrylic party dresses that are dirty and torn in a sad rather than violent way.

The power of the name Timbuktu becomes evident the closer we get to the old town. South African, Dutch, Norwegian, and British aid agencies line the road. Their buildings are white and concrete-heavy with high, tight windows to keep out the sun and sand, but there are small indications of luxury inside: a brand-new SUV idling outside a front door, a generator gently humming in the shade of a thorny tree. Many of the agencies have signs on the road publicizing how they are refurbishing Timbuktu's ancient libraries and gathering up all the old manuscripts from locals. *Look!* the signs seem to say. *We really love Islam. We love the books, the architecture, the ancient, invaluable doodads.* . . . I think of Moussa's scathing comments on the Saudis who came to Mali to build mosques and little else. What would he think of those who only came to build libraries?

When we arrive in the old town I am surprised by the stillness of the place. The buildings in the old town are mostly made of mud, like most towns in this part of Mali, but the sun seems stronger here and some of the buildings have been baked into a kind of flaky crust. Many of the mosques have been visibly softened by the rains and look like melting ice cream that was thrown into a freezer. Others are being pulled down and reconstructed out of harder stones or concrete. The center of town feels like a construction site, with boulders and buckets strewn across the path. Someone is trying to make Timbuktu permanent, as if it needed any such help.

The farther we get into town the quieter it becomes. A kind of simmering beauty, born of pure heat, appears. As we enter the smaller lanes of the old city, the women's voices are pulled in and swallowed by the mud brick houses and small alleys of dunes that slow our feet and seem sometimes to almost send us backward. On a ridge I catch a glimpse of the desert that spreads out before us, harsh and scrubby, and in the haze a man walking beside a camel that is carrying huge slabs of salt. I pause a moment, mystified as to why this mode of transport hasn't been replaced by jeeps. When I look up, the women are gone and I hurry to catch up with them.

They have stopped and gathered under a tree with leaves like small minnows and barely any shade. Each sets her bowl down on the ground and rests a moment, pulling her legs down underneath herself and lying against the wall of a mud house with wooden plinths sticking out of it. I sit down next to them and they smile, but none of them speaks a word of English or French. I buy a couple of mangoes and they seem pleased. One of them points to the door of a house and encourages me to go look.

The doors in this neighborhood are made of wood, an extraordinary indulgence, and embedded with silver studs and door knockers. They glisten in the sun, looking solemn and medieval, like tiny fortresses. These are the only relics of a once wealthy Timbuktu and its ties to the wealthy cities of Marrakesh and Casablanca.

Suddenly a door opens. A man in a purple boubou stands looking at me.

"Hello," he says.

"Hello."

Behind him on the back wall of his entrance hall is a large poster of the leader of Libya, Muammar Qaddafi, who is wearing aviator glasses and smiling.

"Qaddafi," I say, surprised.

The man smiles. "He is a hero to my wife."

Then he closes the door.

The women make for the central market in town and I find

a kiosk, whitewashed in the inside and still glistening from a fresh wipe down, for water. The water comes in small bags that I am invited to drink on the doorstep with the owner. He is about twenty-five years old with high cheekbones and widely spaced eyes.

"How is business?" I ask.

"No one has work here. No one can buy. I have two shops and I don't have enough money to marry," he says.

"It looks like a prosperous town," I say. My mind conjures up Djenné's miserable mud streets and slavelike conditions. Timbuktu doesn't suffer from sewage in the streets or open-air generators belching diesel fumes. This is the benefit of receiving more than the occasional tourist.

"That's the aid workers' cars," he says. "The big Toyotas with the AC. They make Timbuktu look prosperous, but if they left it would look like what it is. Shit."

"Are they helpful, the aid workers?"

"No, not at all. They do nothing."

"They are redoing the libraries," I venture.

He looks annoyed. I suppose the libraries touch on his loyalty to Timbuktu and his fealty to Islam. It's sort of like asking an Eastern liberal whether he supports a monument to Martin Luther King Jr. *Well, when you put it that way, of course I do.*

"What about the government?" I ask.

He smiles slowly.

"There is no road to Timbuktu. There is no money to trade. ATT didn't even give us a second round in the elections. We don't expect help from the government."

"What about Qaddafi?"

This makes him smile broadly. "He is a little crazy," he says fondly. "But he built the water tower. He brings doctors. He is building a canal."

"I'm sure Bamako loves that," I say.

"Oh, he doesn't tell them when he comes," he says. "He just comes."

It strikes me that Timbuktu struggles with a terrible weight. The quiet, the pictures of Qaddafi, the slow decay of its streets leave it without either a past or a future. Despite the poverty of almost every town in Mali, every single one was also energetic and young, forward-looking. Children outnumbered the elderly. Women took on tasks like bartering that men eschewed. Men in turn took on weaving and sewing. Mali seemed until now, if not modern, at least future oriented and a touch iconoclastic. This town, however, feels like a place whose history forces it to always look backward. For would Qaddafi be here, would the Tuareg not demand independence, if they were not enamored of the name as well? How dangerous it is for the inhabitants of this town to live someplace that signals the glory days of the Sahara and Islam when the world is so full of misguided, overzealous people.

I also am guilty of romanticizing Timbuktu, I suppose. I came to Timbuktu for the name, and now I too am burdening the town. I am bringing my baggage to this sunbaked end-of-the-road town and asking it to provide beauty and meaning. I am asking it to be something it is not.

Yet I have also mellowed since I started the trip, laid aside what assumptions I had. It is partly exhaustion, partly surprise. One can carry only so much belief in one's head, and hardened belief, as a mode of thinking, has been drummed out of me. The chance that I will find some new way of living in this town is remote. In some respects it feels like insight, if it is to be had, is had on the road. Caillié might have felt this way too. The goal is attained, but I remain restless. After all this time in buses and cars, I find it hard not to let go of the constant motion.

The women have moved on to the central market and I

find them when I leave the shop. They have spread their mangoes out in front of them under a small tree and are waiting. I wander the market, searching. Merchandise from all over the Sahara is available—wheat and biscuits from Mauritania, cigarettes and milk from Algeria, imported rice all the way from Chad. In one corner, light-skinned Moors in long blue daraas drink tea and sell fabric. In another, a couple of North African Arabs read the Qur'an and sell peanuts, jewelry, and cigarettes. Tuareg men, thin as a curve, pass in twos, their heads and faces hidden by black scarves. Everyone seems to be eyeing each other carefully, even the Fulani women, who are usually the joy and laughter of a market.

I consider going to see the old mosque, and perhaps to see some of the martyr tombs for which the town is famous. I consider the libraries and Caillié's house and all the things I should do in order to make my stay here worthwhile. But all of those things seem so historical, and I want in some way to liberate Timbuktu from its past—as I would like to be liberated from mine. So instead of taking the great tour, I sit in the market. Waiting, watching, and listening like the women who come bearing mangoes, rice, and water. What will happen here today? I think. What does this town in this place have to offer this hot, hot day in May that is different from anything that has happened here before? How shall we start again today, my old Saharan town, in a way that looks to the future?

34

Faking Devotion

I DON'T KNOW HOW long I planned on staying in Timbuktu. I never really considered the equation in that way. I just wanted to get there, have it mean something, and get out. Now that I am here it feels oddly difficult to make any sort of decision at all. It is so remote, transport so unreliable, and the air surrounding the town so heavy and hot that it forces a kind of inertness. *I couldn't leave today even if I wanted to,* I think.

I am also, for the first time in Africa, struggling with my health. I am not sick per se, but chronically lethargic. Nausea greets me with every meal and I frequently have a headache. I spend inordinate amounts of time staring at the wall in my hotel room, drinking Coca-Cola and failing to organize my thoughts. I wonder if I am exhausted or chronically dehydrated or maybe just a touch malnourished.

I remember thinking in Paris that I would pour Africa into me like some kind of magic elixir. Then I would be seen. Then I would exist. I seem now like a naive woman who thought a place or even beauty could make her whole. The place has made me strong. It has made me determined. Mostly, however,

I am stripped of knowingness. The more I am out here in the world, the less I know.

"You need to go out," says the hotel proprietor, a firm and straight-thinking Malian who named his hotel the Hendrina Khan, after the wife of the Pakistani nuclear scientist A Q Khan.

"I will," I say.

"There is much to do in Timbuktu."

This I sincerely doubt, but I would like to at least see René Caillié's house.

"I know what we will do," says the hotel proprietor. "We will call Khalil."

Khalil works for a guy named Mr. Monday, so nicknamed because Monday was the only day he ever went to school. Mr. Monday now owns a couple of Range Rovers and takes tourists out into the desert and seems to be doing well with his meager education.

Unlike a lot of other young Malian boys, Khalil doesn't make pretenses to fashion—no big sunglasses, no low-riding jeans. Just carefully pressed khaki trousers and a blue button-down shirt. He is all about business.

"Shall we rent a four-by-four and spend a few days out in the desert?" he asks me with a completely serious face.

I raise weary, hardened eyes. "No."

"It's not that expensive. Just three hundred dollars."

"No."

"Are you sure?" he persists.

"Yes."

He nods and waves his hand toward the center of town. "Shall we?"

Like most Malians who seem to do well, Khalil is an autodidact. He went to a religious school, where he spent his days memorizing the Qur'an, but at night he went home and taught himself French, English, and a little German. In that respect he reminds me of Mary Kingsley, tackling her father's library, determined to learn and improve herself. Mr. Monday picked him up for his language skills, entrepreneurial spirit, and decided lack of religious fervor.

He is half Tuareg and says he has modern views, but he won't marry until he can buy his mother a house and doesn't approve of women wearing trousers. He has an illegitimate son who lives with his mother, a Bedouin woman, out in the desert, and although he tells me he loves the child's mother he has no intention of marrying her due to her low caste and nomadic ways. I can't even imagine what it's like being a Bedouin woman with an illegitimate child but Khalil shrugs his shoulders and moves the conversation on.

I ask Khalil to show me the houses in which Mungo Park, Gordon Laing, and René Caillié stayed. He nods his head but over the course of the morning ignores the request and keeps the tour to Timbuktu's Muslim, African past and politically strange present.

"Qaddafi is everywhere," I note.

"I know," Khalil says. "People put up his picture because they think he will give them gifts."

"Does he?" I ask.

"Sometimes."

Qaddafi's picture is so omnipresent it feels a little oppressive. It is on the sides of fruit stands, inside private houses, outside mosques. He is known as the true friend of the Tuareg and all desert peoples. Reportedly he shipped arms to the rebels and gave fighters safe haven in Libya during the Tuareg uprising in the late 1990s. In Timbuktu, he has built a brand-new water tower, attractively decorated like a medieval fort, and wants to fund a twenty-five-mile multibillion-dollar canal that will divert water from the Niger River to Timbuktu. He treats northern Mali like his fiefdom, and the hotel owner at the Hendrina

Khan tells me that he will show up unannounced, walk into a hotel, ask the owner about business, have lunch, and walk out again. His presence can be felt all over the town and it isn't a benign one. He empowers the Tuareg, who walk through town as though they own it, nudging aside the market women.

The lawlessness even pervades the market in the center of town. There smugglers who leverage the strong currencies of the CFA zone, which stands for *Communauté Financière Africaine* and includes Mali, Senegal, and Niger, against the weak currencies of Mauritania and Algeria come to make a profit. These countries' porous borders and overlapping ethnic tribes, such as the Fulani and the Tuareg, make things difficult for even the best-funded and well-intentioned governments to police. Thus the traffic in arms, drugs, and illegal immigrants thrives.

"I can make it to Chad in four days if I only stop to piss," a truck driver boasts to me in the market when I ask him where he is from.

"Did you just come from there?"

"I couldn't say," he says, grinning.

Khalil doesn't seem thrilled to have me talking to truck drivers so he urges me on, showing me the mosques and small sand shrines around Timbuktu dedicated to holy men or marabouts that came down from Morocco.

"Here you can pray for a child," he tells me. "Here you can pray for your mother's health." It is interesting, but when he presents the great mosque of Timbuktu for a second time, from a different angle, I'm annoyed.

"Where are the houses where the Europeans stayed?" I ask.

"You can't go inside. You know they are private homes. No one will let you inside. Why do you care?"

Suddenly we walk by a house with a plaque on its side that says in French *René Caillié stayed here.* I pause in triumph outside the house while Khalil kicks the hot white sand with his sneakers and avoids my eye.

"He was a remarkable guy," I say, trying to get the conversation going. "He walked across the desert and learned Arabic."

"He was a liar," Khalil mumbles. "A disgrace. It is a disgrace that he is still honored."

I shouldn't be startled but I am. Caillié wasn't a military man or even much of a colonist. Caillié never developed a fetishistic relationship with the flora and fauna of Africa or took an underage African wife. After finishing his trip he went home and struggled the rest of his life to convince skeptical Europeans that he'd visited Timbuktu and hadn't just made up the whole story.

"What do you mean, he's a liar?" I ask.

Khalil winces and his face loses its softness. Suddenly he seems a lot more Tuareg than Soninke — insufferably arrogant and entitled. Descended from a master race.

"He told everyone he was a Muslim so he could investigate the town. He went to the top of the minaret so he could draw a map of Timbuktu and when people asked him what he was doing he told them he was praying. He's a liar. He's the worst."

But I am stubborn in my admiration of Caillié so I say, perhaps foolishly, "Oh, that's not such a big deal."

Khalil blows up.

"He stood on the top of the mosque and said that he was praying when he was really drawing a map of the town. He *lied* about using the mosque. He *lied* about praying. He lied about being *Muslim.*"

It's the first time anyone in Mali has gotten really angry at me. I take a step back, looking at him. He stares back at me, still angry. It is foolish of me to argue.

"I see," I say. "I'm sorry."

He nods, apology accepted, and walks on.

Even Khalil, who escaped the rigors of his Qur'anic school

and had a baby out of wedlock, feels that Islam is the corner-stone of his life. The sanctity of the religion, its honor, is more important to him than anything else. He rests his identity on it. I know this intellectually, but I still find it hard to relate to. I have never cared for anything that abstract.

It also indicates that Timbuktu is more religious than I pre-viously thought. Beneath the appearance of an easygoing atti-tude toward religion, Mali is sharply divided between a tolerant south, which includes Bamako and Ségou, and a stricter north, which includes Djenné, Timbuktu, and Gao.

When we come to the house of Gordon Laing, Khalil stops, looking very important.

"This British explorer was killed by his guides in the des-ert outside Timbuktu because he couldn't speak Arabic or Tamashek," he says in this weird guide voice.

"I don't speak Arabic or Tamashek," I say solemnly.

"It's that he didn't understand the language," Khalil says with irritation. "You imagine how people felt!"

"He was killed because he wasn't Muslim," I say.

"Yes, that too," he says.

"That's not a great reason to kill someone,"

"Well, times were different," he says airily.

It suddenly strikes me as terribly absurd, the quest for some-thing—a place, a job, the thrill of climbing to the top of Mount Kilimanjaro. The hunt for glory rarely leads to good, or anything at all. I almost hear Mary Kingsley's great sigh of disappointment as she reached the peak of a foggy and freezing cold Mount Cameroon. *Is that it? My goodness.*

Timbuktu, by virtue of its remoteness, held not only mys-tery for me, but also a kind of masculinity to it. Real men try to get to Timbuktu, and I have always, in my own way, yearned to be a real man. I resented the ease with which men traveled to the corners of the world, the way they assumed freedom. Men *took* from the world without guilt, as though it owed them something.

I envied that assumption and I wanted my life to have an immediacy and physicality to it. After several months of traveling in Africa, it most certainly does. Perhaps, at the moment, too much so. Yet so little that I love about traveling through Africa has, up to this moment, standing outside Gordon Laing's house in 120-degree heat, had anything to do with masculinity. I have never really hit on glory. Probably wouldn't even know it if I had.

The victories are smaller and incremental. If I wanted to become a stronger actor in my own life, I suppose I have succeeded, but not through acts of bravery so much as modesty. I have learned to walk along the side of the road with the other women, to pass as discreetly as possible, and to listen to the shopkeeper when he talks about his marriage woes. I have learned to follow the flow of people and to trust people I don't know at all. I have trained my brain away from my own concerns and memories to the stories that I see and hear around me. It is the annihilation of ego, but it is also freedom from the small alleys of my own mind. I am almost entirely outward looking. Strangely enough, in expecting and hoping to not be noticed I feel more relevant in the world and more visible.

René Caillié—poor orphaned child from Bordeaux, spirited traveler, talented Arabist, dogged artist—certainly sought glory. But he wasn't after it in a big-man kind of way. He wanted to see the most remote place in the world, collect his prize, and go home. And after two weeks in Timbuktu he reckoned that he had seen and understood enough to get out. He had his glory, now he wanted the pleasures to be had from returning home.

35

Dogon Country

THE SANDSTORM I WAKE UP TO on the fourth day isn't a storm in the conventional sense, but more like a deep yellow haze that almost entirely blots out the sunlight. The desert around Timbuktu is mostly scrub, acacia trees, and small rolling rocks that catch under your feet. It seems unlikely that this piddling hamada could block out the blue Saharan sky. Then again, this desert is unimaginably vast. For a thousand miles north of Timbuktu there is nothing but sand. In the summer, hikers in the Swiss Alps see in the glaciers red streaks of Saharan sand that has blown across the Mediterranean.

The change in weather makes my stay in Timbuktu immediately, palpably miserable. In the morning when I blow my nose, the snot comes out black and brittle. My ears are coated with grime and my salivary glands seemed leached of moisture. Even Fanta with ice chips begins to lose its appeal. The heat, which previously beat down from on high and could be deflected with a wide-brimmed hat, now gets caught in the dust and creeps into everything. My calloused heels crack and bleed. My lips become bloated and tender.

I consider my maps of Mali and search out Gao. It's three

hundred miles farther east and just a bit south of the northern-most bend in the Niger River. To Malians, Gao is Timbuktu, the absolute end of the earth and a slightly ridiculous place to visit. In Bamako, I had met a Lebanese businessman born and bred in Mali who didn't even think it was part of the same country.

Plus this morning I hear that Tuareg rebels have raided an army post in the desert near Kidal, just north of Gao. They made off with a stash of weapons and killed two border guards. Though I love the remoteness of Timbuktu and its vague air of lawlessness, I find the encroaching war unsettling.

But if I was searching for a reason to leave Timbuktu, for the strength and motivation to make the hard trip back to the road that runs through the center of Mali, this is it.

I hop the morning bus to the big road, a trip that takes four hours, crosses five army checkpoints, and leaves little doubt in my mind that the Malian army would lose a war against the Tuareg. By the time I reach the paved road that runs the spine of Mali, I'm hungry, disoriented, and coated in a film of dust that has even turned my eyelashes white.

It's still four more hours to Gao, and though it's approaching midday I find a car and a driver, a wormy little fellow with a ripped T-shirt and three silver teeth, named—wait for it—Mohammed. His smile is lopsided and wet, as though he's lost muscle control in his face, and his fingers are thick and covered in grease. He owns a garage down the road and will drive me the six hours to Gao in his green Nissan.

"We can't leave now," he says in alarm. "It's far too hot."

"We have to," I say grimly. "If this road is going to get hit by bandits or Tuareg, we don't want to drive it while it's dark."

We drive east into the Sahara, leaving behind the Niger River and its wandering cows. In the haze, Tuareg in black robes and turbans walk among their camels and scrawny goats. This terrain is far drier and more menacing and the dust seems to be getting thicker as well. Even by Saharan standards, the terrain outside Gao is uncommonly harsh. To the north lie the Adrar des Iforas Mountains, which are teeming with Tuareg raiders. Beyond the mountains is the Tanezrouft—four hundred miles of limestone and iron ore flats without water sources, vegeta tion, or any permanent residents. In the winter, midday temperatures in the Tanezrouft rise to the eighties and nineties and plunge to freezing at night. Traders walk roughly thirty-three miles a day to make the crossing in twelve days, which is all the time a camel can live without water. It's like walking from New Canaan, Connecticut, to Richmond, Virginia, in a week and a half, carrying with you every single thing you will consume.

Mohammed, locally called Hamdi, drives at exactly forty miles per hour. Every once in a while he strokes the dashboard with exaggerated concern to see if the engine is overheating. I roll my eyes in the back seat until we pass a broken-down car on the road. Hamdi stops. It's his cousin. They speak briefly as men do, with little eye contact and hands set on hips, and Hamdi comes back.

"What's the story?" I ask.

"*Le moteur a fondu.* The motor melted. There is nothing we can do." He glares at me in the rearview mirror. "We really shouldn't be driving this time of day. I hope our engine doesn't melt either."

The dust in the air thickens again and visibility falls to almost zero. We pass through sheets of sand like sheets of rain, each hotter than the next. The road starts to disintegrate and I'm reminded that the government abandoned this part of its country for nearly ten years during the Tuareg rebellion. Some of the potholes are so deep we have to slow to a crawl to get over them. Hamdi grips the wheel and mutters under his breath the entire time. I hope he's cursing the road and not me.

Suddenly he stops the car and points out his side window.

"Dogon."

I strain my neck to see the top of two black flattopped mountains staring down at us through the yellow haze. Five hundred years ago, when the Muslims began pushing south, the Dogon escaped into these mountains, building their houses and villages into the sides of escarpments and growing crops in the valleys below. Now Dogon artifacts, particularly statues of their god Amma and carved stone doors that depict their creation myth, are among the most sought-after African artifacts in Paris. During Christmas the area is supposedly swarming with tour buses of French retirees foisting kola nuts on the Dogon elders so they'll invite them into their homes and temples.

Hamdi and I stand around the car and take in the mountains for a moment. I see why Muslim armies thought twice before pursuing the Dogon here. This country is harsh. The mountains look like stern black-robed judges prepared to sacrifice my rights for those of the state.

But then, a miracle happens. A cool breeze blows down from the top of the mountains, clearing sand from the air and ushering in a baby blue sky. The massifs glow pink and yellow in the setting sun, and no longer seem menacing at all. Giddy, we take huge gulps of air, spinning just a little to detach our sweaty clothes from our skin. Hamdi turns on the car radio and opens the hood to let out the heat. It's probably still over a hundred degrees, but it feels as brisk as Christmas morning in the Alps.

When the heat lifts, people get hungry, and so we stop at a small hotel near the base of a mountain. The owner has nothing in the pantry but pasta, oil, onions, and dried tomatoes, which he cooks up into a thick stew. Hamdi orders two forty-ounce beers and fields phone calls from a girlfriend in Gao and one in Niafunké. He wants to marry, but to do so he will have to build his own house, which will cost about four thousand euros. This is an incredible sum in a country where the average Malian makes three hundred euros a year, but he insists that no woman would want to live with him either with his family or in any lesser house. The problem of housing is part of the reason so many Africans aren't marrying, he adds, and why they are becoming more and more frustrated with the government. Still, he is optimistic that he can raise that amount of money. I ask him how he plans to do it, and he says that business is looking up since he got a job fixing two Land Cruisers owned by Dutch aid workers. Twice they have driven out alone into the desert and broken their Toyota's axle, and it seems unlikely they'll learn caution anytime soon. Life is good. He shows me his new cell phone that has the ring tone of the telephones on the television show *24*.

Dou dou doou dou. Je suis Jacques Baww-ere.

He's never actually seen *24* but has heard it is a show about a French commando who kills terrorists in American cities. With a big smile he pretends to shoot down enemy combatants with a machine gun. I tell him that Jack Bauer is actually American and more of an intelligence expert than a Rambo figure. He just looks at me and smiles. Crazy white girl.

Hamdi pounds beers while I doze in the corner. When we finally leave it's late, and we don't reach the outskirts of Gao until nine p.m. I'm exhausted, dehydrated, and oniony. Hamdi stops at a customs checkpoint just outside Gao so I can use the bathroom. In the parking lot huge transport trucks idle, covered in waterproof tarps to hide their contents. Truckers from Mauritania, Libya, and Algeria stand around a grass hut chatting in French and holding their import/export papers. A customs officer holds court inside a hut, next to which sits a new black Mercedes lovingly swaddled in palm fronds.

"Mon frère, mon frère," a Mauritanian begs. *"Deux mille c'est trop cher, trop cher. Je traverse ici deux fois par mois.* At this rate I'm really going to be bankrupt."

The customs officer catches sight of me and motions me over to the hut. He's tall with a small paunch to his belly and bloodshot eyes. I pretend not to see him and walk back to the car. Hamdi has disappeared behind a French colonial building that says DOUANE on it in faded red letters.

The customs officer comes right up behind me.

"*Toi, toi. J'ai dit viens ici.* I said come here."

The truck drivers stop their chatting and turn.

"I was calling you. You ignore me? What are you doing here? What is your name?"

His breath falls heavy on my face and I step back in revulsion. He steps forward quickly and swings his hand back. His fingers are oddly bloated and crusted in broken capillaries. For a second I wonder if he's going to hit me. He turns to the Mauritanian.

"Enough, I've had enough. Get out!"

He turns back to me.

"I asked you what you were doing here. I told you to come inside."

He speaks slowly, methodically. "Come inside now."

The hut isn't exactly enclosed, but it's snug. Not safe.

"So why did you ignore me? Why did you think you could ignore me?"

I say slowly with an exaggerated American accent: "*Je ne . . . peut . . . pas parler Français.*"

It was all I could think of, my only possible out. I didn't understand you—not my fault, not yours. Hamdi comes into the hut and takes a chair. The customs official doesn't even acknowledge him when he explains we are going to Gao. He looks straight at me the whole time.

"I think you understand French a lot better than you say," he says.

There is something damaged about this man. When customs officials want bribes, they usually just ask for it, but he seems more interested in playing with me than extorting me.

And he seems sick. As he paces in front of me, I notice his legs are stiff and his feet hit the ground at odd angles. His hands are bloated and the skin around his face falls over his neck in cascading wrinkles. He's too thin for a customs official who sits around all day extracting bribes and drinking sugary tea. When he walks, he rubs his stomach and his eyes as though he's trying to clean them.

"Are you okay? Are you sick?" I ask in English.

He stops his pacing and takes a seat in one of the rattan chairs. Hamdi looks on neutrally. The officer leans his head against the back of the chair and whispers, "Diabetes."

I nod.

"You probably know more than any doctor in Mali about diabetes," he says. "How do I cure it?"

I make a motion as though receiving an insulin shot and he shakes his head. Either he doesn't want to take insulin or doesn't need it or can't afford it.

"I got diabetes five years ago," he says. "I have lost forty kilo. I don't eat sugar. But I feel sick all the time. I need medicine."

He looks at me with the eyes of a small boy, pleading for help. "Do you have medicine?"

If this is a shakedown, it's the most effective one imaginable. Playing on the sympathy and undirected maternal instincts of a thirty-four-year-old woman is just as good as robbing her at gunpoint. Better.

The problem is that I don't have much in the way of medicine, much less a cure for diabetes. Before I left for Africa, my father sent me every conceivable bug-killing, tropical-disease-preventing drug known to man but marked the package MEDI-CINE, prompting French customs to send it back with a stern warning not to import unprescribed drugs again. Thus I only have Band-Aids, Imodium, Pepto-Bismol, and some hand sanitizer that I found in Senegal. As I dig around the bottom of my bag I find some Visine I bought Florent in Corsica.

"I have eye drops for your eyes," I say cheerfully. "And something to make your tummy feel better."

Strictly speaking I don't know that his tummy hurts, but almost everybody feels that his or her stomach could perform better. He takes three packets of Pepto-Bismol and splashes half the eye drops in his eyes before I can stop him. When he sees more Pepto-Bismol in my bag he holds out his hand imperiously, but I tell him it's for me in case I get sick. He scowls and keeps his hand out. I hand over the remaining Pepto-Bismol.

We discuss medical issues for a while and I gradually begin speaking French. Living in Mali as a diabetic is an impossible situation. The diet consists almost entirely of white bread and white rice, with side sauces of oily meat and vegetables. Although I often skip meals and eat ridiculous numbers of mangoes, I have gained about five pounds in the last ten days because, since leaving Ségou, I have only eaten white bread or rice at every meal. Salad, fruit, even chicken is hard to come by. Here the elite can be as malnourished as the poor.

The border guard has given up sugar, but he needs to give up refined carbohydrates, which convert to glucose in his blood almost as quickly as pure sugar. If he was living in America, he would eat plenty of fresh vegetables and meat, with whole grains on the side. I tell him that there is brown rice produced in southern Senegal that is much better for him than the rice imported from Thailand and he looks at me doubtfully. "How about pasta?" he asks.

When we leave he hands me a smart-looking business card and hugs Hamdi. Safely away, I slouch in the back seat and realize how tense the whole thing made me.

"Why did you hug him?" I ask Hamdi, looking for a fight.

"He's my brother."

"This damn cousinage. The whole world is related."

"No, really. We have the same mother. He is really my brother. We grew up in the same house."

I think about my next sentence carefully because I'm close to Gao but Hamdi still holds my life in his hands.

"I thought he was scary."

"He was," Hamdi says simply. "Very scary."

36

Madness and Cocoa Butter

AT A CERTAIN POINT, traveling loses all of its appeal and the traveler who dreamed of discovery and escape becomes a little demented. The purpose is to keep moving rather than enjoy or even absorb the sights around you. *Press on. You must press on.* The intensity and the anxiety is like that of a runner who wakes up at three a.m. to run up and down the football stadium in the rain. She knows it will hurt her. She knows it won't help the race, but she just can't stop.

That's how I end up in Gao.

I just keep going and all of a sudden I am at the edge of Mali, deep in the desert, trapped by the appalling weather. Here it is so hot I can't sit outside the hotel at night to have dinner without my whole body becoming drenched in sweat. I can't sleep or read or write. I feel sick, and normal street smells make me nauseated—sheep fur, fish chips on rice, fried onions are all unbearable. In the afternoons, I lie under the lazy, useless fan and stare at the ceiling. The air conditioning in my hotel doesn't even work anymore; the walls are too hot.

In the morning I walk down to the Niger. It is a long walk,

maybe five miles, and I feel faint by the time I get there. After its dry, tortuous journey through the desert, the Niger here is little more than a slow trickle through a wide, cracked bed of earth. There I meet a Frenchman in red shorts who tells me he is biking from Marrakesh to Cape Town. The back wheel of his bike is held on with duct tape. He walks with me to the old post office, a gargantuan art deco building built by the French, and inside there is a family and a cow living in the ruins. They give me water to drink out of a white plastic can.

All day I stay inside my concrete hotel room, watching French movies from the seventies. The temperature falls so slowly, barely a degree an hour, but by eleven p.m. I can walk around. Everyone comes out at night. It is always hard to see at night because the sandstorm hovers on the edge of town and blots out the moon, and sometimes I get lost. But then out of the darkness, a light will appear around a corner. A man sitting in front of a small store that sells crackers and anchovies and salt, sometimes soap or sugar, points me in the right direction. Then the wind blows out his candlelight and we are again bathed in darkness while he feels for the matches.

I am alone. But I don't feel lonely. That feeling has long since passed. I don't have an ache anymore in my soul. I just feel alone, probably because I am, and because Gao is so far away from everything I know. Even if I decide right now to go home, it would take me days to get back to Bamako. Weeks ago that would have terrified me. Now I feel perhaps a little dazed, but not scared.

I remember being in Dakhla in Western Sahara and feeling like this, but so much more vulnerable. I remember thinking I should go home to France, where life is sad and gray but solid and predictable. That I should go home to my very good husband and our quiet, ordered house; I should start up as a reporter again; I should have babies. The notion frightened me so much that I kept on traveling even though it made no sense and wasn't safe. I was young then, just three months ago. I am older now and these thoughts don't frighten me.

I'm aware of how far gone I am. I live in dirty clothes that I have all but stopped trying to wash. When I bathe at all it is under a tap of either stale hot water or sludge that smells often of sulfur. I have eaten so many mangoes I always have light diarrhea, which means I am always a little dehydrated. My face is bloated and pale despite the sun I am often exposed to. I rarely wear shoes. And I have pretty much stopped trying to talk to the people around me. My mission is to keep moving, keep ahead of the rains and cross the border into Niger before they come. Now at rest stops or on buses or long walks I conserve my energy and keep to myself.

Then one night in Gao, something breaks inside of me. I try for the first time in three weeks to get a comb through my hair. I have long since stopped washing it or even rinsing it and simply tie it back in a bun at the base of my scalp, even sleeping in it like that. When I release it from the rubber band, it doesn't move at all. I don't have any shampoo, and I think dry soap might just make it fall out so I take a dollop of cocoa butter and run it through my hair. Combined with the sand and oil and car fumes and cigarette smoke, the cocoa butter creates a kind of helmet around my face. I try again to get a comb through my hair but it just gets stuck and stands at an angle, like a hatchet buried in my head.

I peer at myself in the mirror in Gao. The bare light bulb swings in a vague breeze and casts dark shadows under my eyes. I think: Well, it wasn't enough that you were an outsider, white and a woman and alone, you now have done something so weird to your hair that old men will stop and stare, little kids will laugh, and women will shake their heads in wonder. It reminds me of what George Orwell wrote in *Down and Out in Paris and London:*

It is a feeling of relief, almost of pleasure, at knowing yourself at last genuinely down and out. You have talked so often of going to the dogs—and well, here are the dogs, and
you have reached them, and you can stand it. It takes off a
lot of anxiety.

I look like hell. I feel like hell. I am in hell. I have tested
myself and managed, in the past couple of months, to free myself of normal constraints. On the plus side, I have lost all physical vanity, and most concern for self. I am walking through the
world as someone who isn't much afraid of anything anymore,
not making a home in Paris or the claustrophobia of marriage
or certainly working long mornings at the newswire. My world
has been pared down to the smallest concerns—decent water, a safe place to sleep, the occasional kind word from a passerby—and I am free in a way I have never been before.

But now I have reached the limits of what I can do without descending into madness. Any further and I will get lost
or get hurt. I will become tormented by the knowledge that
I am losing the things I love and no longer belong anywhere.
For a moment and for the first time since I sat by the ocean in
Dakhla, I let my head drop and I cry. But even the tears are
sparse and painful, as though my body resents the loss of fluids.
Everything in me has been broken down, and now it is time to
rebuild. It seems an impossible, terrifying task, and I think for a
moment of staying in Gao, maybe forever. But then, as though
the gods are responding, I hear the distant roar of thunder. It is
a low, deep sound, filled with promise and relief and change. I
open the door to my room and a cool wind cracks through the
courtyard, stirring up dead leaves. Lightning pierces the purple
sky, and beyond the walls of my hotel, radios and televisions
are turned off as people stop to listen to the weather. The rains
are coming. Finally. And it is time to go home.

Part V

PARIS

37

The Quiet

I SPEND AN HOUR in the bathroom of my apartment assessing the damage. Months in Africa have thinned my cheeks and exposure to the sun has bleached my eyebrows white. I have a liver spot above my right eye and deep wrinkles around my mouth. I look different. Older perhaps. Stronger around the jaw. In any case, there is no semblance of the round-faced Connecticut girl who came to Paris to be with the man she loved. I wash my hair over and over again in the sink to get the dirt and diesel out.

"Why are you washing your hair in the sink?" asks the cleaning lady. "Is the shower broken?"

"No, but this way we won't waste water."

She looks outside at the pelting June rain and raises her eyebrows.

"Waste water?"

My hair is ruined, but I don't cut it. It spreads out like a fog around my head, falling in broken waves around my shoulders. It is startlingly, uncharacteristically blond, and the vegetable sellers on my street don't recognize me. I try to strike up conversation with them, as I had done in the past, but they are truculent and too busy to talk. Some are even rude, looking at me blankly when I ask about the asparagus. *It is fresh,* they huff, *otherwise why would it be here?*

They are not African, though many are from Algeria. They have become brusque and put-upon in Paris, Parisians themselves, and they make me miss the easy conviviality of the African market. Still, there is much on offer here, and I buy things that I had been denied in Mali—pears, lamb, brown bread, and cheese. Gluttony takes over and when I get the food home I eat it all, sitting on the floor of my lemon-smelling apartment. The food feels leaden in my stomach, though, and I wonder, despite myself, when mangoes come back into season.

Florent watches me eat on the floor and keeps his distance. There has been no exuberant reunion, no expressions of remorse or declarations of love. He looks at me intently though, waiting for something. In the meantime he keeps to his routine. He is up again at five forty-five, in the office at seven. He is home at eight, spent but affectionate. He is drinking his gin and tonic and laying his head on my shoulder and we are talking about the things we like to talk about—the French elections, American politics, food.

On the surface everything is the same. Underneath everything has changed. We have been turned off for a few months, rebooted and cleared. The screen is clean. I can't even remember anymore why we fought before I left for Africa, although I realize with a touch of melancholy that perhaps we aren't close enough now to fight again like that. I have seen too much in Africa, gone on to live a different sort of life, while he has struggled alone in Paris.

Yet the distance between us is instructive because I see him again through fresh eyes. Here is a man of wisdom, clarity, and fidelity. Above all he is constant. He never misses a day of work, never gives in to sadness or depression, never neglects to open the car door for his wife or pour her wine. He never stops looking me in the eye and trying to assess my strength and happiness. He is in this marriage for the long haul, and so while he can be distant, even inscrutable, his fidelity means he has time on his side. We will find each other again. I must be patient too.

While Florent works during the week, I write about Africa. I close my eyes and think about Ségou — the wide and silent river, the birds diving for prey above its purple waters. I think about the soft little baby with amulets around his waist that I held in Bamako. I see the silver doors of Timbuktu and the moment the sand cleared above Dogon country to reveal black flattopped mountains. I have these images to hold on to for the rest of my life; they are the most precious things I own. When I am tired and bogged down in Paris, cursing again the coffee machine for its indolence, I can remember the beauty of West Africa and hopefulness will return to me.

When I open my eyes again, the apartment feels empty. After Africa, with its chattering market women and bleating goats, it is abnormally quiet. Soon the stillness seems melancholy and I remember again why I struggled so much with Paris when I first arrived. Even under the summer sunshine, everyone out in sundresses and drinking coffee in outdoor cafés, there is such restraint, such an adult attitude to the city, it's hard to relax. The formality permeates the apartment, creeping under the floorboards, infesting the walls.

"Don't you feel like it's just too quiet . . . this place?" I ask Florent one Saturday. He is sitting in his undershirt watching France versus Italy and looking for all the world like a man who enjoys a bit of quiet.

"This is how we like to live," he says smoothly.

"I know," I say. "It's just . . . soooo quiet."

"Do you want to have people over?" he asks. Socializing is always vaguely exhausting to him, but he'll do it, for me, with enough advance warning.

"No, it's not that," I say. "I feel restless. It feels wrong to live in so much space, just the two of us."

"I have *nothing* to say on that," he says, going back to watching his favorite striker stick it to the Italians.

"What do you mean?" I ask.

"I mean that if you think there should be more people in this apartment, then you need to make up your mind on that. Not me."

"Maybe I just miss Africa," I say.

"Maybe," he says, looking at me steadily. "Though it is possible you are confusing two different issues."

Some people never really adjust to being home again. Mary Kingsley, who blossomed in West Africa, wilted in London. As soon as she landed in Southampton, her health gave out and she spent both winter and summer racked by fever and mysterious coughs. And while she was fearless in Africa, in England she reverted to the Victorian spinster sister, keeping to her outmoded black skirts, spending her evenings fussing over her brother, Charles. Only after he was properly fed, bathed, and tucked into bed did she go up to her office, pull out her notes, and allow herself to write.

When not attending Charles she tried to keep herself busy. Often she was invited to lecture on West African fetish and fish. Her views made her famous for their radical nature. She denounced the missionaries and said that the West Africans had complex religious and commercial institutions that should, under the rubric of colonialism, be left intact. She caught the attention of Rudyard Kipling, who admired her enormously, saying that, "being human, she must have feared some things but one never arrived at what they were." Over time she also made the acquaintance of high-ranking ministers in the British government, becoming wealthy and, to the external eye, independent.

Slowly, however, her success began to slide and her unhappiness became more apparent. She refused to leave Charles, even when it became clear that he would never become the breadwinner and all their financial stability depended on her. Soon she was several years out of the African continent and running low on new material for books. It was at this time she began her first and last foray into love, falling for Mathew Lane. Thereafter she wrote to a friend in 1899 that she "felt lonely despite being in a crowd," and that "none of my own friends and relations up here care for what I am interested in. All the people I meet up here I have to talk about West Africa very carefully to, and very lightly and briefly. They don't understand."

She was claustrophobic and bored, alienated and confined to the drawing rooms and parlors of staid, gray London. Thus in 1900 when an opportunity to go to Africa presented itself, she leaped at it. The war between the British and Dutch in South Africa had reached a cruel and critical point, and nurses were needed. She signed up immediately. No one, not even her weak and needy brother, could blame her for serving her country.

War wasn't killing British soldiers so much as disease—cholera, typhoid, measles, and mumps. A few months after arriving in South Africa, she got typhoid. The doctors cut out some of her stomach to remove the bacteria embedded there—for there were no antibiotics at the time—but she couldn't be saved. Two days after the operation, she died in horrible, excruciating pain at the age of thirty-seven.

In the end she preferred to die ravaged by typhoid in a foreign land than prepare another cup of tea. This seemed extreme, even to me, and somehow disappointing. Kingsley never found a compromise between her independence and the requirements of domestic life. She never made a choice, either accepting her place in the home or flinging off her absurd duties, abandoning her brother, and returning to Gabon. Rather than make these choices she put herself in danger.

I inhaled the lemony smell of my apartment. So privileged. So ordered. The quiet. Always the quiet that wrapped itself around a woman like a cold jungle snake and slowly squeezed the air out of her lungs. The quiet that represented in its decorum the civility and rigidity of life in the West, the structure and banality of one day after the other. That did her in, I thought. The quiet.

No wonder she made such a strange and painful attempt for love with the dashing Mr. Lane, then went to South Africa to die. Having lost the adventure, the chaos, the demanding nature of Africa, she was left with nothing. Nothing except the stark truth that there wasn't enough love in her life, and without that love, no reason to keep alive.

I had Florent to love. Florent could keep me alive, but the quiet ran too deep with him. It was in his bones to the marrow, as it was in mine. Together we would become morose, rootless, peevish, selfish. We were inward-looking people, prone to melancholy, entirely too focused on work.

I lay down on the floor of the apartment and tried to think of one time in my life I had really, truly made a decision. Not been told to go to college or asked to commit to marriage. Not fell sideways into this job or that, or took a house because it was the last one on the market. The last time I really made a choice. All on my own. I suppose the first one was leaving my husband and going to Africa. Now for the second one.

The good thing about going to the dogs is that it takes off a lot of anxiety, said Orwell after working as a *plongeur* in France and ending up a tramp in England. Like me, Orwell had privilege and means. He didn't have to give up material things to wander in foreign lands. He chose to because he knew it would be instructive, and he knew he had a moral obligation to know, exactly, how people lived. It toughened him up, as it did me, and helped me believe there are things I could do that I couldn't do before. I had been to the dogs and now I was back. My eye for life was clear, curiously uncomplicated. Life as it stood unsettled me, even as I appreciated its comforts in a new way. Someone had to bring chaos and change to this house. Someone had to bring more love into the mix, more levity. Someone had to break the quiet. I guessed that it would be a child.

38

A French Doctor

IN AUGUST, TWO MONTHS after getting home from Africa, I become pregnant. In French they say *elle est tombée enceinte,* which means "she fell pregnant." It's a good phrase, for I feel as though I've fallen down a very dark, very black hole.

I planned this child. I wanted it. I lay on the floor of my apartment just a few weeks before and hated the quiet, lemony smell. I despaired at the sheer decadence of an apartment for two people and thought about Africa and how anything was possible if you had the guts to see it through. I thought about how strong I was, having gone to the dogs and back, and how nothing would ever really scare me again. I could make decisions now. I was a warrior, not a housewife.

Yet I lie in bed at night, grappling with nausea, and think about all the charmed lives I know that have been ruined by children. Beautiful women who aged ten years in six months, hopelessly in love couples who descended into incessant squabbling, good and honest men who turned out to be terrible fathers, profitable careers that went down the tubes because in the end no one thinks well on five hours of sleep.

Suddenly it seems a terrible mistake. The only thing I've

ever done that I can never undo and the bridge to a life that will be smaller and more constrained, just as I was figuring out a way to be married and not have it feel like a shackle.

A baby will make me feel crazy, I think. It doesn't help that Florent has no idea what he is getting into.

"We'll play baseball," he says.

"Who?"

"The baby and I."

"In about a decade."

"Nooo."

I fail to hide an irritated look.

"Oh yeah, it takes that long?" he asks.

"It takes them six months to sit up. I don't think they can throw until they are four."

Regardless, he is happy, and I am grateful for his optimism. Gradually I come around to his point of view and I too try to see the positive. Everything I need to live in this world exists in Africa, I think. There is a well of experiences there I can tap into and learn from that will fortify me. Others have the new testament, the Torah, and Qur'an. I have my travels in Africa, my own long life of searching out experience.

What will help me now: I think about the baby I held in Bamako and his young sleepy-eyed mother. She had her child with so little, not even a man. Clearly, if she could deal with having a child with so much less, then I could too. I could have eight children. *Calm yourself, Nina,* I say sometimes out loud, *there is no need to panic.*

Yet I do panic, over and over again. The anxiety is like a stab of pain that strikes out of nowhere in the middle of the day. I'm buying tomatoes from the grocer, talking to a friend on the phone, washing dishes, and the fear rises to the back of my skull, raising the hair on my head, stopping me in my tracks. Every time the fear strikes it takes me hours to recover, leaving me drained and sullen for the rest of the day.

The thing about being pregnant, however, is that your life gets routinized quite quickly and even if you want to sit in your apartment and lose your mind you can't. You are immediately set into a schedule of doctors and tests and diet, especially in France, where medical care is almost free and the state draws in all its citizens. If you have questions the state will appoint you someone to guide you along the thorny path. For me that someone was Dr. Georges Dulaurans.

The doctor-patient relationship in France is pretty similar to that in the United States circa 1952. Doctors are honored, feared, largely unquestioned, and liberal with their opinions. Patients do as they are told, and are no more likely to challenge the OB-GYN than they are to call into question the engineering specs of the Eiffel Tower.

Imposed on that model is the French obsession with beauty and the culture's comfort with sexuality. Paternalistic old white French doctors will ask you (often when you are sitting stark naked in front of them) if your marriage is happy and your sex life vibrant. They will suggest how many children you should have, where you should go on vacation, and whether you need to lose weight or just do sit-ups because your stomach is flabby.

The primary target of their inquiries is stress. Stress is the bogeyman of twenty-first-century France, what germs were in the 1950s or humors in the Middle Ages. French doctors are on a mission to eliminate stress, searching the crevasses around your eyes and the strength of your voice for evidence of strain or tension. The reasoning is that if you are healthy and not stressed you look good. If you look unattractive, you must be stressed. Thus your doctor will treat a bout of acne or puffy eyes with almost the same seriousness as a lump in the breast. Beauty is sober business in France, for a pretty girl is a happy girl, a happy girl is a healthy one, and a healthy girl isn't stressed.

My doctor, Dr. Dulaurans, embodies all these philosophies.

He is in his early sixties, gray and slightly balding, from the best schools with all the attendant lofty degrees. He occupies a huge apartment in the old and rich Sixteenth arrondissement, where he keeps an office in the style of Versailles—gold brocade curtains and busts of the Dauphin everywhere. He takes long lunches, never makes me wait, and his wife, who runs the office, does so in the company of a soberly obedient schnauzer. By French standards, his fees are exorbitant, so he is careful to spend half an hour chatting with his patients and taking detailed medical histories.

I had seen Dulaurans before for routine appointments but wait six weeks before seeing him about the pregnancy. To do so would make it real and I'm not ready for that. I'm not even ready when I finally go, but I bring Florent along, which makes me at least feel like it is an occasion. We sit in his office, holding hands. Supplicant. Sweating.

Dulaurans is pleased by what he finds. The embryo, just eight weeks old, is well placed and well sized. I am healthy and so far the pregnancy is going well. He pats my cheek and says to Florent, *"Vous avez gagné, monsieur. Vous avez gagné.* You have won, sir, you have won."

Then he shuffles papers on his big Louis XIV desk and comes to my chart. "So, I have here the tenth of August as the conception date. Does that make sense?"

He raises eyebrows in anticipation.

"Uh, we were in New York," I whisper.

Florent nods vigorously, "Yes, yes. That's right. I remember. Yes."

Satisfied that the correct father has been identified, Dulaurans turns to his files and starts writing down numbers. Suddenly his face becomes very stern.

"So. I see here, Madame, that you have gained eight pounds in your first month. Is this possible?" He shuffles some papers even more officiously and pulls out a chart.

"I've been feeling very sick and the only thing that makes me feel better is eating. Specifically cheese," I say.

He nods gravely and pulls out his fountain pen like it's a knife.

"Imagine if you gain three kilos a month. Imagine! A catastrophe," he nearly wails.

I am tall and have friends who have gained fifty pounds in the course of a pregnancy so I don't think three kilos is such a big deal, but I try to look stricken.

Dulaurans isn't finished. He pulls out a chart that appears to be some kind of French food pyramid and turns to Florent.

"Madame is to eat small portions, cooked vegetables, a little bit of meat. No bread at night, and no sugar except perhaps on Sundays. Since there seems to be a problem with cheese"—he gives me an arched-eyebrow look—"very little cheese. There is calcium in the vitamin tablets."

Florent nods. "No cheese," he repeats, as though committing the concept to memory. "No cheese."

"No drinking alcohol, except for a glass of champagne now and then. She should try not to smoke, but it can be stressful not to smoke so a cigarette or two now and then is permissible." He thinks a moment. "She should swim but not run."

"But I love to run . . ." I interject.

Florent squeezes my knee.

"No running!" Dulaurans barks.

"Can I travel?"

Florent audibly gasps, but Dulaurans places his fingers together in an arc under his chin and looks at me curiously as though I could be more interesting than he thought.

"Where?"

"Africa."

"Where in Africa?"

"Niger."

He nods slowly and smoothes his eyebrows.

"I was a doctor there once. The situation is explosive."

I wilt a little in my chair.

"You can go. Be safe. Avoid mosquitoes." Then he stands up from the desk, spreads out his hands, and shrugs his shoulders like the godfather.

"Madame, really, next month. Do us all a great service. No weight gain at all."

39

Panic

MY OLDEST FRIEND IS AN emergency medicine doctor at Kings County Hospital in New York. I'm sure if I call her and ask her what she thinks about my traveling to Africa four months pregnant I would get an earful, but I'm smart enough not to make that call. If Dulaurans says I can go to Africa, I can go to Africa. I have spent years putting up with the annoying things about French culture. Finally something is going my way. I'm not going to blow it.

Florent, who believes that Dulaurans's hourly fee and posh office alone give him nuclear scientist status, complies. He thinks traveling is a good idea, but he would like to contribute. This is not always helpful. For the first time, my cool-headed, hands-off, give-her-freedom-and-she'll-come-home husband seems to fret. One afternoon in October I am lying on the bed looking at books on Niger. He comes in with a look of furious determination on his face.

"You've been to Mali, to Timbuktu. . . ." He looks honestly flummoxed.

"Ah, but I haven't been to Zinder. Fascinating caravan town in eastern Niger . . ."

"You need a bigger bag," he says, holding up my beloved and rather worn black book bag that I took with me to Senegal, Mauritania, and Mali. "You can't travel around Niger with that little black suitcase, or whatever it is."

"It's fine," I say way too dismissively, thumbing through my book. "It has served me well, and honestly, I feel so huge and tired, the idea of carrying even more junk with me seems totally . . ."

"No, it is not!" he shouts. "Enough is enough!"

"Enough is enough?"

"Yes, you need a bigger bag. We're going shopping."

"We're going shopping?"

"Yes. To get a bag."

I've never been shopping with Florent, not for clothes or home furnishings or even groceries. I actually would love to go shopping with him; the idea of strolling through the Marais on a Sunday afternoon and looking in shops seems very romantic. I think Florent, as well as many French men, thinks that shopping is a low-down affair, akin to flossing your teeth or pumicing calluses. People should just turn up places looking lovely with clothes that have been selected from shops on their lunch hour. Then it can be said: *Is that new? It is so lovely. It brings out your eyes and skin and hair.* And the other will smile and say thank you and the two will wander off to dinner.

He wants to relax this French ideal of romantic beauty and go shopping, but it's not to the women's department at Bon Marché, but rather GoSport!, a French outdoor activity chain that makes RMI look like Saks. He enters the store looking like one of those mean French schoolmasters from 1970s movies who hunt errant boys.

"Here it is, here," he says gruffly, holding up a huge black backpack. "This should do."

It's called the twenty kilo bag and can apparently carry

around forty-five pounds of weight, which I understand is the standard carrying pack ordinance for a marine.

"What am I going to carry in that?"

"And you need this," he says, holding up a huge malaria net that I am supposed to hang from the ceiling. "And these!"

He scoops up protein bars and hiking boots and fleeces and bug sprays and oral rehydration salts. Everything I would need to hike the Andes. He even goes for a kerosene lamp and binoculars, but I stop him there.

"That stuff will just get me arrested. They'll think I'm a spy."

Thankfully he channels his anxiety into the requisitioning of a bag and doesn't articulate all the things that I'm sure he is thinking. I try to sate his fears by reiterating all the positive things about going to Africa.

In all the time traveling there, I've never caught a virus or cold or gotten sick from the food. Africans are meticulous about caring for their meat, knowing that while flies may look unappetizing they won't kill you, while unwashed hands very well might. West Africa is mellow, ordered, often barely populated. Also, I will be very careful this time, stay in nice hotels, and make sure there is food for me to eat. I will avoid the buses.

I tell him about the slowness of Africa, its hospitality and charm. In the West, pregnant women are supposed to discreetly slip out of meetings to throw up in the bathroom, refrain from napping at their desks, and work until their contractions are four minutes apart. In West Africa, women nap under gao trees in the afternoon, walk barefoot in the sand when their feet swell, and sit down pretty much anywhere they want. Once pregnant, they spend most of their time with their children and other women, oblivious to their husbands.

My vision of Africa has become so much more refined. It

is less romantic and sweeping and more detailed and substantial. When I travel now I am concerned with the grittiness of life—the body, the wallet, the future—but also the community of women, the play of children, the health and well-being of my fellow travelers. My concerns are concrete. And while I originally went to Africa in search of a better life, one in which travel was incorporated into the everyday workings of my marriage, I return there as a kind of resident. Africa is in my blood and I love it too much to give it up because I am pregnant.

With these thoughts the panic finally subsides. My life isn't over, for here I am living it, even with the baby in my belly. I can still go to Africa. I can still be alone and on the road. Nothing has really changed, except my waistline.

Part VI

NIGER

40

Niamey

THE NIGER RIVER HAS grown wide and confident under the summer rains. A man in a pirogue slowly paddles against the current, and another stands by the bank with three white long-horned cows. They nose at tufts of the grass, eating slowly, indolently. Herons and African sandpipers fish the shallow brown waters, rising with small squirming fish in their mouth. In the distance, a marching band starts to play, at first raggedly, then better, reminding me of a small-town Memorial Day parade.

It is the cool season in Niamey but it's already in the high eighties and humid. I feel self-conscious about my size, the way my breasts stretch my bra, the looseness of my thighs. All my body parts seem to hang, jiggle, and slightly ache. My jeans feel sticky and hot, obscene in the way they hug my legs and stomach.

The waiter comes, bringing eggs, toast, sliced tomatoes, and coffee. He hums as he works, setting down napkins and knives and forks in precise and practiced motions. When he is finished the table is set with a clean and threadbare white tablecloth, and a napkin perches jauntily on my plate. A range of silverware is laid out as though I were having a three-course meal. He asks, "Madame. Shall I pour the coffee?"

There was a time my American sense of equality would have rushed forward and I would have waved him away with a friendly smile. *No, no, no, of course I can pour my own coffee. No need.*

Now I am slower to impose my own culture on others. He has a job to do and I should let him do it.

"Please."

He pours the coffee. I drink a little and it is too strong for me.

"Do you have milk?"

He comes forward with milk and pours it into my cup. Then stands a bit behind me while I eat. When I am finished he counts the silverware slowly, meticulously, and puts the milk on the tray. He walks away and before he gets into the kitchen drinks the milk in one fluid motion.

The waiter returns. This time I look more closely at him. He has black eyes set deep into his head and a face that is thin and sharp with bones but otherwise seems to be in good health. I resist the urge to dig into my jacket and give him the crackers I carried with me on the plane.

"Is there anything I can do for you?"

"I will need to go into town," I say. "So I suppose if you have a driver you like, a friend of yours, that would be helpful."

He smiles. Delighted. Soon his friend Mustapha has arrived and a modest amount of money has been passed all around. As usual I am the only person in the hotel, which is huge and concrete, Soviet in character.

"No other customers?" I ask.

"No," says the waiter. "There isn't a famine right now."

He says it simply and directly, as though talking about a UN delegation. I touch the baby in my belly. Even after traveling in Africa for months on end it is hard for me to understand that famine can be integrated into the social fabric of a country.

Niger is a huge country with a small population of fifteen million that is constantly living on the edge of disaster. It is landlocked, nudged at the bottom of the Sahara, and almost entirely dependent on herding animals. It is always very dry but occasionally the rains fail altogether, causing the shrubs in the desert to die. Then the sheep and cows that live off the shrubs expire, and when they go the nomads have nothing to eat, no milk to drink.

Yet drought does not necessarily mean famine is inevitable. In 2005 Niger had some failed rains but basically enough food to feed its people. Famine occurred because the merchants and military men who controlled the grains found they could get a better price outside the country's borders and so were selling it on the market. When some NGOs protested, they pointed out that as owners of the grain they were free to sell it to whom they wished.

Perhaps exacerbating the shortages is the government's attempts to isolate the Tuareg, who like their brethren in Mali want both more autonomy and access to the government trough. They are angry for not being integrated into the Nigerien armed forces, claiming that they are discriminated against by the central government.

Yet the war here is more menacing than in Mali because Tuareg independence hinges on a great prize—yellowcake uranium deposits in northern Niger. The ruling class will go to great lengths to protect this uranium and their contract with France's nuclear producer Areva, even hiring US mercenaries to protect the mines. Their desire to retain control over the one and only export good (and the concentration of power around that commodity) is perhaps why Niger is less democratic than Mali, Senegal, and even Mauritania. It is why the president,

Mamadou Tandja, who was reelected in 2004, is also showing autocratic tendencies, limiting the press and allowing his supporters to harass opposition candidates.

Thus Niger is both poorer and more militarized than any of the countries in West Africa I have visited. According to the United Nations, as of 2011 Niger is 186 on the health and humanitarian index of 187 countries. As I tour around town with Mustapha, buying a phone card, stocking up on beans for my trip across the desert to Zinder, the militarization is evident.

On street corners, soldiers in black uniforms holding AK-47s stand around drinking palm wine out of old milk bottles and leering at schoolgirls. The small market in the center of town lacks vegetables, except for the odd pitted tomatoes and black yams. The market women, usually the lifeblood of a West African city, are thin and dour, selling great baskets of dried tomatoes and palm oil.

There is no modern banking system, no international banks or ATMs, so I must change euros at the market. Mustapha takes me to an old colonial building and we go into a small room in the back. It is closed and airless, with a low ceiling and plaster walls that seem to sweat humidity. Light filters in through a hole in the ceiling, and bits of dust dance in the shaft of the sun. On the earthen floor an enormously fat man lolls on a straw mat while around him stacks of bills from all over the world gather dust. There are euros and dollars, yen and Swiss francs, South African rand, Chilean pesos—hundreds of thousands, maybe millions of dollars worth of currency. As my eyes adjust I see in the corners thinner men with black masks squatting behind the bills. They are carrying AK-47s, staring silently at me. The fat man on the floor take my euros and adds them to the stack behind him. He offers a fair rate, and I thank him, then hurry out. Mustapha, who doesn't speak very much, raises his eyebrows at me and whispers, *Money changers.*

The poverty outside the money changer's house is jarring.

I wander the market alone and pause, fascinated, at a bucket of locusts. An old man walks up next to me, grabs a bug about the size of his finger, snaps off the wings, and pops it into his mouth. He hands me one, grinning, and an old woman slaps his wrist so the locust falls back into the bucket. "You don't eat them like that," she admonishes. "You cook them in palm oil and tomatoes. They are delicious."

Perhaps, but it's not a good sign when people eat bugs. There doesn't seem to be much else to eat, however, or even to buy for that matter. When our car comes to a halt at a light no one comes to sell us anything, not phone cards or break-fast cakes or plastic dolls from China. It is as though the city is frozen in the 1970s, with concrete high-rises and white pre-fab ranch houses. Niamey is so quiet it feels almost deserted, as though the city people have given up and gone back to the countryside to take their chances with the rains.

Plus the pace here is even slower than in Bamako or even Gao. Around noon Mustapha begins to complain that it is too hot and too late to be out. Against my wishes he drives me back to the hotel. "Now it is time to sleep," he says. "I will come back at five."

I lie in bed under a mosquito net, sweating. Even during the day there are mosquitoes here. When I arrived from Paris at three a.m. the air was thick with them. Fattened by the rains that passed through here in July, they drifted from light bulb to light bulb, dragging their tiny legs behind. There were so many that it seemed the night air was gray with them. I sprayed every exposed part of my skin with repellent, including the backs of my ears and the heels of my feet. Then I walked up and down my room, spritzing the air above my bed and the dark cor-ners. I jammed a towel under the door to the bathroom to keep those that lived in the toilet bowl out. I cranked up the air con-ditioning as high as it would go and turned on the corner fan, hoping the wind currents would scatter the survivors. Finally,

I unwrapped my twelve-meter mosquito net, lay down in bed, and draped it across my body, head to toe, like a great white shroud. I fell asleep feeling vaguely as though I were drowning.

Now I wake with a start, the faint taste of metal on my tongue, a souvenir of first trimester nausea. As always in the beginning, I don't know where I am, then the smell of West Africa—diesel, rotting leaves, cooking grease, cayenne pepper, sweet dried tomatoes, human sewage, and camphor—welcomes me back. I lie there in bed a while and breathe it in, feeling the slightest tug in my stomach as though butterflies had taken up residence there.

In minutes the flutter becomes an aching, furious hunger, and I look at the clock by my bed. It's five thirty. I step outside. The sun has begun to set and a thin, distant moon is rising in the opposite sky. It is pale and white, three-quarters whole and hard to see. Not a dramatic moon. Not even very visible, but there. A universal presence.

Mustapha has likely come and gone so I wander out of the hotel, heading for the long white bridge that crosses the river. The only bridge in Niamey. The night is promising soft beauties, fresh air off the river, clear and visible stars. Again in the distance I hear the sound of a marching band.

I always walk in Africa. Even at night. Niger is different, however, and now I am pregnant. My reflexes are slower. I am dreamy and tired. Just feet from the entrance to my hotel a man grabs me by the arm. He has sunken cheeks and bulging eyes, covered in cataracts. I try to pull away but his bony hand holds my wrist with surprising strength.

"What is your name?" he asks. "No," he says, thinking better of it. "What is your room?" Then his thinking becomes muddled. He is hungry and addle minded. "I have things to sell. I am so poor. Look, I have only this shit to eat."

He says *shit* in English and opens up a small plastic bag in his right hand, revealing a fish head so old and decayed it has turned to mush. It stinks and I pull back my head reflexively, thinking I might vomit.

"Niger is dangerous these days, you need me."

I nod my head vigorously.

"Meet me tomorrow morning in the hotel. Come at nine. Bring your things and we will talk," I say.

He nods, both convinced and confused. He wants something now, but he doesn't have anything to sell me, and he doesn't really want to be a thief.

Slowly he releases his grip on my arm, and I turn around to go back to the hotel. When I arrive the waiter who served my coffee is standing on the steps waiting for me.

"You mustn't go out alone," he says, holding out his arms, then slapping his forehead. "No, you mustn't." Then he slaps his head again in a way that is startling, a little disturbing.

"I see that now," I say.

"We will keep him away," he responds fiercely.

"He's starving."

He shrugs. "Many people are starving."

I understand why aid workers and journalists are careful to draw boundaries around themselves. Why they don't give away all the money in their pockets to the first people they meet. They are no use to anyone when they are depleted, financially or morally. I'm not an aid worker though. I am a traveler, however, and my presence here is entirely at the generosity of the Nigeriens I meet. I have untold comforts at home and I don't need to survive here in the long run. Perhaps more important, want has reached a certain extreme in Niger. Even in my relatively comfortable hotel in the capital Niamey, the waiter drinks down the extra milk. I suspect nothing is wasted in the hotel kitchen. It's far worse here than in Mauritania or Mali.

"He could have robbed me of my things outside the hotel and decided not to, despite his hunger and need," I say to the waiter.

"This is no excuse," he says violently.

"I know, but let him through tomorrow. He has things I want to buy."

He comes the next day and I buy a leather case for holding pencils and some statues. I don't bargain with him but he doesn't ask a high price. I hand over the money and I suppose I expect some sort of gratitude, a moment of eye contact, an acknowledgment that I have done him a good turn. He is, however, so hungry, so desperate, he just takes the money and runs, down the drive and into the streets of Niamey.

41

Women of the Book

I GO DOWN TO THE market and order maternity boubous, and when I put one on I feel better about myself than I have in months. The elastic waists and flaring blouses allow air to circulate between my legs and across my belly. The tailor has sewn pleats at the bottom of the skirts, which add volume at the knees and make me feel a little like I'm wearing a crinoline. When I stop walking, I actually need to "fix my skirts," which is fun and girlish, and seems to give meaning to my girth. I never thought I would feel dainty in my second trimester, but I do. Before I go out, I pull the skirt up around my waist, until it is sitting right under my breasts, and pat my stomach affectionately. Baby's first boubou.

When I go to the hotel terrace for lunch, three African women, in glorious purple and gold boubous, are sitting in the shade eating omelets. I give a little twirl to show off the bottom drift of the skirt. The woman at the head of the table pulls her glasses down from the top of her head and whistles.

"Come here," she says.

I walk over to her, feeling shy and proud. She takes the bottom of my boubou between two manicured fingers.

"Not bad," she says, flipping up the bottom of my skirt and studying the lining and the white scalloping. "Did you get it done in town?"

"Yes."

"Who?"

"The cabdriver took me. I dunno. He was nice. Said I could wear it all the way through."

"Maybe," she says, surprised. "But at the end your stomach will show. Trust me. I gained so much weight I had to have a cesarian."

Then, after looking her two friends in the eye for consent, she motions to the empty chair at the bottom of the table. "Sit down, sister. You cannot carry the weight of two."

The woman identifies herself as Fatima, "but everyone calls me Mami." She is the hotel manager, plump like a Moorish woman, with blue eye shadow, blue eyeliner and mascara, and purple lipstick spread just beyond the edges of her lips. She wears gold hoop earrings and gold glasses, and sports a gold front tooth. Even in the hazy morning light, she glows like a small molten sun.

She peers at me through the top lenses of her trifocals, lifts a corner of egg to her mouth, and rests her other hand self-consciously on her stomach.

"Where were you born?" she asks.

I explain as best I can the history of my life, with a nod to African sensibilities. I miss my parents, who live in the States, and I am here in Africa because I want to see these ladies' beautiful country before my baby is born. They smile and nod, as though they are accustomed to meeting pregnant women who come to see Niger before settling down. Only Mami asks follow-up questions.

"What is your profession?" she asks formally.

"I'm still a reporter," I say. "As soon as the baby is born, I'll go back . . . I think. I don't know. I wish I could stay here in Africa."

She smiles a little on the edges of her mouth.

"Why don't you just come shopping with us."

Before I can think to say no we are all piling into her gold Mercedes. I sit wedged between Mami's sister, Adissa, and a cousin whose name I do not catch but who is fat, even by local standards, and a little smelly. Mami drives through the small back streets of Niamey at one hundred miles an hour, but I feel completely safe, protected as I am by several hundred pounds of female flesh. The women pass biscuits and crack jokes in French, English, Hausa, and Arabic.

"When I come to Paris in March I will bother you," Mami says merrily. "You will have to drive me around. You will be sooo round then. Not even your French husband will want you."

Then the woman next to me makes several alarming motions of a man pulling a woman toward him to have sex. The Mercedes dissolves into hysterical laughter, with Mami actually holding her nose in distaste. I blush and Adissa knocks her shoulder into me in solidarity. "I *know*," she whispers. "*Yuck!*"

We spend the afternoon going into supermarkets stocked floor to ceiling with knickknacks made in China and food imported from Dubai. Mami busies herself in the kitchen section, reviewing with Adissa each and every stainless steel knife and fork in the place, even cutting through cardboard to test a butter knife. I am sent to the children's clothing section to find something for the baby to wear. I haplessly comb through frilly pink dresses made of acrylic and satin, little boy jumpers that say NUMBER 1 BABY! and eventually find a big leather chair next to the television section where I settle in for a nap. When Mami is ready she yells "*Nina!*" at the top of her lungs, and we are off to the next store.

Like everything in Niger, these stores were built for a population and a prosperity that never came. There are turnstiles at the entrance and exit to control the flow of people, and one register has a barcode reader. But the shelves are almost bare and covered in dust. When we walk into Niamey's largest supermarket, the manager hurriedly turns on the sound system, playing a rap song that comes on with a violent screech. *You you you you you gonna get fucked.* I wander the aisles, finding things for my trip—baked beans, almonds, pineapple juice, and the French equivalent of Spam. Suddenly, way in the back next to a bin of sunflower seeds, I run into a man in khaki shorts holding a beautiful blond baby. His white skin glows under the neon lights. We exchange startled looks, and hurry off.

At the register Mami is talking to another woman and I plop my goods down in front of the checkout girl. She asks for exact change and I fumble with the currency, looking for ten centimes. Without pausing for breath, Mami comes over and digs through my purse, finds the money, drops it on the counter, and escorts me out.

I settle into the back seat of the Mercedes and Adissa pats my knee as she sits down. At last, I am comfortably ensconced in the company of African women.

Mami's warmth and familiarity is so intoxicating, so rare among African women, that I put off any kind of travel for a week. Mami takes to leaving the door to her office open for me, and in the mornings I go there for tea or a plate of fried eggs, lured as much by the food and company as her German freestanding air conditioner.

Cold air matters when you are pregnant. I generate so much heat just housing the baby that I am constantly pink and sweaty, wiping my brow and fanning the back of my neck to keep the perspiration at bay. Although it's the cool season in Niger, it's still ninety degrees by ten a.m. and one hundred by midafternoon. For three days running, the weatherman on

CNN has informed me that Niamey is the hottest place in the world right now, hotter even than Alice Springs, Australia, where it is the height of summer. In these conditions, the sad little window unit in my room, installed in the 1970s with the rest of the hotel, doesn't stand a chance.

Mami has an air conditioner in her office so powerful, however, it sends seismic shocks through the hotel when she turns it on. Her office is so cold it momentarily blinds you when you walk through the door and opens your tear ducts. Even in the afternoon, we all wear shawls in there, and the children are made to wear wool caps. Mami says she likes it that way, but I suspect she keeps her office so cold to intimidate people, the way a mobster might leave a revolver lying on his desk.

For me the freezing temperature is great, but I also like the office because the air conditioner has driven off the mosquitoes. Every morning, I wake up to the terror of their whine. Like a crazy person, I bat at my ear and lunge across the bed for the bug spray. Although I am hypervigilant, it's hard to keep that many mosquitoes at bay. They covet my swollen, sweaty, hormonal skin. Sometimes when I sleep, I can feel them dancing across my brow, looking for a patch of unsprayed skin upon which to land.

Once I get out of Niamey and away from the Niger River, the mosquito population should plummet. I know that I should at least begin to inquire about transport east to Zinder, a caravan town that hosts one of West Africa's great mosques. No longer can I just hop a bus and hope for the best. I need a driver and a car with air conditioning. For once I'm going to travel in style like the aid workers, but I need a reliable car and a good driver. I go to see Mami, who as usual is holding court in her office under a great purple shawl.

"Hi, Mami," I say. "Can I talk to you for a second?"

She looks up from a pile of carbon copy credit card receipts, the old-fashioned kind that require a handheld machine to imprint the card. Since the hotel has no guests at present, I suppose the receipts are from her other enterprises. She motions for me to sit down in the chair across from her, and her daughter, who has been plucking her eyebrows with the aid of a dusty compact, gets up from the chair and takes a seat on the floor with two other women. Every day she tends to her eyebrows like this and now there is hardly anything left, just two dark pencil lines against skin she has artificially whitened. But she is still good-looking, tall and thin, with carefully ironed hair and newly hennaed feet. I think she likes me too, and has told me several times that she is coming to Paris in March and we should go shopping.

"I need a car to Zinder," I say, unaccountably nervous. "Something reliable and cheap, with a guide. And I prefer air conditioning. In fact I need it."

She picks up the phone. It's so nice to be taken care of this way. "Why you want air conditioning?" she asks, the phone cradled to her ear as she begins to dial. "It's the dry season. Not hot yet."

"It's hot if you're pregnant," I say. "And I'm not used to the heat."

"Oh, you're pregnant!" Mami's daughter says, delighted. "I thought so but then I thought you just got a really unflattering boubou. You know. We thought that you went to a bad tailor." And with that everyone laughs, and one woman in the corner, whom I don't know at all, slaps the floor in mirth.

"Okay, sit down," Mami says. "I'm sure we can find someone."

I find a place on the carpet. Adissa leans over and touches my shoulder.

"You want some eggs? Have you eaten enough today?" She beams as she looks at me, leaving her hand on my shoulder. "You look tired."

She goes to get a pillow and puts it under my head. I find a comfortable spot on my side and look at her, feeling like a very small child. Adissa's much younger than Mami, slimmer and with slightly Arab features, a thin hooked nose, a hint of cheekbone under her eyes. Although they are sisters, I doubt they have the same mother.

"You lived in America, right?" I ask her.

"I did," she says, drawing her hennaed feet under her and considering the question. "I hated it."

"Why?"

"People were cold. I didn't know anybody in America. We don't like it when we don't know anybody. Mami and I have eighteen brothers and sisters. We are used to walking in the street and everyone saying hi."

"New York isn't like that."

"No, the whites aren't like that. They are too busy to say hello. Even here in Niamey. You are the first white person I have ever talked to in Niger."

"Ever?"

"Ever," she says definitively.

"I'm so sorry."

"Yes, it's bizarre. Maybe it's because you are an only child you have to talk to people you don't know." As she says this, she pulls out a wooden stand on which she places a leather-bound Qur'an. Crossing her legs before her, she opens it to a page marked by ribbon and begins to read. She tracks the words with the bottom of her finger and whispers to herself words of God.

She reads rhythmically in that steady cadence and with the musicality that makes a faithful rendering of the Qur'an one of the most beautiful sounds in the world. It is transporting and pure. While the book is often blamed for violence that emerges from the Middle East, to me it is a peacemaker, especially when it is sung by a woman of deep faith.

• • •

There were angry young men in the occupied Palestinian territories in 1997 when I lived there. Even in the lull of the Oslo
Accords, when people believed that a Palestinian state was
years, rather than decades, away, that anger permeated the
streets of Ramallah, making it an unpredictable place to live.
On some days the frustration was obvious and visible; young
men and women would gather near an Israeli settlement on the
outskirts of town and throw rocks at the Israeli soldiers until a
rubber bullet was shot or tear gas was used, causing the anger
to dissipate into fear and sadness or simple confusion. Usually,
however, the anger was less premeditated. It hovered around
the conversations and daily interactions of all Palestinians. Suddenly a chair would upend in a café and a young man, just moments before drinking cappuccino and talking about the poetry of Mahmoud Darwish, would be lunging across the table
at his friend. Or a car would be hurtling toward another on the
road, trying to drive him into a ditch in a random and inex-
plicable game of chicken. The ambient rage of the Palestinians
even affected the expats. One night I returned late from Jerusalem with a friend. We had had dinner, perhaps too much wine,
and he looked up with obvious hostility at the Israeli soldier
who checked our passport. "If you are looking for terrorists returning to Palestine," said my friend, "you are looking on the
wrong road." Then he snatched the passport from the soldier's
hands and drove the car through the checkpoint.

I remember ducking down into the seat so the bullets at
least wouldn't hit my head.

"Are you insane? Are you insane?"

He just muttered to himself, gunning the car and looking
up at the rearview mirror.

"Enough is enough."

These things happened all the time, and I adjusted to them.
I avoided returning late from Jerusalem. When Palestinians began to fight among themselves I joined the crowd of onlook-

ers shouting "Shame! Shame! Brothers shouldn't fight," because societal approbation was often the best way to get angry young men back into their corners. Over time it was stressful, however, and it felt like the Palestinians, people I cared for deeply and whose desire for dignity and independence was just, were spending too much time squabbling with each other.

There was only one time when peace was guaranteed and I could let down my guard a little. The morning was and is still a time of tranquility and unity in Ramallah. Getting to work was both beautiful and an adventure, and in large part this had to do with the Qur'an.

I think people who have never been to Israel and Palestine wonder sometimes why both sides are so insistent about creating a homeland there. It is a narrow strip of land, the size of New Jersey including the West Bank, made up of hard, windswept rock on one side and long sandy beaches on the other. There are fertile valleys around Nazareth and the Jordan River, but much of the country is rocky and barren, able to host only olive trees and goat herders. Tourists get off the plane and stand on the white hills of Judea and Samaria, also known as the West Bank, and think, *This is it? This is the Jewish homeland?*

It takes a week, maybe two, to infect you and then you are infected for life. You stand on those high hills and look out at a thunderstorm rolling in from the Mediterranean. The depthless blue sky becomes a steel gray, rain and hail lash down on you, and you struggle to hold your footing in the violent wind. Rivers arise out of nowhere and rush in the canyons below you, sweeping away everything in their path. Ten minutes later the storm is gone but the world is covered in a glistening dew. The olive and lemon trees glow under the sun and the red earth under your feet throws off the smell of rosemary. God is here, you think. His glory and grace just appeared with might and fire.

I loved the land. I loved the people. I loved the politics. I would get up early and sit in the back of my humid little house, drinking strong Turkish coffee, going through my notes for a day of reporting. Then I was taking the long walk up the hill to the center of town, past stone houses lovingly restored by Palestinian families, new pizza shops, street vendors selling ladies' shoes and snazzy leopard-print hijabs.

The taxi was more like a short bus with three long seats. I would get into the front seat with another woman, usually an old mother type who was round, red-faced, smelled of yeast, and wore a plain white hijab. The passengers on the rest of the taxi were young professionals, young men in black pants and white shirts who worked as administrators or translators for the NGOs in Jerusalem. Each would pass forward three shekels, which the woman next to me would collect, count, and deposit in a little tin next to the driver.

As soon as we started off, the driver would put a recording of the Qur'an in the tape player. A man in low and emphatic tones would begin singing the verses to the Surat Ad-Duhaa.

By the glorious morning light
And by the night when it is stillest,
Thy Lord hath not forsaken thee nor doth He hate thee,
And verily the latter portion will be better for thee than the former,
And verily thy Lord will give unto thee so that thou wilt be content.
Did He not find thee an orphan and protect (thee)?
Did He not find thee wandering and direct (thee)?

The chanter's voice would rise and fall with the import of the verses. Sometimes there was a hollowed-out echo sound that was meant to make things sound even more impressive but tended to recall very bad 1980s techno. Usually, however, the only sound was the clear, strong voice of a young man trained as a chanter.

The taxi would go quiet. Young men would close their eyes. Children would lie against their parent. Then very often the woman next to me, the round maternal woman, would pull out a Qur'an and begin to read, mouthing the words slowly and with the faintest sound. It would feel as though the entire cab was bending toward her, for she was the spiritual leader of us all. The mother who could stand up to an Israeli soldier and cry shame. Who could demand her daughters go to university. She knew better than any of us the holy Qur'an. We were united behind her and she brought peace.

Adissa sings the Qu'ran this way, in a low voice, stumbling a little over the words, stopping occasionally to look one up. She loves her religion in a way I don't think I will ever fully understand. To me it is a book—imperfect, human, confusing—but to her it is transportation to the foot of God. A kind of express elevator to divine joy.

Thus it is lovely to hear her sing the ancient text, to hear the passion in her voice and the surety of her belief. She finishes a long sura, pauses, and drinks some of her soda. Then she turns to me, still lying on the floor like a child, and pats my head thoughtfully. Her hands on my hair make me immediately sleepy.

"I study Arabic every Saturday and Sunday. I want to become perfect at it. I am feeling inspired today. I just returned from the hajj."

"How was it?"

"So relaxing," she says, sighing.

"You make it sound like a spa vacation."

She smiles. "Truly every year it is better than ever."

She returns to her book, drawing her feet under her, the very face of contentment.

I don't remember falling asleep. I never do in these months when the fatigue comes on like a brick to the head. When I wake up, my mouth is cracked dry and I don't know where I am. Mami's grandchild is dropping bits of cooked egg onto the floor in front of me and I guess that someone has ordered a roasted chicken because the whole room smells of it. I sit up, cradling my stomach, feeling vulnerable.

"Whoooo, she's awake," Mami says. "We thought we had to call the doctor."

The light in the room has changed. The shadows are longer and the wall is bathed in yellow. Outside the eucalyptus trees are caught in the afternoon heat that makes their trunks shimmy and swirl. The air conditioner is working furiously, rattling and heaving as though taking a huge hill. I look at my watch. It's four p.m. I've been asleep for four hours.

Adissa pushes a chicken toward me. Her Qur'an is gone and she has changed clothes. She appears to have washed her hair and braided it in a different style. She looks pretty and fresh. On the tip of her left-hand index finger there is still a smudge of ink from where she traced the lines of the book.

"Eat," she says gently. "You must keep up your strength for the baby. For God."

42

Fashion Show

I LIVE IN PARIS, the world center of fashion, and never has the air tingled with the prospect of the season's dresses the way it does in Niamey. Every year, the city hosts the International Festival of African Fashion. All the up-and-coming fashion designers from Cairo to Cape Town swarm the capital to show their ready-to-wear lines in the old soccer stadium. Designers are encouraged to use traditional fabrics as well as African plants and skins, and there is a prize of one hundred thousand CFA for the most beautiful model and the best designer. It is *the* event of the cool season: the president of Niger's wife always shows up, and the French press often covers the event.

"Nina, you are going to love this," Mami says from her desk on the day of the show. I'm lying on the floor, picking at a plate of eggs, snoozing a bit and chatting with Adissa. "All of Niamey will be there."

"Do we have to go?" Adissa asks, resting her head against the wall.

"Yes," Mami says. "You know we do."

"I'm not going," Mami's daughter, Nadia, says. "The children can't take it. It goes so late. We'll watch on TV."

"Well," Mami says, "Nina will come."

Mami's entourage seems excited by the prospect of the dresses but not by going to the event itself. They treat it as some tedious social registry event, necessary and prestigious but painful. Nonetheless, everyone spends considerable time preparing—beautiful boubous are pulled out of closets and even poor Adissa, slightly overwhelmed by the prospect of being away from her language studies, unearths an old Chanel handbag. It will never cease to amaze me the way designer goods make their way into the heart of the Sahara.

I consider buying new cloth for a boubou, but when I catch sight of myself in a full-length mirror, I lose hope. The girlish swing of my skirts has lulled me into a false sense of security, but the constant eating in Mami's office has done me in. In just ten days I must have put on seven pounds, maybe ten. I'm too disheartened to buy new fabric in this state. I probably couldn't even afford the four thousand yards of fabric it would certainly take to cover me.

So while everyone fusses with themselves, I act as the spinster sister with no chance for love at the ball. I loll on Mami's floor, praising their beauty and giving voice to their decadent, spendthrift selves: "Absolutely you should get that new gold bracelet! How can you even think of going without a new silk bra?"

We talk about the fashion show for days, and while we prepare, Mami tries to set me up with a young man named Nicolas.

"Why do I have to hang out with Nicolas?" I whine. I have just been sitting in the corner talking to Adissa about breastfeeding. As a woman without children, she is as horrified as I am by the prospect. "It has to hurt," she whispers. "How could it not?"

"You can't spend all your time here talking to old ladies," says Mami.

"Adissa isn't an old lady," I say, bristling a little.

"You are always wanting to talk about politics," says Mami. "Well, here is your chance. Nicolas will talk to you. He is a journalist too."

I am hot, pregnant, and sleepy but that's not why I want to stay in Mami's office. I sense that more than the soldiers on the street with their AK-47s, or the government bureaucrats, or even the large complex owned by the French nuclear power company Areva, power lies in Mami's office. A country is being run by women out of this hotel and hotels like it all over the city.

At first I almost made the mistake of dismissing Mami and her clan. I liked them but I saw them as trivial, prone to conspiracy theories, perhaps a little mean. They seemed to spend all their time making merciless fun of their husbands and rival female gangs. To my eye too much energy was expended on clothes, gold, and makeup.

Woven into their gossip, however, is a constant flow of information that is vital to the family's prosperity, perhaps even its survival. *Oh, did you hear so-and-so who owns the old sand hotel down the street didn't have enough forks for the Save the Children cocktail party? What a disaster! How hilarious!* Then, after suitable jokes and hilarity have been enjoyed, Mami would beckon her cousin over. *Who do we know at Save the Children? You think they can be brought over?* She was constantly working the angles, constantly trying to improve her family's financial position, because without new sources of income the vagaries of Niger's political climate—from coups to suddenly spiking food prices—could ruin even the most prosperous clan.

One day after I have come back from a walk in town, she calls me over.

"What did you see? Anything new?"

"I don't really know what is new," I answer flatly. Adissa raises her eyebrows at me. Not the right answer.

"Did anything *interest you?*" Mami asks with exasperation.

"I did see a Ferrari. I think it was a Ferrari. I'm not so good with cars . . . Maybe it was a Lamborghini."

"Red or yellow?" she asks swiftly.

"Yellowish," I say. "Why, whose is it?"

She then bends over her desk and says something to Adissa in rapid-fire Hausa. Adissa nods, goes out, and comes back with the driver. Mami hands him the keys and he disappears like a man on a mission.

"What is it?" I ask Adissa.

"Looks like someone in the president's entourage has a new car," she says with tremendous significance.

"And what does that mean?"

"Someone is getting richer," she says ominously.

I am reminded that when Mami's brother died she was chosen of eighteen brothers and sisters to run the hotel. Over the years she has expanded her holdings into various other properties throughout Niamey so that she sits on a closely held empire (its exact contours are unclear to me because she shushes when I ask—"you don't need to know business," she says). This success didn't arise out of sitting in her office alone. She works her network constantly. Blood relatives, especially women, are the pillars of her power. This includes not just her sisters, but also her daughter, Nadia, whom she sees every single day and calls countless times more. After the women there are half brothers and uncles, who are distant but are also the crutches on which Mami and her sisters maintain both their legitimacy and their empire. Beyond the family are women of rival gangs. These are both allies and rivals, tucked into hotels and restaurants throughout Niamey, whom Mami mostly sees at night.

Yet despite this keen interest in business and fearless intrusion into a realm that is considered male territory in Muslim Africa, Mami keeps an air of prim respectability about her. She never leaves the hotel without a clean and pressed boubou. Her alligator handbag is always perched on her arm, and though she drives like a madwoman through the back streets of Niamey she is constantly waiting for a man to open her car door so she can step out, like a lady. Whenever she speaks of her brothers or her father it is with a truly reverential air, almost like a little girl. "I am nothing without them," she tells me.

It reminds me very much of Mary Kingsley, who hated suffragists, said once that every step she took in Africa was due to the grace of a man, and wore black silk skirts and crinoline even as she waded through the black swamp of Gabon's rivers. "You have no right to go about in Africa in things you would be ashamed to be seen in at home," she wrote in what I imagined was a slightly shrill voice.

I suppose it's easy to judge such women, but preserving an air of femininity is a decent way for a woman to protect herself in a man's world. It charms and disarms men. It fends off attacks from other women who have stepped beyond their boundaries. No one is really going to go after a woman in a light blue dress with an alligator handbag. And for both Kingsley and Mami it is a good deal. In exchange for a little coquetry now and then, they get to do exactly what they want.

Hence the importance of the fashion show. It represents not just a business opportunity—Mami explains that the president's second wife will be there and she must say hello—but a chance for Mami to present herself as just another fun-and-fashion-loving woman. Just another one of the gang.

Thus the night of the show is a little rushed, a little frenzied, like a wedding. Mami changes boubous twice and Adissa digs up her own little crocodile handbag. Nadia makes good on her promise not to come along, which makes Mami tight-mouthed with maternal disappointment. She turns her ire on me.

"Tonight Nicolas will take you to the fashion show and you

will sit in the press section and write an article about it," Mami says as we prepare. "You will write about the great Nigerien designers."

"Oh no, Mami," I say before thinking, slight desperation in my voice, "I'd so much rather spend the evening with you and Adissa."

She looks at me, hard.

"Well, suit yourself. This following me around has to stop, though."

Mami is harsh, in her way, but so is my mother, and something about being pregnant makes you miss your mother, so I ignore it. Then it turns out that I have to go with Nicolas because Mami gave away my ticket to a cousin.

"Really? She gave my ticket away?" I ask Adissa, a little heartbroken.

She rubs my arm in sympathy.

"We need this cousin there."

So rather than walking in with Mami and Adissa as my chaperones and immediate entrée in Niamey society, I find myself standing in the alley next to a soccer stadium and talking to a young man named Nicolas, who, if indeed a journalist, isn't a very professional one.

"They are all pedophiles," he whispers. "They traffic our children. They trade them to whites. They are disgusting."

We are looking at the rolls of concertina wire stapled to plywood that are guarding this particular entrance to the stadium. Nicolas, who is about five feet five inches tall and wearing skintight black jeans, is looking at my general heft with uncertainty.

"Can you get through this?" he asks, poking at the wire with a stick.

"No. Can you?"

"Probably not," he admits. "Let's keep going."

We continue to circle the soccer stadium. Clumps of garbage and dried nettles grasp my ankles, cutting them a little.

Mosquitoes round my head. Under a bleacher I see a shadow move.

"I think that if we can't find an entrance soon, we should just buy a ticket from a scalper," I say nervously.

"Look at what they did in Chad," Nicolas continues, ignoring me. "They were behind that. Those kids were going to be turned over to the Lebanese, then to the French."

"What are you talking about?" I ask.

"The group, the Christian group," he says, waving around the stick.

"Zoe's Ark?" I ask him.

"Yes, that's it," he says, pointing the stick at me directly. "Those people."

Zoe's Ark, a French NGO run by a man with little experience in Africa, had tried several months earlier to airlift 103 wounded Sudanese orphans out of Chad. When Chadian soldiers stopped the aid group's convoy near the airport at four a.m., it turned out that the children were wearing bandages to cover nonexistent wounds and were not Sudanese at all. They were poor Chadians whose parents had been told they would be going to school in France on a temporary basis. Six aid workers were convicted for child trafficking and only released after the French government helped repulse a rebel attack on the central government of Chad.

He nods. "Yes, yes, that's it. The Lebanese were behind that. Probably the Tuareg too."

I'd heard people complain about the Lebanese in Africa before, but usually in hushed tones and with a touch of embarrassment. I'd never heard anyone call them pedophiles. "You know they control all the money," he continued. "With the French," he spat.

"That's crazy," I said. "They didn't want to sell the kids, just raise them in French homes. People were going to adopt them."

"Well, that doesn't help," Nicolas said. "A lot of people around here would rather they die than be brought up Christian."

That was true. People could put up with a lot from the West but not their children's souls losing the path to God. Yet I felt the need to defend aid workers' actions in Africa. Just that afternoon I had watched a French-language drama on television showing a middle-aged French couple driving around an African city in a huge SUV, asking officials if they could adopt a baby. A corrupt and fat African man agrees to help them for a large sum of money but has to steal the baby from a poor local woman. In the end, a tall and beautiful lady cop from Burkina Faso breaks up the ring, reunites the child and mother, and slaps the French people in jail. Aid workers could be annoying and useless, but they didn't usually buy and sell children.

"I don't think they had bad intentions," I repeat, stepping over the carcass of what appears to be a dead dog as we come to our third barred door. "They were just arrogant and wrong and lied."

"Well, they better not try it in Niger," Nicolas says. "Because we are prepared."

I want to drop the subject and so does Nicolas, so we continue on in silence. Eventually we come to a small set of stairs that someone forgot to block off and begin to climb. Soon we are inside the soccer stadium, blinded by klieg lights.

The soccer stadium in Niamey was built in the 1970s and, like everything else in the city, was made out of poured concrete. It has just enough size and decay to be menacing—spectators sit on long slabs of concrete under sharp lights that create Halloween shadows—but not enough to dent the air of festivity. I scan the seats for Mami and her gang. Around me hundreds of wealthy, plump, bespectacled and well-dressed African women arrange themselves on the seats. All are wearing bright and shiny boubous and carrying little alligator handbags in the crook of their arms. The clatter of their laughter, the hellos flung across the stadium, is deafening.

Finally I find Mami. She nods hello and Adissa gives me a quick hug. Nicolas goes to sit near the stage with the photographers. He waves good-bye and says, "I hope I have been helpful."

At nine p.m. the show starts. The lights go down and two Moroccan women sing ballads in French and Arabic—sloppy soaring songs that bring the audience to its feet in adulation. They are followed by two Senegalese rappers who bounce across the stage in blue track suits and swear a lot. Their singing brings less ecstasy but Mami nods along to the beat and smiles, surprisingly game.

Then the "Top Model" contest begins. Beautiful women from all over Africa, thin as sticks, with ribs and shoulder blades sticking out from their long dark bodies, strut across the stage in miniskirts and bikini tops. Despite the fact that all the woman in the audience weigh well over two hundred pounds and would no sooner show their ankles than walk down the street naked, they cluck in appreciation at the spectacular beauty before them. A model from Côte d'Ivoire wins and is handed a huge cardboard check for one hundred thousand CFA from the previous year's winner, a Senegalese girl wearing a powdered wig à la Marie Antoinette. The runners-up all get baskets of cloth from Uniwax, from which they can make boubous.

"What exactly is she going to do with a hundred thousand CFA?" asks Mami in a huff. "It's a pathetic amount of money."

Then there is a pause, which lasts an hour, and then the president's second wife arrives. She's wearing a saffron boubou laced with gold thread, a matching headscarf, and saffron eye shadow, and sits in an enormous stuffed chair near the stage.

Mami says that she is much nicer than the president's first wife, but won't elaborate. She also doesn't go and say hello, which is slightly mysterious to me.

Finally, after three hours of prelude, the fashion show looks ready to start. It's already midnight and I'm so tired I slump against Adissa's shoulder as the stagehands douse the runway with sand and rearrange the lights. By the time the fashion show begins, Adissa has pulled out her pocket Qu'ran and is doing a little one a.m. reading.

But once the models arrive onstage, we all agree the wait was worth it.

There is, in no particular order: a model dressed as a witch with a conical hat made of peacock feathers; a straw hoop skirt five feet in diameter made of desert grasses; and a sexy Nazi outfit, complete with jackboots, short-shorts, a riding crop, and a patent leather cap. There are silver spike high-heeled boots and dresses made of braided hay. Throughout the evening there are enough sequins, gold lamé, taffeta, and rhinestones to shame the cast of *Dynasty*. There is even an African designer from Canada who shows the most shocking piece of all—a shearling coat.

It goes on forever. In Paris, fashion shows are over in ten minutes, but this stretches for more than two hours. The outfits get more and more outrageous, with one woman dressed in a leopard-print loincloth and the branches of a baobab tree. Occasionally a small Lebanese man named Alphael who sits at the feet of the president's wife runs onstage and rearranges a model's outfit or fixes a stray peacock feather. He is obviously flamboyantly gay, with a campy walk and flirtatious turns of the head, but no one seems to mind—certainly not the president's wife, who finds him hilarious. By three thirty a.m. the production has completely fallen apart as the sound technicians abandon their posts to sit at the bottom of the stage and look under the models' dresses. Finally, even as the show goes on, the president's wife leaves and the women of Niamey begin to filter out. But Mami, fixed to her seat and eyes glued to the stage, looks completely undeterred.

"Mami, let's go," whines Adissa, who has long since stopped looking at either the dresses or the Qur'an.

"No, Adissa," Mami says firmly. "Once a year we get this show. I will see it to the end."

Adissa leaves in a huff.

"She knows we came here to see this. I'm here to see it," Mami says. "At least I know you're not going anywhere. You have nowhere to go."

It's true. I have no idea where I am and no way to get home. So I spray myself with bug spray (again) and wait with Mami until the very last model has left the stage. At the end of the show, Alphael bestows the top design prize on a woman from Ghana who has created, to my eye, a series of plain black jersey dresses. I can't believe it. Black dresses after the woman who wore a baobab tree.

Once the show is finished Mami goes down to the stage to meet her friends. She chats with the other grandes dames of Niamey, and I curl up in the president's wife's chair and fall asleep. At around five a.m., Mami comes to get me and we go home in her white Mercedes. When I wake up at nine a.m., hungry and unable to sleep, she is already at her desk, going through receipts, eating eggs, and scolding the workers. I realize with a sad heart that I no longer have a good reason to stay in Niamey and that it is time to move on. Out there lies the African savanna, and perhaps my last chance of traveling through it alone.

43

Free from Love

THE WOMEN IN THE HOUSES next door speak in hushed just-awake voices. They begin to boil water for tea, bending at the waist to plump small cakes before putting them on the fire. One woman pinches her friend, who mock slaps her, then laughs gently. Their houses are ordered and clean, the ground swept into swirling rows punctuated by children's footprints. But beyond the confines of the village it feels like the land has been worked to the bone, stripped of fat and laughter. Only the freshness of morning saves it from harshness.

The sun rises huge, soft and cool. My taxi driver prays while I lean out the side of the car and eat a block of cheddar cheese like a candy bar. Nearby a tree with gnarled branches reaching for the sky has been carved out as a cistern for collecting water. I slip off my sandal and run red dust through my toes, considering the scrubland before me. Flecks of straw glitter in the morning haze like gold thread woven into a dress. The earth under my sandal, so fine and light it can barely support life, floats away in the wind.

How many days in the one hundred fifty that I have traveled have I sat in bus stations waiting for something, *anything* to happen? How many hours have I spent waiting for the bus to arrive, suffering stomach-churning, hope-dashing, mind-numbing frustration? And for once, it feels perfect. Completely satisfying. I am in Maradi, the commercial capital of Niger that sits on the Nigerian border, in the clean and shaded bus station while the baby does his summersaults inside me. I'm exhausted and spacey and on my way back to Niamey after three weeks of terrifying travel across the savanna. Even reading seems beyond me. I can't think of anything I would rather do than sit in this bus station for three hours with my shoes off, running my toes through the cool sand.

It's early, about six thirty a.m., and the ticket man is all alone in the station. He finds a chair in the back and puts me under an awning and tells me that a bus for Niamey should be coming in by noon. The station is just a walled compound, with a bus and a floor of red dust. A long-horned cow, chewing its cud, wanders in from the road, then wanders out. A Nigerien customs official, his car heaped floor to ceiling with consumer goods from China that were shipped through Lagos, stops, buys a Fanta, and leaves. As people filter in for the bus, they pull out loaves of yellow bread and cans of condensed milk. Green lizards crawl up the walls.

Yesterday in the market, as I walked around Konni, a Nigerian man pulled out a three-foot-long machete and waved it at me. I could tell he was Nigerian because he wore expensive-looking jeans and a T-shirt that said MUST HAVE THIS. A pharmacist ran in front of me and yelled at the man in French, then in English. *Get away, get away, you wicked, wicked man!* I see the pharmacist now and he nods at me when he walks in to buy his ticket. He told me yesterday that he was going to Niamey to pick up perfume for his shop. You must wear perfume every day, he told me. It will make the baby happy.

Across the station a shopkeeper who works out of a wooden stall opens his shop for the day. He beats dust off his wares—baby dolls, crackers, rock salt, and dates—with a switch made of horse hairs. The bus attendant comes to water some small green vines, and the shoe man arrives to shine people's shoes. A gust of wind blows through the lot and all those inside stop for a moment, turn their back to the wind, and resume their activities once it has passed. When the breakfast man comes in, people gather around to see what he has this morning. He unveils a silver plate of porcupine stomach that has been cut up, gutted, and flattened on the plate. With a knife he scatters the flies and begins to cut meat, which he serves out on little cones of newspaper. People crouch in the dust and eat, fat running down their lips, grunting in pleasure.

"What? Nothing for you, sister?" a woman asks. She is tall and round with high cheekbones and small gold earrings. A respectable woman of moderate means, probably in her thirties.

"No, I'm okay," I say.

"Well," she says, "let me then, keep you company."

It's such a natural gesture. There is no other chair in the train station so we go into the ticket agent's office and sit on long benches tied to the walls. After a while she lies down and so do I, our heads meeting in the corner of the room where we talk in a whisper, without seeing each other's faces. After asking each other where we live and what we do we come around to the business of marriage. She tells me her name is Aminata and that she and her husband were married for sixteen years but he died two years ago. Since then she has gotten a job in the bus station in Zinder and the past two years have been the happiest in her life. She loathed her husband and he seemed to loathe her back. She has only two daughters.

"His first wife was never good. She lied about me all the time. She stole my husband's love. She said I was casting spells on him to make him love me or castrate him. This is jealousy. People in Niger are mean, mean and jealous," she says, sighing, one of those long, dark marriage-is-hard sighs that seem universal among women. "What are your husband's other wives like?" she asks.

This question always shakes me a little. Don't Africans, who see French television and are often educated by French teachers, know anything about European culture?

"It's illegal in France to take two wives."

She reaches over from her bench and pats me on the forehead, indulgently, like I'm a spoiled little girl whose daddy has given her a pony for Christmas.

"This is a better way," she says. "I would not let my daughters be second wives."

"What if they wanted to? If they loved someone?"

"It's her choice. I cannot make this choice for her, but I wouldn't . . . I would be sad."

She sits up and smiles at me. A man selling cloth comes into the ticket room and stares at me, then asks if I was in New York during September 11 and leaves. Aminata slowly gathers her things. She is catching the bus to Filingué to pick up her children, who have spent a week staying with their half brothers and sisters in their old house. Although Aminata hates her dead husband's first wife, she still brings her children to see their siblings every few weeks, because in the end, family is family and that house will always be home to those little girls.

"You know, I have been traveling in Africa for many months," I say. "I have talked to many people, both men and women. On one thing most everyone agrees: two wives in one household is not a good idea. The wives feel jealous and betrayed. The men feel afraid of the women in their house, who are planning ways to get power."

"If women had a choice they would never get married. Me? I have many offers, but never will I marry again," she says, smiling.

"What if you fell in love?"

She emits a sharp laugh.

"I am an old woman, nearly forty years old, lucky to be on this earth for so long. God is good to me. I am not going to fall in love again."

Aminata hugs me for a moment before she takes her many bags and puts herself on the bus. She waves through the window and tells me to stop by the bus station in Zinder next time I am in town to say hello. Even from afar she looks happy. She is going home, and God protects his favorite children from love. There is truth in that.

44

Home

Sometimes when I am alone in my apartment in Paris, the baby is sleeping, and I feel like I am losing my footing again, I take down *Out of Africa* and read a few pages.

There is one section to which I have become particularly attached. It is called "Visitors to the Farm" and mostly talks about the Somalis and Kenyans with whom Dinesen worked. Generally speaking she is too elegant and self-effacing to talk much about the man she loves, but in a few paragraphs of this section, she makes an exception, for sentimental reasons.

Lady Delamere, the wife of a prominent British landowner in Kenya, has come for tea. It's a proper and stately affair, with Limoges china and homemade scones. In my mind, Karen hasn't seen Denys in a long time and is lonely for him—curious to know where he has been on safari, perhaps envious of his freedom. Suddenly his little airplane swoops over her house and he lands on the plain below her plantation. Karen and Lady Delamere go down to get him and he yells over the sound of the propeller.

"The buffalo are out feeding on the hills. Come out and have a look at them."

"I have a tea-party. I have *guests!*"

"Don't worry," he responds. "I will have you back in fifteen minutes."

She cannot resist, and they are up, skirting the green and shaded side of the Ngong Mountains, catching a herd of buffalo and their calves grazing. They are circling the animals, diving in several times, and inadvertently scattering the herd into thunder and dust. When they land, I imagine she runs her hand through her short brown hair, pecks him on the cheek, and runs off to see her friend. "When I came back to my tea-party, the teapot on the stone table was still so hot that I burned my fingers on it," Dinesen writes.

She is casual in the telling of this anecdote. As a writer, Dinesen is more interested in talking about her three-month trek through the bush to bring supplies to British troops, or the evenings she spends chatting with the Somali women on her farm. Yet I find it one of the most instructive tales in her book. For in this scene she has perfectly wed her own search for adventure with a domestic life. Here is a moment of exhilaration and beauty that injects itself into the security and safety of her home, giving it that little jolt of excitement.

I ask myself often if, after traveling in Africa, I am better able to accept the life I have chosen. Have I come anywhere close to wedding this divide between security and adventure? Am I better able to deal with commitments and responsibilities, to squelch wanderlust when it raises its head at inopportune times? Am I a better wife to Florent? Am I a decent mother?

Very often I say yes. I don't recognize the woman who stood crying in the supermarket over her inability to find bread crumbs. I don't recognize the woman who thought that love could compensate for the loss of friends and a job. Love holds a small pocket in a life. It's an important one, but it is small. In the rest of us are the adventures we have lived and fortitude we have built. Our experiences shape us, and if we do not go out and get new ones we will stay static.

Those adventures live in my memory now and they are always at hand. There are times in motherhood when the patience of an African traveler is required. The baby is squirming and crying and trying to put everything in his mouth and I look at the clock and think, "Four hours to bedtime. Worst case scenario five." It isn't unlike waiting for a bus in Maradi. There is at first boredom but then a kind of Zen-like state takes over. Your brain resists the slow ticktock of time. You give in to it, and your submission is rewarded with the lifting of restlessness.

Most of my thoughts on Africa are practical like this. I went there for the resurrection of my childhood dreams, a return to the sense that the world was full of promise and beauties. I went to get closer to the earth and to discover what really mattered to me and whether I could live with less, or with nothing at all. I went to challenge myself as a man might. These were romantic notions, and I found experiences to sustain a whole life. I am tough now in a way I wasn't before. Yet it is the smaller lessons that I live with every day. It is the memory of waiting for a bus, of walking by the road, of sharing crackers with women. It is the good sense of ordering a day with Islam and tea, of making eye contact with strangers, of spending time on hellos and goodbyes. It is the ability to laugh—really laugh with noise and snot and mirth—regardless of circumstances.

The small things stay with me, not the exhilaration of riding through the desert on top of a jeep, though I confess, on occasion, I yearn for that particular freedom too. They allow me to feel that I have experience and adventure in my bones, that it is woven into me, even as I struggle to be a wife and mother.

For I do still struggle. The contradictions of my life still exist. I am an adventurer who often finds herself at home. I am a lover of solitude who is surrounded by people all the time. I am an impulsive romantic thrust into the routine of daily life. It is never easy to grow up and live the life you have chosen, even if it is a good life.

Yet I am far more clearheaded now about how to make for myself the life I crave than I was before I went to Africa. I refuse to see my life in the context of Parisian bourgeois society, and I hold on to the notion that our stay here is temporary.

I have broken the spell of my mother's sadness and my own upbringing. Africa is a living, vital place that holds not just my past but also my future. In this way it is a part of my daily life, rather than a mystical fantasy. I close my eyes and there is the wide, placid Niger River at Ségou and the red clay earth under my naked feet. The heavy gold moon is rising over the desert of Chinguetti, throwing rays of light over a sand dune sea that reaches hundreds of miles beyond my horizon. Now my son Theo is walking to the kitchen door with a bottle of milk and peering out at the mist on the savanna across the river where herons dive for fish. He is at the simple wooden table in our kitchen sampling a corner of manioc root and kicking his legs in pleasure at the chewy, earthy taste. He is pointing out to me a lizard on the wall and speaking to me in a language I don't understand, and when I hold my hands up in confusion he looks at me in pity. *Mama speaks only English and a little French,* he tells his friends. *She doesn't know the language we speak.*

Admittedly, Florent fits oddly into these dreams. It remains hard to see him in Africa and he seems better calibrated to sit by the pool of a big hotel in Miami smoking cigars. Then again, he is able, more than most people I know, to change and adapt for the ones he loves. He has also become a firm believer in the notions of travel. After six years in Paris, he is serious about leaving. He understands that there is happiness in working less and seeing his family more. He also senses that the grinding, never-ending crisis in Europe is eroding his kindness and gentility. "Soon I'm going to turn into one of those American managers who start a conversation off with: let me cut to the chase," he says one evening after a particularly stressful day. "The world doesn't need any more of those guys."

I think sometimes of the fights we had when I first came to Paris. I think of him standing on the balcony smoking cigarettes and the sorrow in his eyes that our young marriage seemed so dangerously off-kilter. I remember him coming to me one night and trying to stop the arguments and remind me what kind of man he was.

"This is unbearable," he said, trying to catch my eye one night.

I looked at him through hazy eyes. I still found him terribly handsome, so adult in his pressed blue suit and faint smell of cigarettes and cologne. He was such a man. How on earth did I get myself such a man?

"I feel like my life here is a slow march towards death," I mumbled. "I feel like I'm not really living at all. I'm suffocating."

He sighed and sat down, rubbed my cheek. His eyes were soft and brown, slightly drooping at the edges like a hound dog. His voice, always high and slightly weak, seemed shy to many people, but underneath he was all determination.

"Sounds horrible. Sounds like prison."

"Isn't it?"

"Nina," he said softly. "I'm not that guy. Don't make me that guy."

I didn't really understand what he was saying, but now I did. He wasn't the one to kill dreams. He wasn't thrusting me into the role of housewife and mother. I still had my freedom. I just needed to pick it up and claim it as my own.

Africa still beckons, more so now than ever because there is change in West Africa as never before. The Tuareg have managed to take over northern Mali, cutting off Timbuktu and Gao from the rest of the country. Senegal is dealing with democratic reforms. Niger is trying to contain famine in the face of rising demand for its uranium. A part of me wants to be there to see if this kind and tolerant part of the world will, as I expect, turn away from radicalism.

But mostly it is the quiet moments I miss. Sitting atop a dune outside Chinguetti. The heavy night air in Bamako. Moonlight drifting over a Saharan sea and making me feel like I am tied to nature in a way I haven't been since I was a little girl. I yearn for the stories of the people who live there. Stories that I have put into my pocket and take with me, wherever I go, of Africa.

ACKNOWLEDGMENTS

First and foremost I'd like to thank all the folks on the road in Africa who took me under their wing when they really didn't need to and probably sometimes wished they hadn't. The kindness and generosity shown me by African men and women is something I still think about every day. I hope the people of Chinguetti, Timbuktu, and Gao find peace and justice in these difficult times.

On the home front I'd like to thank Harper Montgomery, Mariah Quish, Avital Rosenberg Chatto, Eve Herzog, Tyler Schnoebelen, Wendell Steavenson, Digby Larner, and Christina Passariello for reading pages once, twice, sometimes three times.

I'd like to thank my parents, Britt-Marie and Stephen Sovich, for taking the baby so I could work and for holding their tongues (sort of) when I quit the newswire not once but twice.

Thanks also to Brettne Bloom, my agent, who is tough and smart but above all, kind.

To Katie Salisbury at Amazon Publishing, who walks on the sunny side of the street and thinks I should walk there too. Many thanks for having a good eye and ready ear.

To Rebecca Ryan for constant support for not just wandering around the world by myself, but for writing it down on paper before there was an earthly reason.

And of course to Florent, my love. My life would be a wasteland—a wasteland!—without you.

BIBLIOGRAPHY

Alexander, Caroline. *One Dry Season: In the Footsteps of Mary Kingsley.* London: Bloomsbury, 1989.

Battuta, Ibn. *Ibn Battuta in Black Africa.* Trans. Said Hamdun and Noel King. Princeton: Markus Wiener Publishers, 1998.

Birkett, Dea. *Spinsters Abroad: Victorian Lady Explorers.* Stroud, UK: Sutton Publishing, 2004.

Boahen, Adu, Jacob F. Ade Ajayi, and Michael Tidy. *Topics in West African History.* Harlow, Essex, UK: Longman Group, 1986.

Caillié, René-Auguste. *Travels through Central Africa to Timbuktoo; and Across the Great Desert to Morocco, Performed in the Years 1824–1828.* London: Darf Publishers, 1930; reprint 1992.

Collier, Paul. *The Bottom Billion: Why the Poorest Countries Are Failing and What Can Be Done about It.* Oxford: Oxford University Press, 2007.

Dinesen, Isak [Blixen, Karen.] *Out of Africa.* London: Penguin Books, 1937.

Frank, Katherine. *A Voyager Out: The Life of Mary Kingsley.* Boston: Houghton Mifflin Company, 1986.

King, Dean. *Skeletons of the Zahara.* London: Arrow Books, 2005.

Kingsley, Mary. *Travels in West Africa.* Washington: National Geographic, 2002.

Kryza, Frank, T. *The Race for Timbuktu: In Search of Africa's City of Gold*. New York: HarperCollins, 2006.

The Meaning of the Glorious Koran. Trans. Mohammed Marmaduke Pickthall. New York: Plume, 1997.

Meredith, Martin. *The State of Africa: A History of Fifty Years of Independence*. London: Simon & Schuster, 2005.

Orwell, George. *Down and Out in Paris and London*. London: Penguin Books, 1989.

Ousmane, Sembène. *God's Bits of Wood*. Trans. Francis Price. Oxford: Heinemann, 1995.

Park, Mungo. *Travels into the Interior of Africa*. London: Eland Books, 1983.

Popenoe, Rebecca. *Feeding Desire: Fatness, Beauty and Sexuality Among the Saharan People*. New York: Routledge, 2003.

Porch, Douglas. *The Conquest of the Sahara*. New York: Alfred A. Knopf, 1984.

Robinson, Jane. *Unsuitable for Ladies: An Anthology of Women Travelers*. Oxford: Oxford University Press, 1994.

Ross, Michael. *Cross the Great Desert*. London: Gordon & Cremonesi Publishers, 1977.

Thurman, Judith. *Isak Dinesen: The Life of Karen Blixen*. Middlesex: Penguin Books, 1984.

Villiers, Marq de, and Sheila Hirtle. *Sahara: A Natural History*. New York: Walker & Company, 2002.

ABOUT THE AUTHOR

© Ed Alcock

Nina Sovich was born in New Canaan, Connecticut, to a Swedish mother and an American father. Her work has appeared in the *Wall Street Journal,* the *Christian Science Monitor, Reuters, Fortune Small Business,* and the *Patriot Ledger.* She lives in Paris with her husband, Florent, and their two children.